48.95

W9-ART-452

Mobile IP

Mobile IP

Design Principles and Practices

Charles E. Perkins

ADDISON-WESLEY

An Imprint of Addison Wesley Longman, Inc.

Reading, Massachusetts • Harlow, England • Menlo Park, California
Berkeley, California • Don Mills, Ontario • Sydney
Bonn • Amsterdam • Tokyo • Mexico City

The publisher offers discounts on this book when ordered in quantity for special sales. For more information please contact:

Corporate & Professional Publishing Group
Addison-Wesley Publishing Company
One Jacob Way
Reading, Massachusetts 01867

Library of Congress Cataloging-in-Publication Data

Perkins, Charles E.
    Mobile IP : design principles and practices / Charles E. Perkins.
        p.   cm.
    Includes bibliographical references and index.
    ISBN 0-201-63469-4
    1. Mobile computing. 2. TCP/IP (Computer network protocol)
I. Title.
QA76.P425   1997
004.6'2—dc21   97-35781
                                                          CIP

ISBN 0-201-63469-4
Text printed on acid-free paper
1 2 3 4 5 6 7 8 9—MA—0100999897
First printing, October 1997

C O N T E N T S

LIST OF FIGURES

Two technological advances in recent years have radically altered the nature of computing for most computer users. The first is mobility. Laptop computers now represent the fastest growing segment of the computer market. Most observers expect that laptop computers, palmtop computers, networked personal digital assistants, and other such mobile computers will eventually represent the majority of the stations connected to the Internet. The advantage of mobile computing is that users may access all their applications from any location, whether they are in another building or a different state. The second advance is the widespread use of the Internet for communication, file transfer, and World Wide Web connectivity. This book describes how to make a mobile computer user a citizen of the Internet and how to access everything the information superhighway has to offer.

The goal of this book is to provide you with an introduction to the design and implementation of Internet protocols that are useful for maintaining network connections even while moving from place to place. We look at several protocols including Mobile IP, route optimization, IP version 6, the Dynamic Host Configuration Protocol, encapsulation, source routing, and some related miscellaneous topics still under development.

To take full advantage of the information in this book, you should be familiar with basic Internet protocols such as the Transmission Control Protocol (TCP)/IP. Rich Stevens' book *TCP/IP Illustrated, Volume 1: The Protocols* (Stevens 1994) and Douglas Comer's *Internetworking with TCP/IP* (Comer 1991) both provide excellent introductions to TCP/IP. As a developer of hardware and software products for the Internet, you should have these books on your shelves.

By the time you finish *Mobile IP: Design Principles and Practices*, you will be able to implement Mobile IP, and will have a clear understanding of the system impact of mobility. You will also understand the relevant protocols, and the traps and pitfalls that you are likely to encounter along the way.

As you read this book you will notice many italicized terms, some of which have conventional meanings that may be different than one's first impression (for example, *foreign agent*). These terms are defined in the Glossary: Please check definitions there, and be sure that you understand a term's meaning before moving on in the text.

ACKNOWLEDGMENTS

Much of the material in this book has been adapted from protocol specifications text. In particular, Chapters 3 and 4, which detail the base IETF Mobile IP specification (RFC 2002 (Perkins 1996b)), are similar to the relevant part of that protocol specification. As editor of the Mobile IP drafts, I gratefully accepted text for inclusion from a number of people, all of whom have contributed to the success of this effort. Dave Johnson and Jim Solomon are undoubtedly the two biggest contributors.

Chapter 5, which deals with encapsulation, was largely drawn from RFC 2003 (Perkins 1996a) and RFC 2004 (Perkins 1996c), with material added from the base specification to describe the ways that Mobile IP routes various types of datagrams. Thanks to Tony Li for his generous permission to allow me to use the general record encapsulation documentation (Hanks et al. 1994a, Hanks et al. 1994b) to prepare the relevant text in Chapter 5. Parts of Sections 5.2 and 5.6 were taken from portions (authored by Bill Simpson) of earlier versions of the Mobile IP Internet draft (Perkins 1995). The original text for Section 4.9 was contributed by Bob Smart. Good ideas have also been included from RFC 1853 (Simpson 1995).

Thanks also to Anders Klemets for finding mistakes and suggesting improvements. Again, Dave Johnson contributed a great deal of time grooming the drafts, finding mistakes, improving consistency, and making many other improvements to the numerous Internet drafts.

Chapter 8 expands on a paper that I coauthored with Dave Johnson and presented at Mobicom '96 (Perkins and Johnson 1996). Dave also collaborated on Route Optimization (Chapter 6). The multicast preference extension described in Chapter 7 was originally presented as an Internet draft (Bhattacharya, Patel, and Perkins 1996), coauthored with Baiju Patel and Partha Bhattacharya from IBM.

Thanks to Steve Deering (Xerox PARC), along with Dan Duchamp and John Ioannidis (JI) (Columbia), for forming the working group, chairing it, and putting so much effort into its early development.

Thanks also to Kannan Alaggapan (DEC), Greg Minshall (Novell), and Tony Li (Cisco) for their contributions to the Mobile IP effort, as well as for their many useful comments. Thanks to Greg Minshall, Phil Karn (Qualcomm), and Frank Kastenholz (FTP Software) for their generous support in hosting interim working group meetings.

Special thanks to my friend Andrew Myles, who not only battled with me for long hours via telephone and electronic mail about the right ways to do things, but delighted my children and enlivened our wireless systems lab with his insight, hard work, and working code. Thanks to Pravin Bhagwat (IBM) and Felix Wu (IBM) for their diligent work in helping to implement our early Mobile IP specifications. Thanks to Tangirala Jagannathan (IBM) for persisting through the ever-more-detailed implementation requirements imposed by later drafts, for having the willpower to become expert in the vagaries of our previous implementations, and for handling the battle against the Dynamic Host Configuration Protocol so well. Thanks to Hui Lei (Columbia) for his efforts to make Mobile IP compatible with ad hoc network protocols, and to Kavitha for her efforts in creating last ditch demos. I'm happy that developing and implementing the Mobile IP specifications has enabled me to enjoy the added bonus of counting these people as my friends.

CHAPTER ONE

Introduction

Computing in the 1990s is being transformed by an inexorable march toward greater user convenience, greater processing power, more storage, and better display technologies. From humble beginnings with small diskette-based systems with only a few kilobytes of memory, the personal computer has grown to become a truly transportable device with dozens of megabytes of main memory, gigabytes of disk storage, orders of magnitude more processing power, and beautiful color displays that seemed unimaginable in the early 1980s. Laptop computers should no longer be considered the poor cousins of workstations or even mainframes, but should be thought of instead as another choice in a wide spectrum of available computer resources.

Just as there has been an unstoppable trend toward having additional computing power at one's fingertips, the world of networked computing has similarly advanced at an amazing pace, approximately doubling in connectivity and reach every year. In other words, the number of computer users connected to the network next year is likely to exceed the total number of network-connected people in each previous year added together. This rate of growth is causing revolutionary changes in network technology development and indeed has necessitated social, business, and legal advances for integrating the technology into everyday life.

This book furthers such revolutionary changes by demonstrating new ways to view the connections between laptops and the ever-growing worldwide network of computing resources. As people move from place to place with their laptop, keeping connected to the network can become a challenging and sometimes frustrating and/or expensive proposition. The goal is that with the widespread deployment of the mobile networking technologies described here, automatic communications with globally interconnected computing resources will be considered as natural for people on the move as it is for people sitting at a high-performance workstation in their office. In the near future, communicating via laptop should be as natural as using a telephone.

The day will arrive, hastened by Mobile IP, when no person will ever feel "lost" or out of touch. Indeed, with sufficient connectivity (and a network of trusted friends and family), one could issue an alarm at the first sign of impending violence or danger. Even today, global positioning system (*GPS*) systems are used to assist in quickly determining personal location, and knowing one's current location is a first step toward getting help sent to where it is needed. Combining GPS data with access to Internet data relevant to the coordinates of the mobile computer user means the possibility of more effective action and a greater sense of personal security. Moreover, one can obtain information from Internet data sources about events that have recently affected an area. Similarly, the likelihood of preventative action may have a revolutionary effect on the incidence of violent crime. Mobile IP can also further enhance today's pagers and cellular telephones by allowing natural access to Internet data.

In this introductory chapter, after a short overview of the relevant, existing network protocols, the essential problem solved by Mobile IP is described. The two conflicting requirements for a changeable network address (for routability) and a stable network address (for identification purposes by transport protocols, notably TCP), are reconciled by introducing a level of indirection in the network that addresses structure, which then introduces a need to maintain associations between the two network addresses involved. After this discussion, an abstract model of mobile networking is presented that shows in abstract terms the nature of the mobile networking problem and allows an abstract description of some possible solutions. The abstract functions needed for managing the addresses are then described in abstract terms, and particular instances are identified by analyzing some sample designs.

Mobile networking fits in the larger context demanded by the need for total solutions to the problem of nomadic computing and the system support envisioned for solving the needs of nomadic users. Nomadic computer users bring new requirements that affect every layer of the network protocol stack. Some new application-level requirements are described, including

- Dynamic resource and service discovery
- Coping with dynamically changeable *link* conditions
- Profile management
- Environment management
- Proxy services

A glossary is provided at the end of the book to define unfamiliar terms.

1.1 Laptop Computing

Although computers can be embedded in a wide variety of mobile systems, the first and most important mobile computer system of interest is undoubtedly the laptop computer, which is rapidly becoming indispensable for the business traveler. A typical laptop system can be equipped with a high-resolution color display, multiple gigabytes of disk space, high-fidelity audio output supported by a digital signal processor, a pointing device, high-speed network connections, a battery with enough electrical storage to last an entire business day, and a wireless communications adapter.

There are many kinds of communications adapters that allow convenient access to modern computer networks, and laptop computers typically come equipped with networking software to transmit and receive data over those networks. For access to the Internet, laptops must have the correct protocols, namely TCP/IP and the various auxiliary protocols associated with electronic mail, Web browsing, and other Internet functions. With this in mind the current goal is for laptop computers to operate TCP/IP as easily as desktop computers, because the basic equipment in a laptop is as capable as a desktop computer. The fact that this is not yet a reality is the result of insufficiencies in Internet protocols, not the result of inadequate computing power in the laptop.

1.2 Wireless Technologies

With wireless communications systems (and battery-powered operation) laptop computers can be completely tetherless and still have full connectivity to the Internet. New technologies are available that boast faster and faster transmission speeds that approach those of the wired networks of only a few years ago. Wireless telephone communications provide almost complete coverage of most populated areas within the United States and Europe. Of particular interest to readers of this book are the local area network (*LAN*) attachment devices, which typically use infrared light or radio frequency signals in particular bands to establish links to a wired LAN. Cellular telephone technology (which is also a radio frequency technology) is also of interest to mobile computer users, but cellular phone users rely on the telephone company to maintain connectivity and usually pay a substantial premium for that service. In contrast, radio or infrared LAN attachments are typically made without charge, as long as the LAN administrator is willing to accommodate the user's wireless link.

Here is an example of how a laptop computer might be used with an infrared communications adapter. Suppose that an installation has infrared access points installed in a user's office, in the hallways, and in the conference rooms. When the appointed time comes for an important meeting and the user has just finished completing the presentation materials for the meeting, the user can safely carry the laptop computer to the conference room without shutting down and then restoring the communication links in the new room.

To move within a building, operation at the network layer means that Mobile IP eliminates any concern about which network of the many interconnected networks is closest to the user's current connection point to the building infrastructure. Mobile IP also does not depend on the physical nature of the connection between the laptop computer and the rest of the Internet. That is, it does not matter whether the computer is connected via radio LAN, infrared, wireless telephone, or indeed whether the computer is hooked up directly to an Ethernet or token ring network. Physical-layer independence is very powerful in practice. Once the network-layer protocol can automatically track the mobile computer, each new wireless or network adapter that becomes available may be used for mobile computing.

Indeed, a kind of multimodal operation is possible whereby all the software on the laptop computer can maintain connections to the Internet even though the user has changed the physical medium by which the connection is made. For instance, a user may wish to use infrared or even Ethernet links while inside a building, may switch to radio LAN connections when leaving the premises, and may use a cellular telephone to maintain connectivity when out of range of all enterprise base stations, as demonstrated by experimental programs carried out at the University of California at Berkeley (Katz 1994). Such convenience truly deserves the name *seamless roaming*, more than any other products available today.

1.3 Information Superhighway

Much has been written recently about the emergence of the Internet as the long-sought-after information superhighway. From its humble beginnings as the Arpanet of the 1970s (Cerf 1978), populated by a few dozen huge computers of the day, the Internet has been doubling in size to become a democratic and very noisy harbinger of the future of world communications. The information resources available on the Internet are as vast and varied as humanly imaginable. This is demonstrably true, because as soon as someone imagines a new computer resource that could be available on the network, it seems that resource soon emerges.

For years, communication via the Internet seemed possible only for computer specialists. Electronic mail, file transfers, and even on-line multiplayer games were almost unknown to most nontechnical people. However, the emergence of the World Wide Web and tools such as Netscape, which make the Internet accessible to everyone, have introduced another stage of tremendous expansion.

Recent traffic analyses of Internet packet flows show that a substantial majority (over seventy-five percent) of all Internet traffic is indeed caused by requests from Web browsers. Moreover, most of the Web traffic consists of image transfers. This trend is bound to continue and probably increase in the near future. In fact, once the necessary routing protocol details are worked out for improving the delivery of video clips, the denizens of the Internet (*netizens*) will likely find ways to combine video, audio, and text into ever-more dazzling (and ever-more bandwidth-consuming) amalgamations of network-retrievable information. Judging from the continuing emergence of new magazines and television shows, there is no limit to humanity's appetite for new visual (and cerebral) stimulation. As technology improves, prices for interconnection drop, and available storage for network information continues to grow, the Internet's role in satisfying these visual needs will continue to expand.

The Internet is also playing an ever-increasing role in the dissemination of technical reports, mail, design documents, and many other aspects of professional communications including videoconferencing. Indeed the whole nature of technical publication is changing rapidly. Reports that formerly had to wait many months before appearing in refereed journals are now distributed worldwide as preprints to anyone who may find them of interest. Professional computer engineers are among the first to equip themselves with the kind of powerful and portable laptop computer that maintains access to the Internet, and access to computer resources is a powerful motivator for improving the network connectivity for laptop computers. Now more than ever it is easier to find information on almost any subject, but one needs to learn which search engine to use, which keywords to filter, and which buttons to click.

1.4 Mobility versus Portability

This book distinguishes between two similar terms—*mobility* and *portability*. Up until now most mobile computer users have had to be satisfied with portable operation. In other words, the computer can be operated at any of a set of points of attachment, but not during the time that the computer changes its point of attachment. If the computer is moved from one place to another, then its network connections have to be shut down and reinitialized at the new point of attachment to the network. Future mobile users will not be satisfied with this mode of operation, especially if they know that the network *could* support uninterrupted connectivity between application and resource.

This book describes protocols that allow truly mobile operation, so that the laptop can remain in almost continuous contact with the network resources needed by its applications. Using these protocols, neither the system nor any of the applications running on the system need to be reinitialized or restarted, even when network connectivity is frequently broken and reestablished at new points of attachment.

Considerable effort has been put into expanding the sphere of applicability of certain existing protocols such as Point-to-Point Protocol (*PPP*) (Simpson 1994), Dynamic Host Configuration Protocol (*DHCP*) (Alexander and Droms 1997), and Domain Name System (*DNS*) (Mockapetris 1987a, Mockapetris 1987b) to support the portable mode of operation for mobile computers. This book shows that by solving the mobility problem at the network protocol layer, solutions requiring other complex protocols (such as DHCP, and extensions like those requiring modifications to critical enterprise subsystems like DNS) can be largely superseded by less expensive and more general technology.

It's worthwhile to point out that nomadic users of today's Internet are often satisfied with portable computing. For such users all that is needed is a temporary connection to the Internet that is broken when the time comes to move to a new place. For them maintaining connections doesn't matter much, because the connections are short lived. Moreover, often for Web-based information retrieval, the network address of the recipient does not matter. In these cases, the assumptions made about the IP network address being closely related to identity are not very strong, and thus Mobile IP does not provide much benefit.

Another factor that promotes solutions that minimize connection lifetime is expense. For instance, a nomadic connection maintained over a telephone link from an airplane costs well over $1 per minute. This is a great disincentive to keeping idle logins on remote computers. In an office setting no one would think twice about the expense, and the company experiences productivity gains as a result of having the additional network resources available.

It is my strong belief that as wireless computing becomes more prevalent and less expensive, and especially as wireless *cells* shrink in size to promote frequency reuse and greater cumulated bandwidth, Mobile IP will be viewed increasingly as a necessity, and the concessions made to today's realities of portable computing will be viewed more as bugs rather than necessities.

1.5 Quick Overview of IP and Routing

The Internet is largely built using software that relies, unsurprisingly, on the Internet Protocol suite, and specifically on IP (Postel 1981b). It is assumed in this book that you are somewhat familiar with IP and understand in some detail the *catenet model* (Cerf 1978) it provides, by which routers forward datagrams from one network to another by selecting the next hop that the datagram must traverse (Steenstrup 1995). For each datagram, each router in the Internet determines the next hop by finding the entry in its routing table that best matches the destination IP address of the datagram.

1.5.1 IP Addresses

The purpose of routing protocols within the Internet is to allow routers to exchange information about the networks they are connecting. As the routing information flows across the Internet, each router will eventually learn enough to send any datagram along the correct route to its destination. *Nodes* that are not routers typically accomplish this objective simply by sending all of their outgoing datagrams to a default router.

Routers have a difficult task because they have to decide how to forward each packet they receive, a decision that involves selecting from several outgoing network interfaces to forward a packet. Even so, most routers only need to keep track of a small proportion of the total number of routes within the Internet. Routers can try to find a route (that is, a network interface) appropriate for delivering a datagram, and if their attempt does not meet with success they can send the datagram along to another default router for further handling. In this way, datagrams proceed until (as usual) they either arrive at the correct network in few a local hops or they have to go out over the national and international routers (the backbone routers), which have full (if aggregated) knowledge of all high-level routes within the Internet. As one might expect, there is a great deal of interest in finding ways to minimize the number of routes that each router, even on the backbone, needs to maintain.

IP network address allocation and administration have historically assumed that there is a close relationship between a computer's IP address and its physical location. This proceeds naturally from the assumption that a network is easily modeled by a wire (say, an Ethernet cable), and thus to a great extent can be localized. This model works equally well even if multiple cables are connected to a bigger network (say, by repeaters or bridges) (Perlman 1994). As far as the routers are concerned, the mass of cables hooked together by such devices still operates as if it were a single cable and is considered by IP to be a single network. That network is addressed by a single IP prefix (Stevens 1994), and all computers hooked together along that network are assigned addresses that use that same prefix. Among other things, this implies that any two computers connected to that network can communicate directly, without using the services of any router. Computers not on that network will have a different prefix, which can be used to locate the network to which they are attached.

IP addresses (Figure 1.1) have two parts:

1. The *routing prefix* (often determined by the *netmask*) defines the network on which the address resides.

2. The host number fits in the least significant remaining bits of the IP address following the routing prefix bits.

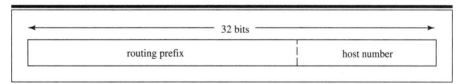

Figure 1.1 IP address structure.

1.5.2 Routing

Effectively all IP addresses are split into subnet prefixes and host numbers. The Internet is far too big to use flat addressing, which is when each host has its own entry in every Internet router. Instead, router entries refer to much larger sets of hosts, namely those that are located together on a subnet. Thus, the routers use a kind of topological addressing and make the assumption that hosts with common routing prefixes can share a common route.

In the past, the routing prefix could be either class A, B, or C. The class was determined by the number of bits in the prefix. One might say that the netmask was implicitly encoded in the high-order bits of the IP address. More recently, to preserve as best as possible the remaining IP address space, routing prefixes have been assigned according to the architecture prescribed in classless interdomain routing (*CIDR*) (Rekhter and Li 1993, Fuller et al. 1993). With CIDR, the netmask is explicitly given separately from the IP address, which allows previous class A and B networks to be carved up into a much larger number of smaller networks. Furthermore, the smaller networks are usually aggregated so that fewer router advertisements are needed overall at the highest levels of the routing infrastructure.

From the point of view of routing, the problem with mobility is that mobile computers move from one IP subnet to another, but have the wrong subnet prefix for the destination subnet. For instance in Figure 1.2, the mobile computer from subnet 132.4.16 is shown attaching to a subnet with routing prefix 128.8.128. This is going to cause trouble because no datagrams for network 132.4.16 will arrive on 128.8.128.

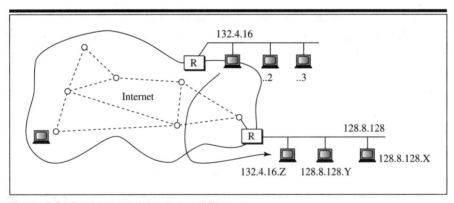

Figure 1.2 IP subnet model versus mobility.

1.5.3 Source Routing

Even though routers maintain practically all the necessary routing information used within the Internet, there are cases in which nonrouter hosts must specify certain routing information, including

- Point-to-point connections
- Multihome hosts
- Source routing

In this book, the first two routing variations are not considered in detail. However, *source routing* has had a large and continual effect on the development of mobile networking protocols, and is briefly described in this section.

In general, source routing means the insertion of routing information into a datagram by the node that originates the datagram (the source node). This routing information can be inserted for a variety of reasons, such as

- Policy routing

- Enabling new routes that are not otherwise advertised

- Debugging

Policy routing is a general term that means selecting a route different from the usual route to suggest or enforce a desired policy for the traversal of the datagram across the Internet. Debugging was the original motivation for the design of source route options. The second use of source routes is the one that has attracted the attention of the designers of mobile networking protocols.

In IP, source routes are specified in the IP options compartment of the IP header. There are two kinds of source routes available: strict source routes and loose source routes.

Strict source routes specify every intermediate routing point that a datagram must visit. If the datagram ever arrives at an intermediate routing point that is not directly adjacent to the next hop in the list of intermediate points in a strict source route, the datagram cannot be forwarded. In that case, an Internet Control Message Protocol (*ICMP*) (Postel 1981a) error message (parameter problem) is returned to the sender and points to the node in the list after which routing was prohibited.

Loose source routing (*LSR*), on the other hand, does not prohibit the further delivery of a datagram when the next hop in the source route list is not adjacent to an intermediate hop. Thus, LSR is more flexible for normal use in routing Internet datagrams. In short, the idea that occurred to several researchers in mobile networking was to define and use a current IP address associated with a *mobile node* as an intermediate hop in a loose source route accompanying all datagrams destined for that mobile node (Johnson 1994, Perkins and Bhagwat 1993, Johnson 1994).

1.6 TCP Connections

A network application often has to identify the communication endpoints that are receiving data by way of some connection over the network. For instance, if an application running on a network client needs to send a file to its remote server, the protocols invoked by the application need to format the data according to spec-ifications so that the protocol processing on the remote node can make sense of the data and digest it at a convenient rate. Every data transfer between network endpoints has to be tightly controlled by conformance to interoperable network pro-tocols such as TCP (Postel 1981c), the User Datagram Protocol (*UDP*) (Postel 1980), or the Real-time Transport Protocol (*RTP*) (Schulzrinne et al. 1996).

This is usually done by maintaining the IP address of both endpoints as part of a *protocol control block*, which stores all of the information needed for the higher level network protocols to manage the connection between the endpoints. TCP makes available a number of *ports* to network endpoints and uses the port numbers along with the IP addresses of the endpoints to identify its protocol control blocks. Consequently, for transport protocols such as TCP, the IP addresses of the network nodes serve to identify the endpoints of the communications channels used for the data transfers, as illustrated in Figure 1.3. Figure 1.3 also shows that a routing path between the two endpoints and at alternate paths may be possible.

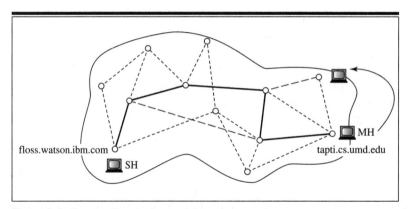

Figure 1.3 Connections between Internet computers.

1.7 Two-level Addressing

As shown in the previous sections, applications use IP addresses to identify routes by which datagrams may be exchanged between two network nodes, namely the nodes performing the actions needed for the application. On the other hand, it is also clear that the IP address used by the applications is also used to identify the endpoints themselves. This dual use of the IP address by the application endpoints causes problems that are encountered when trying to use the application while changing one's point of attachment to the Internet. Clearly, applications need an unchanging way to identify the communication endpoints, but just as clearly the routes between the endpoints must change as they move from place to place within the Internet.

In Figure 1.4, the mobile node named FOO has moved from subnet 132.4 lb to another subnet, 128.8.128. As suggested by Figure 1.4, Mobile IP solves this quandary by maintaining two addresses—one for each of the dual uses of the IP address. Subsequent chapters detail the various mechanisms for acquiring and associating the two addresses; for now, however, the important point is that one IP address is available for *locating* the mobile computer and another is available for *identifying* a communication endpoint on the mobile computer.

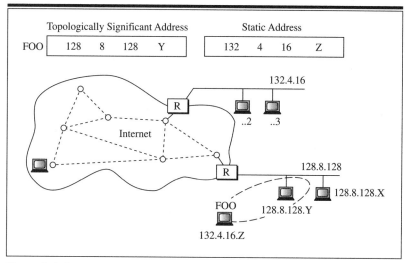

Figure 1.4 Two-tier IP addressing.

1.8 Abstract Mobility Management Model

Mobile IP protocol is described in this book, as well as other related protocols that have been proposed by identifying the necessary functions for managing the IP addresses used for locating and identifying the mobile node. There have been quite a number of proposals (Ioannidis and Maguire 1993, Perkins and Myles 1994, Perkins, Myles, and Johnson 1994, Teraoka and Tokoro 1993, Wada et al. 1993), and it is possible to identify the necessary functions by studying the elements that these proposals have in common. Consult the article by Myles and Skellern (1993) for a detailed analysis of several of these proposals. For the purposes of this book, it is enough to describe the abstract functions and how they are represented by the functions provided by Mobile IP.

Since there are typically two IP addresses associated with each mobile node, there is a clear need for one or more directories to store the associations. Typically the directory should be indexed by the IP address used to identify the mobile node to the Internet at large. Each entry should contain the associated IP address, which can be used to locate the mobile node. This associated address is known as the *care-of address*.

As mentioned, Internet nodes typically use the IP address of a destination node when searching for connections to that destination. Thus the IP address of a remote endpoint also serves to identify the endpoint. Internet protocols use the address identifying the remote endpoint of a network connection as the destination address in the IP header. The IP header precedes the higher level protocol headers and pay-load. Moreover, the destination address carries with it the indication of a particular network (that is, uniquely specifies a particular network's prefix), and the destination address is typically unchanged during transit (disregarding source routes for the moment). Therefore, the network toward which a datagram is routed usually directly depends on the identity of the desired remote endpoint, as known to the source of the datagram.

For mobile computers this destination network is known as the *home network*. Since the mobile node appears to the rest of the Internet as if it were actually located on the home network, we can rightfully call its IP address the *home address* of the mobile node. If the source of the packet is assumed to be an Internet node with no special modification for mobility support, the source will be unaware whether anything special happens when the datagram arrives at the home network. Indeed, if the mobile node is located at the home network, nothing special needs to happen. The datagram will be delivered to its home address and thus to the intended recipient, namely the mobile node.

However, if the mobile node is not attached to its home network, then the datagram somehow needs to follow it to its care-of address. Since the datagram can only follow the mobile node by utilizing the existing Internet infrastructure for the intervening hops, it seems clear that the addressing of the datagram needs to be changed before the datagram is able to follow the mobile node off the home network.

This operation of changing the address of the datagram for further routing is known as *readdressing*. The operation of readdressing a datagram transforms its original destination IP address (the home address, which identifies the mobile node) into a different destination IP address (namely, the care-of address, which locates the mobile node).

The other abstract function needed for supporting mobility is just the inverse of the readdressing function. Basically, if one agent applies an address translation function to a datagram destined for a mobile node, it seems prudent (at least in the abstract) to provide for the possibility of the inverse function so that the original datagram can be presented to the mobile node. The inverse operation is required if the higher level protocols in the mobile node and the nodes with which it corresponds are to operate in a symmetrical manner. Otherwise, the mobile node's home address identifying the higher level protocol connection status control blocks would not be available in the same way as expected by the node that originally sent the datagram. Higher level protocols do operate in this symmetric fashion, and any reasonable Mobile IP architecture must be built with the intention of reducing or eliminating any modifications to existing higher level protocols.

Stated simply, the inverse readdressing function transforms the datagram so that the care-of address (having fulfilled its role in life) is replaced by the home address (used originally by the source node as the destination IP address). It is not absolutely necessary, of course, that these individual abstract functions be performed by physically distinct Internet nodes. The exact ways in which the functions are located in various nodes and networks distinguish the various approaches.

To summarize, the following abstract functions are needed to support mobility:

- Readdressing at the home network

- Associating (in the location directory) the home address and the care-of address of the mobile node (and maintaining up-to-date values for the association)

- Delivering the datagram to the care-of address

- Inverting the readdressing operation once the datagram arrives at the care-of address

These functions are depicted in Figure 1.5. As shown, the readdressing function *f* consults the location directory (*LD*) to retrieve the care-of address of the mobile node before performing the readdressing operation and attempting further delivery of the datagram. When the datagram arrives at the care-of address, the inverse readdressing function *g* is applied and the recovered datagram is delivered to the mobile node for processing by its higher level protocols. Figure 1.5 assumes that the inverse readdressing does not need to consult another directory. This is typically true because the readdressed datagrams contain sufficient information to allow the inverse operation to proceed.

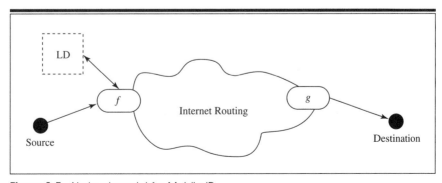

Figure 1.5 Abstract model for Mobile IP.

1.9 Remote Redirection

A common feature of all instances of the abstract architecture is the need to update the LD when the mobile node moves to a new attachment point within the Internet. The update message sent to the LD has the effect of directing traffic from the home network to the mobile node's new location. This redirection operation is known generically as a *remote redirection*, and it introduces stringent security requirements for the realistic deployment of any workable protocol. Security (in particular, authentication) is required so that the LD manager can be assured that the mobile node itself has authorized the delivery of all location update information for the LD. If bogus, counterfeit, or otherwise malicious location updates were accepted, the mobile node could be cut off from future communications with the Internet. The uncontrolled propagation of remote redirects must be avoided to eliminate such well-known problems (Bellovin 1989).

Unfortunately, the requirement for remote redirection surfaces quite often with protocols that aid nomadic computer users. Once the bond of static attachment has been severed, there is always the question whether control messages relevant to the mobile computer are authentic. For every network service that may be employed by nomadic users (for example, Mobile IP, DNS, or DHCP), authorization depends on some method (usually cryptographic) for verifying the identity of the requester. Location maintenance ranks high on the list of services requiring assurance of authorization, and the mobile node itself is usually considered (by mobile networking protocols) the highest authority on its location.

1.10 Example Architectures

Two examples of the foregoing abstract model are briefly described in this section. The first is Mobile IP (Perkins 1996b), as defined by the Internet Engineering Task Force (*IETF*). The second is a previous version of Mobile IP experimentally defined by researchers at Columbia University (Ioannidis and Maguire 1993), which has had substantial effects on the evolution of the IETF protocol.

1.10.1 Architectural Model of the IETF Protocol

In the IETF Mobile IP protocol, the LD is present at the same node on the home network that implements the readdressing function. The readdressing node on the home network is called the *home agent*. Correspondingly, a *foreign agent* fulfills the inverse readdressing function when the datagram is delivered to the care-of address. The intention is that the care-of address is owned by the foreign agent, and after the inverse readdressing function is performed, the foreign agent delivers the resulting datagram to the mobile node.

However, for sufficiently capable mobile nodes, it is quite reasonable to dispense with the foreign agents and allow the mobile nodes to perform the inverse read-dressing function themselves. Notice that this also requires the mobile nodes to be able to acquire a suitable care-of address by some means. The only real constraint is that the care-of address be appropriate to the network to which the mobile node is currently attached, because the datagram cannot be delivered to the current location of the mobile node unless the care-of address is appropriate for that current location. One suitable mechanism (DHCP) by which a mobile node can acquire such a care-of address is detailed in Chapter 9.

Foreign agents can use a single care-of address to serve a number of mobile nodes. In contrast, mobile nodes that acquire their own care-of addresses will each require distinct addresses. This introduces the new requirement for further managing the multiplicity of care-of addresses at each network to which a mobile node might wish to attach.

Figure 1.6 shows an overview of the IETF protocol, with functions labeled according to the abstract model.

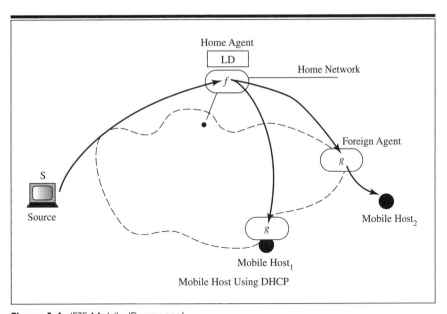

Figure 1.6 IETF Mobile IP proposal.

1.10.2 Columbia Mobile IP

Researchers at Columbia University were among the first to begin experiments in mobile networking. They aimed to provide campus mobility for mobile nodes, partially as an outgrowth of the Student Electronic Notebook (*SEN*) project. Columbia's

Mobile IP (Ioannidis, Duchamp, and Maguire 1991, Ioannidis and Maguire 1993) relied on the configuration of a collection of *mobile support routers* (*MSRs*) that conspired to create a *mobile subnet* (comparable to a home network, but having no physical instantiation) of IP addresses administered for use by the mobile nodes. As mobile nodes moved, they detected *beacons* emitted by the MSRs according to the Mobile Internet Control Protocol (*MICP*), comparable to ICMP, which was the protocol by which the beacons were delivered.

As mobile nodes moved from place to place, they informed their current MSR about their needs and requested that the current MSR inform their previous MSR of their movement. In this way all MSRs could remain up to date regarding the movement of the mobile node. The MSRs communicated by way of a new multicast address, which they had to join. See Figure 1.7 for an illustration of the Columbia protocol.

In terms of the abstract model, several functions in the Columbia protocol are distributed to all the cooperating MSRs supporting the mobile subnet. In particular, each MSR performed the following functions:

- Location directory
- Forward address redirection
- Inverse address translation

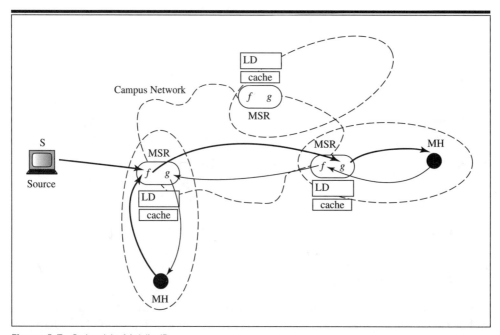

Figure 1.7 Columbia Mobile IP.

The Columbia protocol was very successful for many reasons, including its

- Elegant and simple design
- Symmetric architecture
- Low system impact at small-scale deployment
- Efficient implementation
- Historical precedence compared with other freely available implementation
- WaveLAN wireless interface
- Mach operating system platform

Since the mobile subnet was effectively a virtual subnet, no support for existing hosts on the mobile subnet was necessary. The Columbia protocol also served as the basis for numerous other research efforts into mobile networking at Rutgers and Brown universities, as well as further efforts at Columbia during the early 1990s, especially important first attempts to provide network-layer security (Ioannidis and Blaze 1993). Concerns about scalability, however, drove attempts to avoid distributing the functions to a variable population of symmetric agents maintaining location information for the mobile nodes. With centralized location information, the use of multicast was no longer warranted, gaining possibly further improvements in scalability. This was especially true given the insufficient multicast protocol availability and deployment of the times. See Miles and Skellern (1993) for additional points of comparison between the IETF protocol and the Columbia protocol.

1.11 Where Mobile Networking Fits

This book explores ways to provide for node mobility by making the appropriate modifications to the networking protocol (IP) layer. One might ask why the networking layer should be the layer chosen to implement support for mobility when in fact it is possible to implement mobility at other layers. Socket support can be written so that applications using the augmented sockets work well (Bhagwat and Maltz 1997). TCP can be changed so that the TCP connection is broken into two parts (Indirect TCP), and the connection state passed off from one support station to another as the mobile unit moves. Other strategies are also possible. But providing mobility support at the IP layer fits most naturally, because as previously mentioned the mobility problem can be transformed into a routing problem in a natural way. This naturalness is evident in the simplicity of the protocol and the relatively small amount of code needed to implement the necessary changes to the route table handling at the home agent and foreign agent. Even so, mobility has other effects on protocols at every level of the network protocol stack, as described in the following sections.

1.11.1 Physical- and Link-Layer Protocols

The physical- and link-layer protocols have received the most attention (IEEE 802.11 Committee 1997, Rappaport 1996) for the purposes of mobile networking. This has been driven largely by the needs of mobile voice communications and military applications. Mobile networking needs that have been solved (with various degrees of success) below the network layer include

- Adaptive error correction

- Low detectability

- Data compression

- Data encryption

- Power minimization

- Ad hoc networking

- Isochronous communications

See the draft standard by IEEE 802.11 Committee (1994) for a detailed consideration of such techniques. Managing ad hoc networks below the network layer seems to be a mistake, since routing protocols are inevitably involved in the maintenance of any dynamic topology of interconnections between the nodes populating the ad hoc network. Moreover, operations such as compression and encryption must be coordinated with higher level control software usually operating at the transport or application level. Lastly, protocols supporting *isochronous communications* (communications for which tight delay bounds and reliable bandwidth are needed) are not fully developed at the time of the writing of this book. It seems very likely that there will have to be close coordination between link management and the needs of the application programs (or transport protocol mechanisms) to have a sensible approach for providing isochronous communications capabilities. Thus, it seems premature to build such mechanisms into the link-layer protocols before the higher level needs are better understood.

The mobile node may use link-layer mechanisms to decide that its point of attachment has changed. These mechanisms are specific to the particular link-layer technology. Typically when the mobile node detects a change in its point of attachment by such means it is not necessary for the mobile node also to determine the subnet prefix for the new point of attachment. This is good, because the broadcast range of wireless subnets may not be very well defined. For cases when subnets are relevant when determining the point of attachment, extreme care has to be exercised in the way that subnet numbers are associated with the various wireless cells. For instance, if two wireless cells overlap, they may be unable to share the same subnet prefix. A mobile node moving from one cell into another partially overlapping cell would almost always consider them to be two separate subnets as far as Mobile IP is concerned, unless link-layer mechanisms are in use such as those defined for the Institute of Electrical and Electronic Engineers (*IEEE*) 802.11 (1994) or cellular digital packet data (*CDPD*) (CDPD Consortium 1993).

When making comparisons to identify the nature of its current point of attachment, the mobile node should first attempt to specify its home address so that if the mobile node is attaching to its home network, the unrouted link will function correctly. If a transient IP address is dynamically assigned to the mobile node, and the mobile node is capable of supporting a colocated care-of address, the mobile node may register and use the transient address as a colocated care-of address.

1.11.2 TCP Considerations

TCP Timers

Most hosts and routers that implement TCP/IP do not permit easy configuration of the TCP timer values. When high-delay (for example, SATCOM) or low-bandwidth (for example, high-frequency radio) links are in use, the default TCP timer values in many systems may cause retransmissions or timeouts, even when the link and network are actually operating properly with greater than usual delays because of the medium in use. This can cause an inability to create or maintain TCP connections over such links, and can also cause unneeded retransmissions that consume already scarce bandwidth. Hopefully, mobility-aware vendors will begin to make TCP timers more configurable. Vendors of systems designed for the mobile computing market may have to pick default timer values more suited to low-bandwidth, high-delay links; otherwise, users of mobile nodes may have to be sensitive to the possibility of timer-related difficulties.

TCP Congestion Management

Mobile nodes often use wireless media, which are more likely to introduce errors, effectively causing more packets to be dropped. This introduces a conflict with the mechanisms for congestion management found in modern versions of TCP (Comer 1991, Stevens 1997). Currently, when a packet is dropped, the TCP implementation at the *correspondent node* (that is, the node passing information back and forth to the mobile node) is likely to react as if there was network congestion. This initiates the slow-start (Stevens 1997) mechanisms designed for controlling that problem. However, these mechanisms are inappropriate for overcoming errors introduced by the links themselves and they have the effect of magnifying the discontinuity introduced by the dropped packet. This problem has been analyzed by Caceres and Iftode (1995). There is no easy solution available, and certainly no solution is likely to be installed soon on a majority of IP nodes. This problem illustrates that providing performance transparency to mobile nodes involves understanding mechanisms outside the network layer (Kleinrock 1995). It also emphasizes the need to avoid designs that systematically drop packets. Such designs might otherwise be considered favorably when making engineering trade-offs.

1.12 Middleware Components

Once sufficient capabilities are available in the network protocol stacks to support mobile networking, the need for other capabilities will become more evident. There are a great many services needed by nomadic computer users that have not received much attention yet because the lack of basic protocol support has made the further requirements somewhat of a moot point. These *nomadic services* are likely to be arranged as a set of *middleware* components; that is, service modules that run external to the basic network protocols, but which are viewed as system services by the applications that need to invoke the services to support nomadic users.

Several types of middleware components have been identified as part of a *nomadic architecture* being developed by the Cross Industry Working Team (*XIWT*) group effort for nomadic computing (Corporation for National Research Initiatives 1994). The following list is far from complete, but at least seems likely to be part of any future list. Moreover, further consideration of how the components interact is likely to produce additional needs and the identification of specific new middleware components. Identified middleware components include those that enable the

- Ability to locate network resources
- Ability to adapt to changing link conditions
- Management of profile options and context awareness
- Configuration of local environmental agents

In this section some of the characteristics and uses of these middleware components are briefly considered. Along a somewhat different track, one can consider proxy services and intelligent agents, which can also provide nomadic services, but which are usually too self-contained to be considered middleware. Middleware services are likely to be viewed as part of the operating system by nomadic applications, whereas intelligent agents would be considered entirely separate entities.

1.12.1 Service Location Protocol

The Service Location Protocol (*SLP*) (Veizades et al. 1997) is a new Proposed Standard protocol for discovering and contacting network services, thereby avoiding the continued need for static preconfiguration of all such services that currently plagues mobile computer users. SLP defines the protocol actions required for *user agents* (UAs) to determine the network access points dynamically for network services, which themselves are known by their corresponding *service agents* (SAs). In the most general setting, SAs advertise their services and presence by establishing database entries with a suitable (usually local) *directory agent* (DA). SLP defines the messages exchanged by UAs, SAs, and DAs. In addition, each specific service will define the access mechanisms and descriptions (*attributes* and *keywords*) by which it is made known to UAs. SLP defines the ways that the agents communicate their needs and offerings, not the service-specific descriptions.

SLP may be generally described as specifying the following kinds of operations:

- Service request and reply
- Service registration
- DA discovery
- Attribute enumeration

Each UA uses a *service request* to obtain a *service reply*, which indicates the network address of the appropriate SA. Such service request messages ask for a generically named service, and a specific instance of that service is expected in return. In addition to requesting the generic service, a user will typically need to specify certain desired characteristics that must be available from the SA. For instance, a UA requesting a printer service might need to be sure that the printer can handle PostScript files.

To simplify administration and enhance the scalability of the protocols, a DA should be made available to user clients, because it manages the database of known services for all users. The DA accepts *service advertisements* from service agents; the advertisement messages are expected to contain enough descriptive data (attributes and keywords) to enable the DA to determine when the advertised service will meet the needs specified in the service requests.

One of the main contributions of SLP is to define a general set of mechanisms for discovering DAs. Both UAs and SAs need to identify any DAs that might be available to serve them. Managing the DAs will likely be the main administrative burden imposed by SLP. UAs and SAs will naturally evolve to use DAs as they become available, so that the UAs and SAs can be deployed without the need for any preconfiguration. For instance, DAs can be discovered by use of DHCP, so that the entire administrative load of DA discovery then centers on the ways to classify and organize them in the DHCP server database.

Lastly, SLP defines mechanisms by which UAs can collect sets of available services and service attributes that are available locally. This presumably would be under user control, and the user would be able to satisfy application requirements interactively according to the set of available services that is discovered. In general, SLP has been defined so that it is equally well suited for interactive or noninteractive use.

The benefits provided by SLP for nomadic users should be clear. Nomads are quite likely to be inconvenienced by any need to perform lengthy configuration sequences manually. Both the information-gathering and administrative aspects of the configuration procedures can be arbitrarily difficult and error prone. Any doubt on this point can be banished by a moment's reflection on current means of establishing printer service or groupware connections, finding mountable file systems, or operating dial-up services. All of these services can be simplified by the use of SLP, and all are of interest to nomadic users. As the future unfolds, and the network truly does replace the computer as the center of computing interest, network services are likely to proliferate wildly, as the Internet already has.

1.12.2 Link Adaptivity

There has been a great deal of recent recognition and investigation that shows that the optimal network response to user applications depends heavily on the conditions affecting the link between the computer and the network to which it is attached. For instance, a Web user would like to have new pages presented in a timely fashion no matter what the current link conditions. If speed of presentation requires the replacement of high-resolution graphics with less fascinating markers, then that trade-off is almost always preferred by users experiencing network congestion. Moreover, since protocol implementations can have an internal state indicating congested situations, users can rightfully expect that the Web applications should be able to adjust to link conditions dynamically and make the appropriate trade-offs automatically.

Unfortunately, current network protocol support does not usually offer this capability. Indeed, the problem is multifaceted and will require progress along several fronts:

- Link information will have to be classified so that it can be presented according to some standardized format.

- A standardized application programming interface (*API*) is needed, analogous to the near-ubiquitous and famously useful *sockets API* originated at the University of California at Berkeley.

- Link information at all network protocol levels (physical interface, link-layer, IP, and transport protocols) will have to be made available to the API routines, again indicating the need for a standardized programming interface at the systems programming level.

Some link characteristics of interest to nomadic-aware applications include

- Available bandwidth

- Latency

- Cost (and cost structure)

- Availability of security and privacy

- Error rate

- Quality of service promises

The emergence of wireless interfaces has had the effect of emphasizing the need for this information, since it is particularly wireless communications that make it more difficult to obtain any sort of static characterization of the relevant parameters. Recent work in defining extensions to the Network Device Interface Standard (*NDIS*) device interface (*NetDev* (Stardust Technologies 1996)) represents first efforts to provide link adaptivity information. Designers are also referred to work done at CMU to classify the kinds of link information needed according to various dimensions of *fidelity* (Satyanarayanan 1996).

1.12.3 Profile Management

As the population of nomadic users grows, mobile computers will be seen in an ever-increasing variety of social situations. It will become more and more important to exercise control over the way that applications respond, depending on the social situation surrounding the nomadic use of the application. This differs from link adaptivity in two important respects:

1. The required information is not easily available by inspecting the internal state of the network protocol engines.

2. The same physical setting can correspond to a number of different social situations, depending on the time of day, time of year, identity of the nomadic user, and indeed an indeterminable number of other factors as diverse as society itself.

The middleware component presumed to provide assistance in managing application response in accordance to the context in which the application is used is called the *profile manager*. The profile manager is expected to maintain a set of application-specific profiles and to retrieve stanzas of the profile in accordance with user preferences. The user preferences could be established interactively or by reference to various *environmental variables*. Today, environmental variables are commonly set whenever the computer is initialized or rebooted. But to fulfill the needs of nomadic users it is anticipated that such environmental information will also become much more dynamic.

1.12.4 Environment Manager

One can visualize the need for yet another middleware component—an *environment manager*—that would manage a set of dynamic environmental variables in response to signals detected from active agents within the effective range in the nomad's local environment. Work with active badges (Want et al. 1992) already indicates a strong need for adapting the behavior of various applications in response to the presence (or absence) of active environmental agents, and in accordance with the state of those agents. For instance, in a conference room a nomadic user would most likely wish for paging applications to operate differently than if the user were alone. This adaptation on the basis of external, non-link-related environmental factors represents a new challenge for nomadic-aware applications that has only begun to be addressed.

1.13 Proxies versus Mobile-aware Applications

Nomadic users will create a new need for proxy services that can help perform appropriate translations or other support services for mobile computers (Samara et al. 1997). For instance, a mobile computer that most easily understands a particular kind of video encoding may still wish to receive multicasts from sources of video data that use different encodings. In particular, certain hardware platforms accelerate the display of video data encoded in particular formats (Amir, McCanne, and Zhang 1995), and some compression algorithms offer much higher and effective bandwidths if utilized correctly in the hardware. Computers that do not employ compatible hardware may well wish to avoid the transmission of video data in the wrong compression format or encoding.

Alternatively, proxies can be useful to perform authentication for mobile computers, which are sometimes quite performance limited. Today's software encryption techniques, to achieve the cryptographic strength needed to protect digital commercial transactions, may require a computational speed unavailable in the low-power devices characterizing *personal digital assistants* (PDAs), which are designed for simple appointment management, expense accounting, and other pocket calendar tasks for which efficient battery power management is essential.

Another example of the power of proxy agents may be seen with the proposed *intelligent agents* (e.g., Kraster 1995) that may roam the World Wide Web according to a schedule mostly independent of the actions of the nomadic user. When the nomadic user chooses to contact the intelligent agent, or when the intelligent agent can establish connectivity to indicate the need for a transaction, the nomad will then acquire and process any buffered (stored) data that may have become available. Proxy agents may also be able to store buffered data for mobile users in case data is lost during transmission over a wireless medium.

For all of these reasons—special hardware capabilities, additional processing power, availability of proprietary software, overcoming connectivity problems, and buffering data to correct errors—proxy services and intelligent agents are likely to be designed and made available for nomadic users of mobile computers.

It should be noted that the widespread use of proxies to support nomadic computer users may introduce a new kind of rigidity in the overall network architecture. With proxies, a mobile node always has to remain compatible with the software running on the proxy service. Since a proxy server is likely to be assisting a large and diverse population of mobile clients, it seems unlikely that the server and the clients could all be updated together. Thus, the presence of proxies adds to the number of software components that need upgrades, and could make it more awkward to update software on the mobile computers themselves. Perhaps the proxy server will be maintained efficiently enough so that many different software versions of the same service can be invoked depending on the needs of particular clients. This effect of proxy service should be watched carefully and compared against the possible benefits of allowing the mobile node to operate independently of any proxy. Use of SLP (Section 1.12.1) to locate proxies with special features may improve the chances for their widespread development.

Lastly, note that the forwarding of datagrams through a proxy server before they are delivered to a mobile node represents another routing irregularity, and another possible point of failure in a data transaction. These disadvantages will, hopefully, be more than compensated for by the increased computing power of the proxy service.

1.14 Summary

This chapter explained the need for mobile networking to support the requirements of today's new class of Internet users as they roam about with sophisticated laptop computers and digital wireless data communication devices. The exponential growth of the Internet and the inexorable increase in native computing power of laptop computers have brought the need for mobile networking into sharp focus. As network services proliferate and become available ubiquitously, every network device will take advantage of mobile networking technology to offer maximum flexibility to the customers needing those devices.

The problem solved by Mobile IP is the use of IP addresses for both identifying an IP node and selecting the route to that node. An abstract model was shown that clarifies the need for manipulating the care-of address, which provides the level of addressing indirection needed for routing to the mobile node, while still allowing the mobile node to use its home address, by which it is identified.

Mobile IP, while useful as a general technique to solve a number of problems caused by mobility, nevertheless does not solve all the problems. In fact, some problems that are obvious while roaming with a mobile computer were previously unrecognized, especially those having to do with reconfiguring network access to resources and dealing with variable network connections. New features will be demanded for the further simplification of the nomadic computer user's location-independent interaction with the Internet and its information space.

CHAPTER TWO

Mobile IP Overview

This chapter discusses the main concepts and operations of the IETF Mobile IP protocol. The basic protocol procedures fall into the following areas:

- Advertisement
- Registration
- Tunneling

The functional entities performing these procedures are illustrated, along with the typical interactions among them. Two different ways to acquire care-of addresses are described. Lastly, a brief introduction to the IETF, which hosts the Mobile IP Working Group, is presented to establish an important context that clarifies the procedure by which Mobile IP has ultimately been promoted as an Internet standard protocol.

2.1 What Is Mobile IP?

Mobile IP is a modification to IP that allows nodes to continue to receive datagrams no matter where they happen to be attached to the Internet. It involves some additional control messages that allow the IP nodes involved to manage their IP routing tables reliably. Scalability has been a dominant design factor during the development of Mobile IP, because in the future a high percentage of the nodes attached to the Internet will be capable of mobility.

As explained in the last chapter, IP assumes that a node's network address uniquely identifies the node's point of attachment to the Internet. Therefore, a node must be located on the network indicated by its IP address to receive datagrams destined to it; otherwise, datagrams destined to the node would be undeliverable. Without Mobile IP, one of the two following mechanisms typically must be employed for a node to change its point of attachment without losing its ability to communicate:

1. The node must change its IP address whenever it changes its point of attachment.

2. Host-specific routes must be propagated throughout the relevant portion of the Internet routing infrastructure.

Both of these alternatives are plainly unacceptable in the general case. The first makes it impossible for a node to maintain transport and higher layer connections when the node changes location. The second has obvious and severe scaling problems that are especially relevant considering the explosive growth in sales of notebook (mobile) computers.

Mobile IP was devised to meet the following goals for mobile nodes that *move* (that is, change their point of attachment to the Internet) more frequently than once per second. Even so, the protocol is likely to work quite well until the frequency of movement of the mobile node begins to approach the round-trip time for Mobile IP protocol control messages. The following five characteristics should be considered baseline requirements to be satisfied by any candidate for a Mobile IP protocol:

1. A mobile node must be able to communicate with other nodes after changing its link-layer point of attachment to the Internet, yet without changing its IP address.

2. A mobile node must be able to communicate with other nodes that do not implement Mobile IP. No protocol enhancements are required in hosts or routers unless they are performing the functions of one or more of the new architectural entities introduced in Section 2.2.

3. All messages used to transmit information to another node about the location of a mobile node must be *authenticated* to protect against remote redirection attacks.

4. The link by which a mobile node is directly attached to the Internet may often be a wireless link. This link may thus have a substantially lower bandwidth and higher error rate than traditional wired networks. Moreover, mobile nodes are likely to be battery powered, and minimizing power consumption is important. Therefore, the number of administrative messages sent over the link by which a mobile node is directly attached to the Internet should be minimized, and the size of these messages should be kept as small as possible.

5. Mobile IP must place no additional constraints on the assignment of IP addresses. That is, a mobile node can be assigned an IP address by the organization that owns the machine, as is done with any other protocol engine administered by that organization. In particular, the address does not have to belong to any globally constrained range of addresses.

Mobile IP is intended to enable nodes to move from one IP subnet to another. It is just as suitable for mobility across heterogeneous media as it is for mobility across homogeneous media. That is, Mobile IP facilitates node movement from one Ethernet segment to another as well as accommodates node movement from an Ethernet segment to a wireless LAN, as long as the mobile node's IP address remains the same after such a movement.

One can think of Mobile IP as solving the *macro* mobility management problem. As long as node movement does not occur between points of attachment on different IP subnets, link-layer mechanisms for mobility (that is, link-layer handoff) may offer alternative solutions with different engineering trade-offs compared with Mobile IP. For instance, the IEEE has recently standardized such an alternative solution for wireless mobility in their IEEE 802.11 Committee (1994).

Note that Mobile IP does not place any requirement on the layer-2 (link-layer) operation of a mobile node. This means that it is equally suitable to manage the mobility of a node no matter what the physical nature of the node's link to the Internet. Mobile IP works as well for nodes moving from one Ethernet to another as it does for nodes moving from one base station to another with a radio connection, as long as the link itself is established equally well. Some layer-2 protocols handle node mobility in restricted ways. Mobile IP can still work with those layer-2 protocols to provide wider area mobility, since it is difficult for layer-2 protocols to provide mobility across IP subnets.

2.2 Terminology

Mobile IP introduces the following new functional entities:

Mobile node—A mobile node is a host or router that changes its point of attachment from one network or subnetwork to another. A mobile node may change its location without changing its IP address. It may continue to communicate with other Internet nodes at any location using its (constant) IP address, assuming link-layer connectivity to a point of attachment is available.

Home agent—A home agent is a router on a mobile node's home network that *tunnels* datagrams for delivery to the mobile node when it is away from home and maintains current location information for the mobile node.

Foreign agent—A foreign agent is a router on a mobile node's *visited network* that provides routing services to the mobile node while registered. The foreign agent detunnels and delivers datagrams to the mobile node that were tunneled by the mobile node's home agent. The foreign agent may always be selected as a default router by registered mobile nodes.

A mobile node is given a long-term IP address on a home network. This home address is treated administratively just like a permanent IP address provided to a stationary host. When away from its home network, a care-of address is associated with the mobile node and reflects the mobile node's current point of attachment.

The mobile node uses its home address as the source address of all IP datagrams that it sends, except during registration if it happens to acquire another IP address (as described in Section 4.6.1).

Looking back at Figure 1.6, recall that the home agent should be thought of as the combination of an LD for the mobile node's care-of address and a readdressing/redirecting function *f* for packets that arrive at the home network. Conversely, the foreign agent should be considered to be the inverse readdressing function *g* to restore the datagram to its original form after manipulation by the home agent, followed by delivery to the mobile node.

As a matter of adherence to the protocol specification, in this book the phrase *is required to* means that the implementor is required to abide by the stated condition to be considered in compliance. The word *should*, on the other hand, indicates that some implementations may omit the suggested operation or condition; however, this should only be done in particular cases when the designer of the implementation is well aware of all the implications of the omission. The Mobile IP protocol was specified with the expectation that implementations would in fact support all the features indicated by *should*.

On the negative side, the phrase *not allowed* means that an implementation that permits the indicated condition or operation does *not* comply with the protocol specification. The phrase *should not* means that any designer should be very wary of allowing the operation or condition under consideration. Lastly, the word *may* usually means that the specified operation or condition is purely optional and is allowed but not required. All implementation entities are required to handle messages requesting optional features without malfunctioning, even if the entities cannot support the option features.

2.3 Protocol Overview

Mobile IP is, in essence, a way of doing three relatively separate functions:

1. *Agent discovery*—Home agents and foreign agents may advertise their availability on each link for which they provide service. A newly arrived mobile node can send a solicitation on the link to learn if any prospective agents are present.

2. *Registration*—When the mobile node is away from home, it registers its care-of address with its home agent. Depending on its method of attachment, the mobile node will register either directly with its home agent or through a foreign agent, which forwards the registration to the home agent.

3. *Tunneling*—In order for datagrams to be delivered to the mobile node when it is away from home, the home agent has to *tunnel* the datagrams to the care-of address.

When away from home, Mobile IP uses protocol tunneling to hide a mobile node's home address from intervening routers between its home network and its current location. The tunnel terminates at the mobile node's care-of address. The care-of address must be an address to which datagrams can be delivered via conventional IP routing. At the care-of address, the original datagram is removed from the tunnel and delivered to the mobile node.

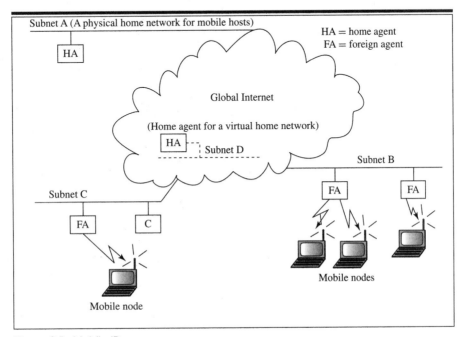

Figure 2.1 Mobile IP.

An overall illustration of the entities of Mobile IP and several home and *foreign networks* is shown in Figure 2.1. In the diagram there are two foreign networks, B and C, with foreign agents; two home networks, A and D, with home agents; and mobile nodes that are attached to the various foreign networks by way of radio and infrared attachments. The tunnels go from the home agents, across the global Internet, and finally arrive at the foreign agents for final delivery.

Mobile IP provides two ways to acquire a care-of address:

1. A foreign agent care-of address is a care-of address provided by a foreign agent through its *agent advertisement* messages. In this case the care-of address is an IP address of the foreign agent. In this mode, the foreign agent is the endpoint of the tunnel and, on receiving tunneled datagrams, decapsulates them and delivers the inner datagram to the mobile node. This mode of acquisition is

advantageous because it allows many mobile nodes to share the same care-of address and therefore does not place unnecessary demands on the already limited Internet Protocol version 4 (*IPv4*) address space.

2. A colocated care-of address is a care-of address acquired by the mobile node as a local IP address through some external means, which the mobile node then associates with one of its own network interfaces. The address may be dynamically acquired as a temporary address by the mobile node, such as through DHCP (Droms 1993), or it may be owned by the mobile node as a long-term address for its use only while visiting some foreign network. For instance, a mobile node may use its CDPD (CDPD Consortium 1993) address as a care-of address while it is within range of the CDPD cellular telephone network. When using a colocated care-of address, the mobile node serves as the end-point of the tunnel and performs decapsulation of the datagrams tunneled to it. An additional advantage of a colocated address for mobile nodes that are equipped to use the address in this fashion is that they can be used for connections that are not long lived and thus will never need the services of any home agent.

With these operations in mind, a rough outline of the operation of the Mobile IP protocol follows:

1. *Mobility agents* (that is, foreign agents and home agents) advertise their presence via agent advertisement messages (Section 3.1). A mobile node may optionally solicit an agent advertisement message from any local mobility agents by using an agent solicitation message.

2. A mobile node receives an agent advertisement and determines whether it is on its home network or a foreign network.

3. When the mobile node detects that it is located on its home network, it operates without mobility services. If returning to its home network from being registered elsewhere, the mobile node deregisters with its home agent through a variation of the normal registration process.

4. When a mobile node detects that it has moved to a foreign network, it obtains a care-of address on the foreign network. The care-of address can either be a foreign agent care-of address or a colocated care-of address.

5. The mobile node, operating away from home, then registers its new care-of address with its home agent through the exchange of a registration request and registration reply message, possibly by way of a foreign agent (Sections 4.3, 4.4).

6. Datagrams sent to the mobile node's home address are intercepted by its home agent, tunneled by the home agent to the mobile node's care-of address, received

at the tunnel endpoint (either at a foreign agent or at the mobile node itself), and finally delivered to the mobile node (Chapter 5, Section 5.9.3).

7. In the reverse direction, datagrams sent by the mobile node may be delivered to their destination using standard IP routing mechanisms, without necessarily passing through the home agent.

Using a colocated care-of address has the advantage of allowing a mobile node to function without a foreign agent; for example, in networks that deploy DHCP or some other means of acquiring an IP address. It does, however, place an additional burden on the IPv4 address space because it requires a pool of addresses within the foreign network to be made available to visiting mobile nodes. There aren't any widely available means to maintain pools of addresses efficiently for each subnet that mobile nodes may visit.

It is important to understand the distinction between the care-of address and the foreign agent functions. The care-of address is simply the endpoint of a tunnel. It might indeed be an address of a foreign agent (a foreign agent care-of address), but it also might be an address that is temporarily acquired by the mobile node (a colocated care-of address). A foreign agent, on the other hand, is a mobility agent that provides services to mobile nodes.

It is the job of every home agent to attract and intercept datagrams that are destined to the home address of any of its registered mobile nodes. Using the *proxy ARP* (Address Resolution Protocol) and *gratuitous ARP* mechanisms described in Section 5.13, this requirement can be satisfied if the home agent has a network interface on the link indicated by the mobile node's home address. However, Mobile IP does not make any requirements in this regard. Other placements of the home agent relative to the mobile node's home location are possible, using other mechanisms for intercepting datagrams destined to the mobile node's home address. Three obvious candidates for placement of the home agent on the home network are illustrated in Figure 2.2, as follows:

A = a home agent as a separate system on the home network,

B = a home agent included with a router to the home network, and

C = a virtual home network.

Similarly, a mobile node and a prospective or current foreign agent must be able to exchange datagrams without relying on standard IP routing mechanisms; that is, those mechanisms that make forwarding decisions based on the network prefix of the destination address in the IP header. This requirement can be satisfied if the

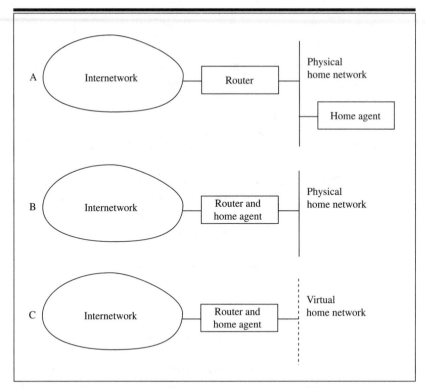

Figure 2.2 Ways to put a home agent on a home network.

foreign agent and the visiting mobile node have an interface on the same link. In this case, the mobile node and the foreign agent simply bypass their normal IP routing mechanism when sending datagrams to each other, addressing the underlying link-layer packets to their respective *link-layer addresses*. As before, Mobile IP allows any placement of the foreign agent relative to the mobile node, using other mechanisms to exchange datagrams between these nodes, as long as the basic protocol is followed.

Of course, if a mobile node is using a colocated care-of address (as described at the beginning of this section), the mobile node is required to be located on the link identified by the network prefix of this care-of address. Otherwise, datagrams destined to the care-of address would be undeliverable.

Figure 2.3 illustrates the routing of datagrams to and from a mobile node away from home, once the mobile node has registered with its home agent. In this figure the mobile node is using a foreign agent care-of address as follows:

1. A datagram to the mobile node arrives on the home network via standard IP routing.

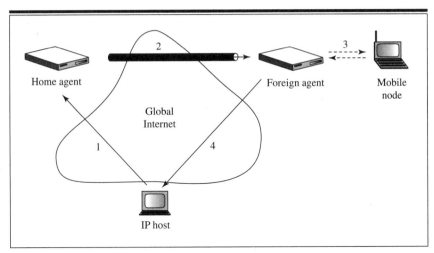

Figure 2.3 Mobile IP datagram flow.

2. The datagram is intercepted by the home agent and is tunneled to the care-of address.

3. The datagram is detunneled and delivered to the mobile node.

4. For datagrams sent by the mobile node, standard IP routing delivers each datagram to its destination. In Figure 2.3, the foreign agent is the mobile node's default router.

2.4 Message Format and Protocol Extensibility

To handle registration, Mobile IP defines a set of new control messages sent with UDP (Postel 1980) using well-known port number 434. Currently, the following two message types are defined:

  1   Registration request

  3   Registration reply

Up-to-date values for the message types for Mobile IP control messages are specified in the most recent *Assigned Numbers* (Reynolds and Postel 1994).

For agent discovery, Mobile IP modifies the existing router advertisement and router solicitation messages defined for ICMP router discovery (Deering 1991), as described in Section 3.3.

Mobile IP defines a general extension mechanism to allow optional information to be carried by Mobile IP control messages or by ICMP router discovery messages. Each of these extensions (with one exception, the *pad extension*) is encoded in what is conventionally called the *type-length-value* (*TLV*) format shown in Figure 2.4, where the *value* is the data following the *length*.

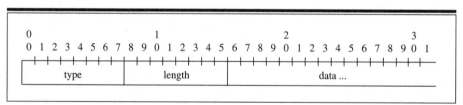

Figure 2.4 The TLV extension format.

The *type* indicates the particular type of extension. The *length* of the extension, counted in bytes—or, more technically in octels, which are groups of 8 bits—does not include the type and length bytes, and may be zero or greater. The format of the data field is determined by the type and length fields. Extensions allow variable amounts of information to be carried within each message. The end of the list of extensions is indicated by the total length of the IP datagram.

Two separately maintained sets of numbering spaces, from which extension type values are allocated, are used in Mobile IP. The first set consists of those extensions that may appear in Mobile IP control messages (those sent to and from UDP port number 434). Currently, the following types are defined for extensions appearing in Mobile IP registration messages:

32   Mobile—home authentication

33   Mobile—foreign authentication

34   Foreign—home authentication

The second set consists of those extensions that may appear in ICMP router discovery messages. Currently, Mobile IP defines the following types for such extensions:

0   One-byte padding (encoded with no length or data field)

16   Mobility agent advertisement

19   Prefix length

Each individual extension is described in detail later in a separate section. Up-to-date values for these extension type numbers are specified in the most recent list of *Assigned Numbers* (Reynolds and Postel 1994) from the Internet Assigned Numbers Authority (*IANA*).

Due to the basically independent nature of these sets of extensions, it is conceivable that two unrelated extensions that are defined at a later date could have identical type values. One of the extensions could be used only in Mobile IP control messages and the other only in ICMP router discovery messages.

The value of the extension number is important when trying to determine the correct disposition of unrecognized extensions. When an extension numbered in either of these sets within the range 0 through 127 is encountered but not recognized, the message containing that extension is required to be silently discarded. When an extension numbered in the range 128 through 255 is encountered but unrecognized, that particular extension is ignored, but the rest of the extensions and message data are still required to be processed. The length field of the extension is used to skip the data field in searching for the next extension.

2.5 Role of the IETF

Mobile IP has been standardized through the efforts of the Mobile IP Working Group organized under the jurisdiction of the IETF. The IETF is a collection of approximately 70 working groups, according to the last count. The working groups themselves are organized into a number of areas, and each area is supervised by an area director. The groups are created by petition, presented to the area director, often after a birds of a feather (*BOF*) session that gauges community interest. Each working group is also supervised by one or more working group chairpersons, and often a document editor is selected by the working group chair to facilitate the production of any Internet Drafts that are needed. The draft documents are intended to be working documents, subject to change at any time, and subject to expiration after being made available for six months in a collection of repositories (called *shadow directories*) maintained around the world. The documents are available free of charge and can be obtained by using a Web browser pointed at http://www.ietf.org, or by *anonymous File Transfer Protocol* (FTP) from the repositories, conventionally in a file system subdirectory named *internet-drafts*. The currently available shadow directories include

- ftp.is.co.za (Africa)

- nic.nordu.net (North Europe)

- ftp.nis.garr.it (South Europe)

- munnari.oz.au (Pacific Rim)

- ds.internic.net (US East Coast)

- ftp.isi.edu (US West Coast)

The history of the IETF helps to explain the evolution and final status of Mobile IP. The original working group was created by researchers Steve Deering (then with Xerox Palo Alto Research Center), and Chip Maguire, John Ioannides, and Dan Duchamp (then of Columbia University). The Columbia protocol described in Chapter 1 was already in the process of being finalized when researchers from other institutions began to show a high degree of interest in the working group. In particular, I had been working on an alternative design that concentrated the LD in a single entity (which has since evolved into the home agent). Other efforts, notably the Mobile Host Routing Protocol (*MHRP*) (Johnson 1994) and the Virtual Internet Protocol (*VIP*) (Teraoka and Tokoro 1993) by Sony were introduced and debated intensely. At some point, suitable terminology had finally come into use, but seemingly endless discussions ensued with little clear indication of which operations might end up in a deployable protocol. After orders from the area director and working group cochairs, proponents of various approaches began to find consensus and the working group at large determined that the deployment of Mobile IP should probably proceed in at least two stages. The first deployment would be the *base protocol*, which allows for operation with no changes to existing Internet computers, but which suffers from problems with suboptimal routing (remedied in Chapter 6). Later deployment questions were at that time thought to center around finding the best ways to modify existing computers to find better routes for mobile nodes. Now, however, even though the base protocol is standardized, deployment questions are centering around *firewall issues* (Section 7.1) instead of route optimization.

2.6 Summary

Mobile IP uses a straightforward protocol to supply the needed routing information to a mobile node's home agent so that it can do the work needed to redirect traffic from the home network to the care-of address. The protocol relies on the foreign agent to advertise its presence, and to relay registration messages back and forth between the mobile node and the home agent. The advertisements fit within extensions to the ICMP Router Advertisement protocol, and the registration messages are carried in UDP packets with retransmission specifications, avoiding some of the complexity of TCP.

The IETF Mobile IP Working Group has shepherded the protocol through the IETF processes until it is now finally a Proposed Standard. Future and continued work on the Mobile IP standard will proceed within the working group, and can be expected to define and refine other extensions to the basic ICMP messages and UDP registration messages that make up the base protocol. Some of the proposed extensions that are not yet standard are described later in this book.

CHAPTER THREE

Advertisement

This chapter presents the detailed message formats used by mobile computers and mobility agents to discover each other's presence. These messages are communicated by way of ICMP, according to the original protocol specification for *router discovery*. The router discovery protocol is, therefore, described in some detail so that this book is relatively self-contained. The extra information required to initiate the Mobile IP registration procedures is contained in message extensions to the Router Advertisement message, which is then called an *agent advertisement* message.

Agent discovery is the method by which a mobile node (1) determines whether it is currently connected to its home network or to a foreign network and (2) detects when it has moved from one network to another. This chapter describes the message formats and procedures by which mobile nodes, foreign agents, and home agents cooperate to realize agent discovery. The methods specified in this chapter also allow the mobile node to determine the care-of addresses offered by each foreign agent on any network to which it might connect.

3.1 Agent Solicitation and Discovery Mechanisms

An agent advertisement is formed by including a mobility agent advertisement extension (Section 3.3) in an ICMP Router Advertisement message (Section 3.2). An *agent solicitation message* is very similar in format to an ICMP router solicitation.

Agent advertisement and solicitation may not be necessary for link layers that already provide this functionality. The method by which mobile nodes establish link-layer connections with prospective agents can be different for each kind of link-layer. For instance, with Ethernet, nodes obey the proper framing and timing specification and obtain the appropriate IEEE 802.2 address for the destination (which can be handled by higher layers) (Metcalfe and Boggs 1976). For the typical wireless link layer, however, there are other considerations. These may include getting an appropriate radio channel, avoiding the *hidden terminal problem* (Bantz and Bauchot 1994) by using a reservation-based media access control (*MAC*) layer protocol (for instance, MACAW (Bharghavan et al 1994)), or any of several other protocol problems that are specific to particular media. The procedures described in this chapter assume that such link-layer connectivity has already been established. Refer to other publications for details on how to establish the link (IEEE 802.11 Committee 1997).

No authentication is required for agent advertisement and agent solicitation messages. As far as Mobile IP is concerned, any agent that advertises its service and performs the needed functions to carry out the service is a bona fide mobility agent. This essentially allows any imposter to pretend to be a foreign agent, and the Mobile IP protocol has been designed with this fact in mind. Impersonating a home agent is typically more difficult given that the home agent and mobile node share a private *mobility security association*.

3.2 Router Discovery Protocol

Mobile IP extends ICMP router discovery as its primary mechanism for agent discovery. Therefore, it is important to understand the relevant details of ICMP router discovery, and a short explanation is included here for that purpose. The following material is taken from RFC 1256 (Deering 1991).

Hosts on a link typically must use the services of a directly attached router to deliver their datagrams to hosts on any other link. In fact, it is quite often the case that hosts send all such datagram traffic through a single router—the *default router*.

Determining the IP addresses of the locally attached router or routers was historically a matter for manual configuration. Later, efficient administrators typically ran locally developed programs to set up the router addresses as part of the machine configuration when the operating system was first loaded. Both of these strategies (especially the former) are likely to offer little help for the problems caused by reconfiguration, when a computer is moved or (less often) when a router is no longer available at the expected address.

Router discovery provides the means by which IP hosts can determine automatically the local routers' IP addresses and can monitor their continued presence. This is done by using two simple ICMP messages—one transmitted by the routers and another that may be transmitted by the hosts themselves. Since the router discovery protocol included enough features to allow Mobile IP hosts to discover foreign agents, it was used as the basis for the mobility agent discovery mechanisms described in this chapter. At the time, it seemed reasonable to avoid the creation of new protocols when previously existing protocols might serve just as well. If this decision were revisited today it would almost certainly be reversed, and a new protocol would be created just for the purposes of Mobile IP (see Section 3.7).

More recently it has become feasible to configure IP hosts with router addresses by using DHCP. However, DHCP is quite a large protocol, and it was (wisely) determined that Mobile IP should not rely on the existence of another more complicated protocol, especially one not widely available at the time the working group started.

It should be noted that the router discovery messages do not constitute a routing protocol. They enable hosts to discover the existence of neighboring routers, but not which router is best used to reach a particular destination. If a host chooses a poor first-hop router for a particular destination, it should receive an ICMP redirect from that router, which identifies a better one.

3.2.1 Router Discovery ICMP Message

Typically, a router implementing RFC 1256 will periodically multicast or broadcast a router advertisement to those links to which it is connected and to which it wishes to offer routing services. Then, each host equipped to understand the protocol will listen for the advertisements and be able to select a router address (typically only one is necessary) to use as a default router. The speed with which such hosts can choose a default router is then determined by the advertisement period. If a host fails to detect several consecutive Router Advertisements, the host can infer that the router is no longer offering service and can try to obtain service from a new router by listening for new advertisements.

One feature of these Router Advertisements is that the routers are allowed to denote, by setting *preference levels*, how eager they are to have new hosts using their services. A route that is advertised with a high preference level should be selected instead of another route that is advertised with a low preference level.

The message format for the Router Advertisement message is shown in Figure 3.1. The fields have the following meanings:

Type	9
Code	0
Checksum	the 16-bit one's complement of the one's complement sum of the ICMP message, starting with the ICMP type. To compute the checksum, the checksum field is set to 0.
Num addrs	the number of router addresses advertised in this message
Addr entry size	the number of 32-bit words of information for each router address (2, in the version of the protocol described here)
Lifetime	the maximum number of seconds that the router addresses may be considered valid
Router Address(i)	i = 1...num addrs, the sending router's IP addresses on the interface from which this message is sent

Preference level(i)	i = 1...Num Addrs, the preferability of each correspond- ing router address as a default router address relative to other router addresses on the same subnet. The value is a signed, two's complement value; higher values are more preferable.

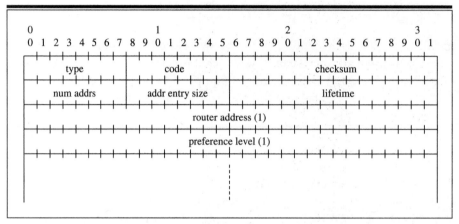

Figure 3.1   Router Advertisements (from RFC 1256).

Since this is an ICMP message, it is preceded by an IP header. In the IP header, the fields are set to mostly natural values. If the destination address is chosen to be the multicast address 224.0.0.1 (the all-systems multicast address), then the *TTL* (time to live) field is required to be set to 1.

3.2.2 Router Solicitation ICMP Message

When an IP host needs timely information about local default routers, it can multicast or broadcast a *router solicitation* message. Any routers in the vicinity that obey the router discovery protocol will respond with a unicast router advertisement message sent directly to the soliciting host. After receiving the advertisement, the host then responds just as if the advertisement were unsolicited and received at the broadcast or multicast address.

In Figure 3.2, the fields have the following meanings:

Type	10
Code	0

Checksum   The 16-bit one's complement of the one's complement sum of the ICMP message, starting with the ICMP type. To compute the checksum, the checksum field is set to 0.

Reserved   Sent as 0; ignored on reception.

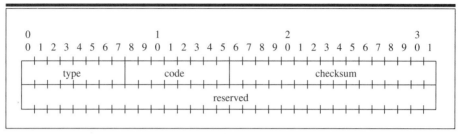

Figure 3.2 Router solicitations (from RFC 1256).

A host sending a solicitation is required to set the TTL field to 1. The only permissible values for the IP destination are the all-routers multicast address, 224.0.0.2, or the limited-broadcast address, 255.255.255.255.

3.3 Agent Advertisement

An agent advertisement is an ICMP Router Advertisement (as described in Section 3.2.2) that has been extended also to carry mobility agent advertisement extension (Section 3.3.1). A mobility agent transmits agent advertisements to advertise its services on a link. Mobile nodes use these advertisements to determine their current point of attachment to the Internet. The advertisement may also carry other extensions, notably the prefix-length extension (Section 3.3.2), one-byte padding extension (Section 3.3.3), or other extensions that might be defined in the future. Unquestionably the most important extension is the mobility agent extension. Within an agent advertisement message, ICMP Router Advertisements include the following link-layer, IP, and ICMP header fields:

- **Link-layer fields**

    Destination address   The link-layer destination address of a unicast agent advertisement is required to be the same as the source link-layer address of the agent solicitation that prompted the advertisement.

- **IP fields**

    TTL   The TTL for all agent advertisements is required to be set to 1.

Destination address	As specified for ICMP router discovery the IP destination address of an agent advertisement is required to be either the all-systems-on-this-link multicast address (224.0.0.1)(Deering 1989) or the limited-broadcast address (255.255.255.255). The subnet-directed broadcast address of the form <prefix>.<-1> cannot be used because mobile nodes will not generally know the prefix of the foreign network.

- **ICMP Fields**

Type	9
Code	The code field of the agent advertisement is interpreted as follows:

	0	The mobility agent handles common traffic; that is, it acts as a router for IP datagrams not necessarily related to mobile nodes.
	16	The mobility agent does not route common traffic. However, all foreign agents are required to (at least) forward (possibly to their default router) any datagrams received from a registered mobile node (Section 5.9.2).

Lifetime	The lifetime is the maximum length of time that the advertisement is considered valid in the absence of further advertisements.
Router addresses	The usual router addresses present in any Router Advertisement may also appear in this portion of the agent advertisement (Section 3.5.1).
Num addrs	Num addrs is the number of router addresses advertised in the message.

Note that in an agent advertisement message, the number of router addresses specified in the ICMP Router Advertisement portion of the message may be set to zero. See Section 3.5.1 for details.

If sent periodically, the nominal interval at which agent advertisements are sent should be one third of the advertisement lifetime given in the ICMP header. This allows a mobile node to miss three successive advertisements before deleting the agent from its list of valid agents. The actual transmission time for each advertisement should be slightly randomized (Deering 1991) to avoid synchronization and subsequent collisions with agent advertisements sent by other agents, or with

Router Advertisements sent by other routers. Note that this field has no relation to the registration lifetime field within the mobility agent advertisement extension defined in the next section.

3.3.1 Mobility Agent Advertisement Extension

The mobility agent advertisement extension, illustrated in Figure 3.3, follows the ICMP Router Advertisement fields. It indicates that an ICMP router advertisement message is actually an agent advertisement being sent by a mobility agent.

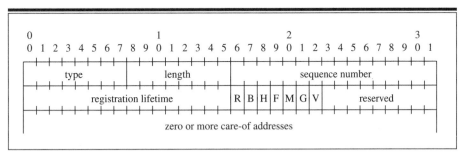

Figure 3.3 Mobility agent advertisement extension.

The individual fields of the mobility agent advertisement extension are defined as follows, with the bit fields denoted by their single-letter name:

Type	16
Length	(6 + 4*N), where N is the number of care-of addresses advertised
Sequence number	The count of agent advertisement messages sent since the agent was initialized (Section 3.5.2)
Registration lifetime	The longest lifetime (measured in seconds) that this agent is willing to accept in any registration request; A value of 65,535 indicates infinity
R	Registration required. Registration with this foreign agent (or another foreign agent on this link) is required rather than using a colocated care-of address.
B	Busy. If this bit is set, the foreign agent will not accept registrations from additional mobile nodes.
H	Home agent. If this bit is set, this agent offers service as a home agent on the link on which the agent advertisement message is sent.

F	Foreign agent. This agent offers service as a foreign agent on the link on which the agent advertisement message is sent.
M	Minimal encapsulation. This agent implements receiving tunneled datagrams that use minimal encapsulation (Section 5.3).
G	Generic record encapsulation (GRE). This agent implements receiving tunneled datagrams that use GRE (Section 5.4).
V	Van Jacobson header compression. This agent supports use of Van Jacobson header compression (Jacobson 1990) over this link with any registered mobile node.
Reserved	Sent as 0; ignored on reception
Care-of addresses	The advertised foreign agent care-of addresses provided by this foreign agent. An agent advertisement is required to include at least one care-of address if the F bit is set. The number of care-of addresses present is determined by the length of the extension.

A home agent must be prepared to serve its mobile nodes. In other words, the home agent should never claim to be too busy to serve the mobile nodes on its home network. To avoid overload, it is possible to configure mobile nodes and home agents so that there are multiple home agents on a home network, and so that the mobile nodes are divided into disjointed populations that report to the different home agents. Even in this case, however, an advertisement from any of the home agents on the same home network will suffice to inform the mobile node that it is indeed attached to its home network.

A foreign agent may at times be too busy to serve additional mobile nodes; even so, it must continue to send agent advertisements so that any mobile nodes already registered with it will know that they have not moved out of range of the foreign agent and that the foreign agent has not failed. A foreign agent may indicate that it is too busy to allow new mobile nodes to register with it, by setting the B bit in its agent advertisements. An agent advertisement message is not allowed to have the B bit set if the F bit is not also set. Either the F bit or the H bit is required to be set in any agent advertisement message.

When a foreign agent wishes to require registration even from those mobile nodes that have acquired a colocated care-of address, it sets the R bit to one. Because this bit applies only to foreign agents, an agent is not allowed to set the R bit to 1 unless the F bit is also set to 1.

Note that the registration lifetime field has no relation to the advertisement lifetime field within the ICMP router advertisement portion of the agent advertisement. The latter field specifies the length of time before which the receiving node should consider that advertisements have been lost. Note also that the maximum registration lifetime permitted by the packet format is 65,534 seconds, which is slightly more than 18 hours.

3.3.2 Prefix-length Extension

The prefix-length extension may follow the mobility agent advertisement extension. It is used to indicate the number of bits of network prefix that apply to each router address listed in the ICMP Router Advertisement portion of the agent advertisement. Note that the prefix lengths given do not apply to the care-of addresses listed in the mobility agent advertisement extension.

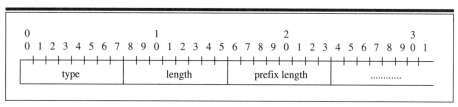

Figure 3.4 Prefix-length extension format.

The prefix-length extension is defined as shown in Figure 3.4, where

Type	19
Length	N, where N is the value of the num addrs field in the ICMP Router Advertisement portion of the agent advertisement
Prefix length	the number of leading bits that define the network number of the corresponding router address listed in the ICMP router advertisement portion of the message

The prefix length for each router address is encoded as a separate byte in the order in which the router addresses are listed in the ICMP Router Advertisement portion of the message. See Section 7.5.2 for information about how the prefix-length extension may be used by a mobile node when determining whether it has moved. There are some extremely important implementation details that must be kept in mind when using this extension; these are also detailed in Section 7.5.2.

3.3.3 One-byte Padding Extension

Some IP protocol implementations insist on padding ICMP messages to an even number of bytes. If the ICMP length of an agent advertisement is odd, this extension may be included to make the ICMP length even. Note that this extension is not intended to be a general-purpose extension to be included to word align or long align the various fields of the agent advertisement. An agent advertisement should not include more than one one-byte padding extension, and if present this extension should be the last extension in the agent advertisement.

Note that unlike other extensions used in Mobile IP, the one-byte padding extension is encoded as a single byte, with no length or data field present. The one-byte padding extension is defined in Figure 3.5, where type is set to 0 to denote one-byte padding extension.

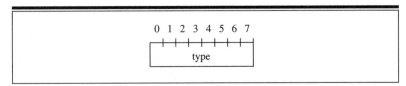

Figure 3.5 Pad extension format.

3.4 Agent Solicitation

The format of an agent solicitation is the same as an ICMP router solicitation, as shown previously in Figure 3.2. However, the way in which it is used is slightly different. For one thing, any agent solicitation used with Mobile IP is required to have the TTL field set to 1. There are other operational differences; see Section 3.6 for more details.

3.5 Mobility Agent Operation

Any mobility agent (home agent or foreign agent) that cannot be discovered by a link-layer protocol is required to send agent advertisements. An agent that can be discovered by a link-layer protocol should also implement agent advertisements so that it can respond to agent solicitations. However, the advertisements need only be sent when the site policy requires registration with the agent (that is, when the R bit is set) or as a response to a specific agent solicitation.

The same procedures, defaults, and constants are used in agent advertisement messages as specified for ICMP router discovery (Section 3.2), except for the following.

- A mobility agent is required to limit the rate at which it sends broadcast or multicast agent advertisements. A recommended maximal rate is once per second.

- A foreign agent must accept router solicitations even when the IP source address appears to reside on a different subnet than the mobility agent's interface on which the solicitation was received.

- A mobility agent may be configured to send agent advertisements only in response to an agent solicitation message.

Refer again to Figure 2.3. Since the home address owned by a mobile node is typically not able to be located on any network attached to a foreign agent, the solicitation mechanism could not possibly work if the foreign agent disallowed solicitations from an apparently off-link IP address.

If the home network is not a *virtual network*, then the home agent for any mobile node should be located on the link identified by the mobile node's home address, and agent advertisement messages sent by the home agent on this link are required to have the H bit set. In this way, mobile nodes on their own home network are able to determine that they are indeed at home. If the home agent is attached to multiple links, it transmits agent advertisements with the H bit set only on those links for which it is willing to serve as a home agent.

If the home network is a virtual network, then it has no physical realization external to the home agent itself. In this case there is no physical network link on which to send agent advertisement messages advertising the home agent. Mobile nodes on a virtual home network are always treated as being away from home.

On a particular subnet, either all mobility agents are required to include the prefix-length extension, or none of them are allowed to include this extension. Equivalently, if any mobility agents on a given subnet include the extension, then all of them are required to include it. Otherwise, one of the move detection algorithms designed for mobile nodes will not function properly (see Section 7.5.2).

3.5.1 Advertised Router Addresses

The ICMP Router Advertisement portion of the agent advertisement may contain one or more router addresses. Thus, an agent may include one of its own addresses in the advertisement. A foreign agent may discourage use of this address as a default router by setting the preference to a low value and by including the address of another router in the advertisement (with a correspondingly higher preference). Nevertheless, a foreign agent is required, in every circumstance, to be able to route datagrams it receives from registered mobile nodes (Section 5.9.2). Note that the mobile node is disallowed from broadcasting ARP packets on foreign networks; this is explained in Chapter 5, but the basic reason is to prevent the creation of ARP cache entries within other nodes on the foreign networks. ARP cache entries in other nodes will be incorrect after the mobile node moves again, and no protocol is established for the correction of such stale ARP cache entries. Without ARP it is difficult for the mobile node to discover link-layer addresses for the other routers in the advertisement, so the use of this feature is questionable at the present time.

3.5.2 Sequence Numbers and Rollover Handling

The sequence number in agent advertisements ranges from 0 to 65,535. After booting, an agent is required to use the number 0 for its first advertisement. Each subsequent advertisement is required to use the sequence number one greater, with the exception that the sequence number 65,535 is required to be followed by sequence number 256. In this way, mobile nodes can distinguish reductions in sequence numbers that result from reboots, from reductions that result in rollover of the sequence number after it attains the value 65,535. Since the mobile node can tell the difference, it does not have to register again with its home agent just because the sequence number from the foreign agent has rolled over. However, if the foreign agent reboots and thus reinitializes its sequence numbers starting from 0, then obviously the mobile node should reregister so that the foreign agent can be notified again of the mobile node's presence. It is expected that mobile nodes would never accidentally fail to detect 255 consecutive advertisements.

3.6 Agent Discovery by Mobile Nodes

Every mobile node is required to implement agent solicitations. Solicitations should only be sent in the absence of agent advertisements and when a care-of address has not been determined through a link-layer protocol or other means. The mobile node uses the same procedures, defaults, and constants for agent solicitation as specified for ICMP router solicitation messages, except that (1) the mobile node may solicit more often than once every three seconds and (2) a mobile node that is currently not connected to any foreign agent may solicit more times than MAX_SOLICITATIONS (as defined in RFC 1256). In fact, a mobile node can continue to send out solicitations indefinitely until a suitable foreign agent finally comes within range.

A mobile node is required to limit the rate at which it sends solicitations. The node may send three initial solicitations at a maximum rate of one per second while searching for an agent. After this, the solicitation rate is required to be reduced so as to limit the overhead on the local link. Subsequent solicitations are required to be sent using a binary exponential backoff mechanism, doubling the interval between consecutive solicitations up to a maximal interval. The maximal interval should be chosen appropriately based on the characteristics of the media over which the mobile node is soliciting. According to the base mobile IP specification, this maximal interval should be at least one minute between solicitations, but it seems likely that for many uses this is too infrequent.

While still searching for an agent, the mobile node is not allowed to increase the rate at which it sends solicitations unless it has received a positive indication that it has moved to a new link. After successfully registering with an agent, the mobile node should also increase the rate at which it will send solicitations when it next begins searching for a new agent with which to register. The increased solicitation rate may revert to the maximal rate, but then is required to be limited in the manner described in the previous paragraph. In all cases the recommended solicitation intervals are nominal values. Mobile nodes are expected to randomize their solicitation times around these nominal values as specified for ICMP router discovery.

Mobile nodes process agent advertisements to discover a care-of address (and a foreign agent)—an event crucial to the successful operation of Mobile IP. A mobile node can distinguish an agent advertisement message from other uses of the ICMP Router Advertisement message by examining the number of advertised addresses and the IP total length field. When the IP total length indicates that the ICMP message is longer than needed for the number of advertised addresses, the remaining data is interpreted as one or more extensions. The presence of a mobility agent advertisement extension naturally identifies the advertisement as an agent advertisement.

When multiple methods of agent discovery are in use, the mobile node should first attempt registration with agents that include mobility agent advertisement extensions in their advertisements, in preference to those discovered by other means. This preference maximizes the likelihood that the registration will be recognized, thereby minimizing the number of registration attempts. Otherwise it might be possible, for instance, to attempt registration with a wireless access point that was not offering any care-of address.

3.6.1 Registration Required

When the mobile node receives an agent advertisement with the R bit set, the mobile node should register through the foreign agent, even when the mobile node might be able to acquire its own colocated care-of address. This feature is intended to allow sites to enforce visiting policies (such as accounting), which require exchanges of authorization. The intention is to simplify matters for mobile nodes in such domains, and to eliminate one possible cause for rejection and delay.

3.6.2 Returning Home

A mobile node can detect that it has returned to its home network when it receives an agent advertisement from its own home agent. If so, it should deregister with its home agent (Section 4.3). Before attempting to deregister, the mobile node should configure its routing table appropriately for its home network (Section 5.9.1). In addition, if the home network is using ARP (Plummer 1982), the mobile node is required to follow the procedures described in Chapter 5 with regard to ARP, proxy ARP, and gratuitous ARP.

3.6.3 Sequence Numbers and Rollover Handling

If a mobile node detects two successively transmitted values of the sequence number in the agent advertisements from the foreign agent with which it is registered, the second of which is less than the first and inside the range from 0 to 255, then the mobile node should register again. Otherwise, if the second value is less than the first but is greater than or equal to 256, the mobile node should assume that the sequence number has rolled over past its maximum value (65,535), and that reregistration is not necessary (Section 3.5).

3.7 Second Thoughts on Using RFC 1256

As stated, the original motivation for using the Router Advertisement protocol with Mobile IP was to simplify development. Router Advertisement was not originally designed to handle mobile nodes, but it seemed like such a natural fit, given that the purpose was to provide a means by which a mobile computer could discover a foreign agent (called for the purposes of this discussion, its *default router*). However, the attempted reuse has had the opposite effect. In the first place, router discovery defines a collection of *configuration variables*, which any implementation has to set and use correctly. Unfortunately, there have been frequent technical debates on whether the configuration variables appropriate for general router discovery were also appropriate for discoverying mobility agents. For instance, consider the configuration variable MinAdvertisementInterval. In RFC 1256, this variable is required to be set to no less than three seconds. Such a value would render the advertisement feature almost useless for many wireless mobile nodes.

For instance, suppose a mobile node makes a cell switch. To detect the movement at the network layer (as detailed in Section 7.5), the mobile node has to hear a mobility agent advertisement from another foreign agent. If the mobile node has to wait three seconds to discover that its previous foreign agent is out of reach, an unacceptably jerky response time will be observed. Worse yet, a mobile node will not typically make a cell switch just because a single advertisement was lost. Especially with wireless communications, there is a high probability that the foreign agent is still available but that the advertisement has experienced a collision during its transmission to the communications medium. Consequently, following the stated values in RFC 1256 would typically lead to waiting at least six seconds to determine that a cell switch should occur.

The result of obeying that requirement would be that all mobility agent discovery operations would proceed by way of using solicitations. This is an undesirable result, especially since each mobile node might issue a solicitation each second, consuming bandwidth unnecessarily.

Even with solicitations, however, there are other problems involved with following the dictates of RFC 1256. For instance, there is another protocol constant (MAX_SOLICITATIONS) that limits how many times a soliciting IP host can request a Router Advertisement. In the wired world, this makes sense because there is little point to continuing to stimulate dead routers on a wire that could be supporting a great deal of routerless local traffic. Furthermore, if the solicitations are sent to the broadcast address 255.255.255.255, every other host on the network would in that case be interrupted to process a meaningless packet.

Contrast this with the case for wireless. A wireless mobile node, out of range of every foreign agent, is likely to issue solicitations indefinitely until a base station or other wireless access point becomes available. And it is less likely (although not completely unlikely) that this behavior will take away from the effectiveness of other IP hosts.

Within the Mobile IP Working Group, the issue of preferences for mobility agent discovery was among the most hotly debated topics. With the unmodified router discovery, a case (albeit weak) could be made for the use of preferences, which allow routers to be selected in a particular order. With Mobile IP a mobile node typically looks for exactly one foreign agent. Even though some commentators thought that a mobile node in the presence of multiple foreign agents should be able to select one with the highest preference, no one was ever able to describe just how the foreign agents would be able to adjust their preference levels dynamically. The ways that were suggested seemed unable to promote interoperability and avoid possible oscillatory behaviors. Moreover, even when preferences were in use, from the beginning it was prohibited for mobile nodes to move away from a foreign agent purely for the reason that it had begun to issue advertisements with lower preferences. Combined with various other perceived difficulties, these points eventually motivated the Working Group to eliminate the use of preferences entirely from the Mobile IP protocol. They have not been missed.

It might seem that foreign agents should be able to advertise the IP addresses of other routers that are attached to the same link as the mobile node. In fact, for these other routers (which are likely not to have care-of addresses) the foreign agent could, just as always, specify preferences so that the mobile node could make an informed selection. However, as detailed in Section 5.13, the mobile node is expressly forbidden to broadcast any ARP packets. Therefore, it is not clear how the mobile node could ever discover the link-layer address of any other router besides the foreign agent, and Mobile IP does not specify a method for doing so. In other words, currently it is useless for the foreign agent to advertise any other routers in its agent advertisement messages.

One additional inconvenience of using RFC 1256 has only recently surfaced. In some commercial TCP/IP product, there is no easy way for user (nonoperating system) code to issue or receive ICMP datagrams. In other words, such commercial products unfortunately do not offer a suitable API for ICMP. Since some Mobile IP products would typically be sold as nonoperating system applications to be added after the initial purchase, this restriction is a problem that has a substantial effect on the design and implementation of such mobility software.

3.8 Summary

The ICMP Router Advertisement protocol is modified to enable mobile nodes to detect Mobile IP home agents and foreign agents. The model is appropriate on one level, since the functions of home agents and foreign agents can be carried out by specialized routers. Much of the mechanism defined for ICMP Router Advertisement is, however, unnecessary for Mobile IP, and vice versa. In particular, the preferences are not used for care-of addresses, and a mobile node is prevented from putting its home address in any ARP requests used to discover link-layer addresses for other default routers besides the foreign agent. Mobile nodes may solicit for service using roughly the same procedures as defined for ICMP Router Advertisement, except the procedures are allowed to be carried out more often as necessary.

The agent advertisement extension is the most important extension defined for Mobile IP, but there is also a prefix-length extension that is useful especially with mobile nodes connected to wired networks. Mobility agents use the agent advertisement extension to make themselves detectable to mobile nodes, and foreign agents include one or more care-of addresses in the advertisement. The availability of other services is indicated by bits in the extension header, including various encapsulations and Van Jacobson header compression. The agent advertisement is also used for other proposed extensions to the basic Mobile IP protocol, some of which are described in later chapters.

This chapter also described the relevant operational procedures and rules by which ICMP messages are to be used by mobile computers and mobility agents. This lays the informational groundwork for the Mobile IP registration procedure, which forms the subject of the next chapter.

CHAPTER FOUR

Registration

Mobile IP registration provides a flexible and reliable mechanism for mobile nodes to communicate their current reachability information to their home agent. It is the method by which mobile nodes

- Request forwarding services when visiting a foreign network

- Inform their home agent of their current care-of address

- Renew a binding that is due to expire

- Deregister when they return home

Registration messages exchange the mobile node's current binding information among a mobile node, its home agent, and (possibly) a foreign agent. Registration creates or modifies a mobility binding at the home agent, associating the mobile node's home address with its care-of address for a certain length of time, called the *registration lifetime* (or usually just *lifetime* when there is no chance for confusion with the lifetime associated with the periodic arrival of an agent advertisement).

Several other optional capabilities are available through the registration procedure, which enables a mobile node to

- Discover the address of a home agent if the mobile node is not configured with this information

- Select certain alternative tunneling protocols (minimal encapsulation or GRE)

- Request the use of Van Jacobson (Jacobson 1990) header compression

- Maintain multiple simultaneous registrations so that a copy of each datagram will be tunneled to each active care-of address

- Deregister certain care-of addresses while retaining others

4.1 Registration Overview

A mobile node is required to be configured with its home address and a netmask (as described in Section 1.5.1), and a mobility security association for each home agent. In addition, a mobile node may be configured with the IP address of one or more of its home agents; otherwise, the mobile node may discover a home agent using the procedures described in Section 4.6.3.

Mobile IP has two variations of its registration procedures—one by means of a foreign agent that relays the registration to the mobile node's home agent and one without any such intermediary. The following rules determine which of these two registration procedures to use in any particular circumstance.

- If a mobile node is registering a foreign agent care-of address, the mobile node is required to register via that foreign agent.

- Under any circumstances, if a mobile node receives an agent advertisement from a foreign agent with the R bit set, the mobile node should register via a foreign agent.

- If a mobile node has returned to its home network and is deregistering with its home agent, the mobile node sends the registration addressed directly to its home agent.

- Likewise, if a mobile node is using a colocated care-of address, the mobile node naturally sends the registration addressed directly to its home agent.

Both registration procedures involve the exchange of registration request and registration reply messages (Sections 4.3 and 4.4). When registering by way of a foreign agent, the registration procedure requires the following four messages, as illustrated in Figure 4.1.

1. The mobile node sends a registration request to the prospective foreign agent to begin the registration process.

2. The foreign agent processes the registration request and then relays it to the home agent, whose address is provided by the mobile node in the registration request.

3. The home agent sends a registration reply to the foreign agent to grant or deny the request.

4. The foreign agent processes the registration reply and then relays it to the mobile node to inform it of the disposition of its request.

When the mobile node registers directly with its home agent, the registration procedure requires only the following two messages.

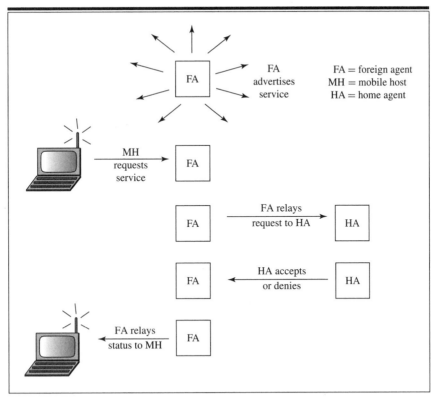

Figure 4.1 Mobile IP registration overview.

1. The mobile node sends a registration request to the home agent.

2. The home agent sends a registration reply to the mobile node that grants or denies the request.

Mobile IP registration messages use the User Datagram Protocol (UDP) (Postel 1980). The overall data structure of the registration messages is shown in Figure 4.2. A nonzero UDP checksum should be included in the header, and is then required to be checked by the recipient. UDP is specified instead of TCP for transporting registration messages, because Mobile IP does not need the windowing, renumbering, congestion control, or flow control that TCP provides. Mobile IP defines its own retransmissions to handle cases of dropped packets. Moreover, and especially in the case of wireless communications, TCP can perform poorly when packets are dropped because of noisy or lossy channels.

Registration messages contain a lifetime field that indicates the amount of time (in seconds) for which the registration information should be considered valid. A value of 0 indicates that the mobile node has been deregistered. A value of 65,535 indicates infinity.

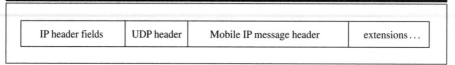

IP header fields	UDP header	Mobile IP message header	extensions . . .

Figure 4.2 General Mobile IP registration message format.

4.2 Authentication Overview

Each mobile node, foreign agent, and home agent is required to be able to support a *mobility security association* for mobile entities, indexed by their *security parameters index (SPI)* and IP address. In the case of the mobile node, the latter must be its home address. Section 4.9.1 discusses requirements for supporting authentication algorithms. Registration messages between a mobile node and its home agent are required to be authenticated with the mobile-home authentication extension (Section 4.5.1). This extension immediately follows all nonauthentication extensions, except those foreign agent-specific extensions that may be added to the message after the mobile node computes the authentication.

If a malicious agent were able to snoop on a mobile node during its registration process, it could collect all the necessary data for that registration, including the necessary authentication data. This registration data could be replayed at some future date, and since the authentication was computed by the mobile node it would still be valid. Thus, something has to change to make the registration data different each time; this change is found in the identification field of the registration request. Replay protection in Mobile IP is accomplished by using a different (fresh) value in the identification field of each registration message.

The registration reply also contains an identification value, and it is based on the identification field from the registration request message from the mobile node. The reply identification also depends on the style of replay protection used between the mobile node and its home agent. Each such security selection is associated with one entry of the mobility security association between the mobile node and the home agent. The particular selection is indicated by the SPI value in the mobile-home authentication extension. Note that SPI values 0 through 255 are reserved and cannot be used in any mobility security association. The authentication procedures are fully described in Sections 4.9.4 and 4.9.6.

4.3 Registration Request

A mobile node registers with its home agent using a registration request message so that its home agent can create or modify a *mobility binding* for that mobile node (for example, additional lifetime). The request may be relayed to the home agent by the foreign agent through which the mobile node is registering or it may be sent directly to the home agent when the mobile node is registering a colocated care-of address. Fields in the various headers of the request message are set as listed.

- **IP fields**

Source address	Typically the interface address from which the message is sent
Destination address	Typically that of the foreign agent or the home agent

- **UDP fields**

Source Port	Variable
Destination Port	434

- **Mobile IP fields**

    The UDP header is followed by the Mobile IP fields shown in Figure 4.3, with the fields defined as follows.

Type	1 (registration request)
S	Simultaneous bindings. By setting the S bit, the mobile node is requesting that the home agent retain its prior mobility bindings.
B	Broadcast datagrams. By setting the B bit, the mobile node requests that the home agent tunnel to it any broadcast datagrams that it receives on the home network, as described in Section 5.10. See also Section 7.3.1 for some more recent efforts.
D	Decapsulation. By setting the D bit, the mobile node informs the home agent that it will decapsulate datagrams that are sent to the care-of address. That is, the mobile node is using a colocated care-of address.
M	Minimal encapsulation. By setting the M bit, the mobile node requests that its home agent use minimal encapsulation (Perkins 1996c) for datagrams tunneled to the mobile node.
G	GRE encapsulation. By setting the G bit, the mobile node requests that its home agent use GRE encapsulation (Hanks et al. 1994a) for datagrams tunneled to the mobile node.
V	Van Jacobson header compression. By setting the 'V' bit, the mobile node requests that its mobility agent use Van Jacobson header compression (Jacobson 1990) over its link with the mobile node.
rsv	Reserved bits; sent as 0, ignored on reception

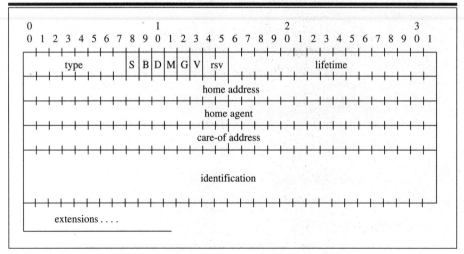

```
 0                   1                   2                   3
 0 1 2 3 4 5 6 7 8 9 0 1 2 3 4 5 6 7 8 9 0 1 2 3 4 5 6 7 8 9 0 1
+-+-+-+-+-+-+-+-+-+-+-+-+-+-+-+-+-+-+-+-+-+-+-+-+-+-+-+-+-+-+-+-+
|       type      |S|B|D|M|G|V| rsv   |            lifetime     |
+-+-+-+-+-+-+-+-+-+-+-+-+-+-+-+-+-+-+-+-+-+-+-+-+-+-+-+-+-+-+-+-+
|                          home address                        |
+-+-+-+-+-+-+-+-+-+-+-+-+-+-+-+-+-+-+-+-+-+-+-+-+-+-+-+-+-+-+-+-+
|                           home agent                         |
+-+-+-+-+-+-+-+-+-+-+-+-+-+-+-+-+-+-+-+-+-+-+-+-+-+-+-+-+-+-+-+-+
|                         care-of address                      |
+-+-+-+-+-+-+-+-+-+-+-+-+-+-+-+-+-+-+-+-+-+-+-+-+-+-+-+-+-+-+-+-+
|                                                              |
|                         identification                       |
|                                                              |
+-+-+-+-+-+-+-+-+-+-+-+-+-+-+-+-+-+-+-+-+-+-+-+-+-+-+-+-+-+-+-+-+
| extensions . . . .
+--------------------------------
```

Figure 4.3 Registration request packet format.

Lifetime	The number of seconds remaining before the registration is considered expired
Home address	The IP address of the mobile node
Home agent	The IP address of the mobile node's home agent
Care-of address	The IP address for the tunnel endpoint
Identification	A 64-bit number constructed by the mobile node and used for matching registration requests with registration replies, as well as for protecting against replay attacks of registration messages. (Sections 4.9.4 and 4.9.6)
Extensions	What follows the fixed portion of the registration request

See Sections 4.6.1 and 4.7.2 for information on the relative order in which different extensions, when present, are required to be placed in a registration request message.

4.4 Registration Reply

As described, mobility agents return a registration reply message to a mobile node that has sent a registration request message. If the mobile node is requesting service from a foreign agent, that foreign agent will receive the reply from the home agent and subsequently relay it to the mobile node. If, on the other hand, a mobile node has a colocated care-of address, it will receive the registration reply from its home agent. The reply message informs the mobile node of the status of its request and indicates the lifetime granted by the home agent, which may be smaller than the original request.

The foreign agent is not allowed to modify the lifetime selected by the mobile node in the registration request, because the lifetime is covered by the mobile-home authentication extension, which cannot be correctly computed by the foreign agent. The home agent is not allowed to increase the lifetime selected by the mobile node in the registration request, because doing so could increase it beyond the maximal registration lifetime allowed by the foreign agent. If the lifetime received in the registration reply is greater than that in the registration request, the lifetime in the request is required to be used. When the lifetime received in the registration reply is less than that in the registration request, the lifetime in the reply is required to be used.

The following lists present the fields in the IP header, the fields in the UDP header, and the fields in the registration request message itself.

- **IP fields**

Source address	Typically copied from the destination address of the registration request to which the agent is replying. (See Sections 4.7.3 and 4.8.3 for details.)
Destination address	Copied from the source address of the registration request to which the agent is replying

- **UDP fields**

Source port	variable
Destination port	Copied from the source port of the corresponding registration request (Section 4.7.1)

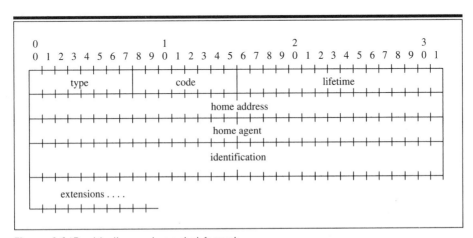

Figure 4.4 Registration reply packet format.

The UDP header is followed by the mobile IP message illustrated in Figure 4.4, with fields as follows:

Type   3 (registration reply)

Code   A value indicating the result of the registration request.

Lifetime   The duration for which a binding is valid. If the code field indicates that the registration was accepted, the lifetime field is set to the number of seconds remaining before the registration is considered expired.

Home address   The IP address of the mobile node

Home agent   The IP address of the mobile node's home agent

Identification   The 64-bit number used for matching the registration request with an eventual registration reply, and for detecting future replay attacks of the registration message

Extensions   What follows is the fixed portion of the registration reply, placed according to the rules in Sections 4.7.2 and 4.8.3.

The value of the code field often indicates some action on the part of the mobile node. Some responses to selected values are described in Section 4.6.2. Up-to-date code values are specified in the most recent *Assigned Numbers* (Reynolds and Postel 1994). If the code indicates that the registration was denied, the contents of the lifetime field are arbitrary and required to be ignored when received. The following code values are currently defined:

Registration successful

0   Registration accepted

1   Registration accepted, but simultaneous mobility bindings unsupported

Registration denied by the foreign agent

64   Reason unspecified

65   Administratively prohibited

66   Insufficient resources

67   Mobile node failed authentication

68   Home agent failed authentication

69   Requested lifetime too long

70 Poorly formed request

71 Poorly formed reply

72 Requested encapsulation unavailable

73 Requested Van Jacobson compression unavailable

80 Home network unreachable (ICMP error received)

81 Home agent host unreachable (ICMP error received)

82 Home agent port unreachable (ICMP error received)

88 Home agent unreachable (other ICMP error received)

Registration denied by the home agent

128 Reason unspecified

129 Administratively prohibited

130 Insufficient resources

131 Mobile node failed authentication

132 Foreign agent failed authentication

133 Registration identification mismatch

134 Poorly formed request

135 Too many simultaneous mobility bindings

136 Unknown home agent address

4.5 Registration Extensions

Three registration extensions are defined in the base Mobile IP protocol, all of which allow additional security measures to be applied to the registration process. The names indicate the nodes that are involved in performing the authentication, as follows:

- Mobile-home authentication extension
- Mobile-foreign authentication extension
- Foreign-home authentication extension

Each extension includes an SPI that indicates the mobility security association that contains the secret and the other information needed to compute the authenticator (also contained in the extension). Exactly one mobile-home authentication extension is required to be present in all registration requests and registration replies. The location of the extension also marks the end of the data authenticated by the mobile node. When a mobility security association exists between the mobile node and the foreign agent, they have to include exactly one mobile-foreign authentication extension in their registration messages. When a mobility security association exists between the the foreign agent and the home agent, they have to include exactly one foreign-home authentication extension in their registration messages.

4.5.1 Computing Authentication Extension Values

The default authentication algorithm uses keyed Message Digest 5 (*MD5*) (Rivest 1992) in *prefix + suffix* mode, which means that the secret is put both before and after the data to be authenticated. The result of the default computation is a 128-bit *message digest* of the registration message, computed as the MD5 checksum over the the following stream of bytes in the order indicated:

1. The shared secret defined by the mobility security association between the nodes and by the SPI value indicated in the authentication extension

2. The registration request or registration reply header fields

3. All prior extensions in their entirety

4. The type, length, and SPI included within the extension itself

5. The shared secret again

Note that the authenticator field itself, the UDP header, and the IP header are not included in the computation of the default authenticator value. See Section 4.9.1 for information about support requirements for message authentication codes, which are to be used with the various authentication extensions.

The SPI within any of the authentication extensions defines the security context that is used to compute the authenticator value and is used by the receiver to check that value. In particular, the SPI selects the authentication algorithm, mode, and secret (a shared key or appropriate public/private key pair) used in computing the authenticator. To ensure interoperability between different implementations of the Mobile IP protocol, an implementation is required to be able to associate any SPI value greater than 255 with any authentication algorithm and mode that it implements. In addition, all implementations of Mobile IP are required to implement the default authentication algorithm (keyed MD5) and *prefix + suffix* mode defined earlier.

4.5.2 Authentication Extension Format

Each extension has the format illustrated in Figure 4.5, with fields defined as follows:

Type	32	Mobile-home authentication extension
	33	Mobile-foreign authentication extension
	34	Foreign-home authentication extension
Length		4 plus the number of bytes in the authenticator
SPI		Four bytes; an opaque identifier
Authenticator		Variable length, depending on the SPI

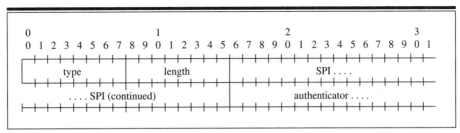

Figure 4.5 Mobile-home authentication extension packet format.

4.6 Mobile Node Registration Procedures

For each pending registration, the mobile node maintains the following information:

- The link-layer address of the foreign agent to which the registration request was sent, if applicable

- The IP destination address of the registration request

- The care-of address used in the registration

- The identification value sent in the registration

- The originally requested lifetime

- The *remaining lifetime* of the pending registration

A mobile node should initiate a registration whenever it detects a change in its network connectivity. See Section 7.5 for methods by which mobile nodes may make such a determination. When it is away from home, the mobile node's registration request allows its home agent to create or modify a mobility binding for it. When it is at home, the mobile node's deregistration request allows its home agent to delete any previous mobility bindings for it. A mobile node operates without the support of mobility functions when it is at home.

There are other conditions under which the mobile node should reregister with its foreign agent, such as when its current registration lifetime is near expiration or when the mobile node detects that the foreign agent has rebooted. In the absence of link-layer indications, a mobile node should not register more often than once per second. The mobile node should allow plenty of time for new registrations to make the round-trip to the home agent, taking into account possible packet losses along the way and required retransmissions. So, for instance, the mobile node may decide to send the new registration when there is enough time remaining in the existing registration equal to three to five round-trip times to the home agent. Of course, this requires measuring the round-trip times. If this is undesirable, the mobile node could reregister when there are only three minutes or so remaining in the existing registration. That should cover almost any reasonable round-trip times.

A mobile node may register with a different agent when transport-layer protocols indicate excessive retransmissions. On the other hand, a mobile node is not allowed to consider reception of an ICMP redirect from a foreign agent that is currently providing service to it as a reason to register with a new foreign agent. Within these constraints, the mobile node may reregister at any time.

Later in this chapter (Section 4.11) examples are presented that show proper values for the registration message fields in some typical registration scenarios.

4.6.1 Sending Registration Requests

This section details the values used by the mobile node in the fields of registration request messages. First the rules by which mobile nodes pick values for the IP header fields of a registration request are discussed.

IP Fields

IP source address

- When registering on a foreign network with a colocated care-of address, the IP source address is required to be the care-of address.
- In all other circumstances, the IP source address is required to be the mobile node's home address.

IP destination address

- When the mobile node has discovered the agent with which it is registering, through some means (for example, link layer) that does not provide the IP address of the agent (that is, the IP address of the agent is unknown to the mobile node), then the all-mobility-agents multicast address (224.0.0.11) is required to be used. In this case, the mobile node is required to use the agent's link-layer unicast address to deliver the datagram to the correct agent.

- When registering with a foreign agent, the address of the agent as learned from the IP source address of the corresponding agent advertisement is required to be used.

- When the mobile node is registering directly with its home agent and knows the unicast IP address of its home agent, the destination address is required to be set to that address.

- If the mobile node is registering directly with its home agent, but does not know the IP address of its home agent, the mobile node may nevertheless be able to determine the IP address of its home agent automatically. In this case, the IP destination address is set to the subnet-directed broadcast address of the mobile node's home network.

IP TTL

- The IP TTL field is required to be set to 1 if the IP destination address is set to the all-mobility-agents multicast address as described. Otherwise a suitable value should be chosen in accordance with standard IP practice (Postel 1981b).

In addition, when transmitting this registration request message, the mobile node is required to use a link-layer destination address copied from the link-layer source address of the agent advertisement message in which it learned this foreign agent's IP address. Broadcast ARP is disallowed.

Note that the directed broadcast address on the home network cannot be used as the destination IP address if the mobile node is registering via a foreign agent. The directed broadcast can always be used as necessary in the home agent address in the body of the registration request.

Registration Request Fields

This section describes how mobile nodes pick values for the fields within the fixed portion of a registration request.

A mobile node may set the S bit to request that the home agent maintain prior mobility bindings. Otherwise, the home agent deletes any previous bindings and creates the new binding indicated in the registration request. Multiple, simultaneous mobility bindings are likely to be useful when a mobile node, using at least one wireless network interface, moves within wireless transmission range of more than one foreign agent. IP explicitly allows duplication of datagrams. When the home agent allows simultaneous bindings, it will tunnel a separate copy of each arriving datagram to each care-of address, and the mobile node will receive multiple copies of datagrams destined to it.

A mobile node may set the B bit to request its home agent to forward to it a copy of broadcast datagrams received by its home agent from the home network. To receive broadcast packets, the mobile node must be able to decapsulate them. Thus a mobile node may only set the B bit in its registration request if it is capable of decapsulating datagrams. The method used by the home agent to forward broadcast datagrams depends on the type of care-of address registered by the mobile node, as determined by the D bit in the mobile node's registration request.

The mobile node should set the D bit when it is registering with a colocated care-of address. Otherwise, the D bit is never set. This is especially important for broadcast and possibly multicast packets, as described further in Sections 5.10 and 5.11.

The mobile node may request alternative forms of encapsulation, described in Chapter 5, by setting the M bit and/or the G bit, but only if the mobile node is decapsulating its own datagrams (that is, the mobile node is using a colocated care-of address) or if its foreign agent has indicated support for these forms of encapsulation by setting the corresponding bits in the mobility agent advertisement extension of an agent advertisement received by the mobile node. Otherwise, the mobile node is not allowed to set these bits.

The lifetime field is chosen as follows.

- If the mobile node is registering with a foreign agent, the lifetime should not exceed the value in the registration lifetime field of the agent advertisement message received from the foreign agent. When the method by which the care-of address is learned does not include a lifetime, the default ICMP Router Advertisement lifetime (1,800 seconds) may be used, or any other lifetime acceptable to the mobile node.

- The mobile node may ask a home agent to delete a particular mobility binding by sending a registration request with the care-of address for this binding, with the lifetime field set to 0 (Section 4.8.2).

- Similarly a lifetime of 0 is used when the mobile node deregisters all care-of addresses, for example when it returns home.

The home agent field is set to the address of the mobile node's home agent if the mobile node knows this address. Otherwise, the mobile node may use dynamic home agent address resolution to learn the address of its home agent (Section 4.6.3).

The care-of address field is set to the value of the particular care-of address that the mobile node wishes to register or deregister. In the special case in which a mobile node wishes to deregister all care-of addresses, it sets this field to its home address.

The mobile node chooses the identification field in accordance with the style of replay protection it uses with its home agent. This is part of the mobility security association the mobile node shares with its home agent. See Section 4.9.6 for methods by which the mobile node may compute the identification field.

Ordering Rules for Extensions

The ordering of the extensions that a mobile node appends to a registration request must be (1) the IP header, the UDP header, then the fixed-length portion of the registration request, followed by (2) any nonauthentication extensions, if present, expected to be used by the home agent (which may or may not also be used by the foreign agent), followed by (3) the mobile-home authentication extension, followed by (4) any nonauthentication extensions, if present, used only by the foreign agent, followed by (5) the mobile-foreign authentication extension, if present.

Note that items (1) and (3) are required to appear in every registration request sent by the mobile node. Items (2) and (4) are optional. Item (5) is only required to be included when the mobile node and the foreign agent share a mobility security association.

4.6.2 Receiving Registration Replies

Registration replies will be received by the mobile node in response to its registration requests. Registration replies generally fall into three categories:

1. Acceptance

2. Denial by the foreign agent

3. Denial by the home agent

Validity Checks

Registration replies with an invalid, nonzero UDP checksum are required to be discarded silently.

The low-order 32 bits of the identification field in the registration reply are compared with the low-order 32 bits of the identification field in the most recent registration request sent to the replying home agent. If they do not match, the reply is required to be discarded silently.

The mobile node is required to check for the presence of a valid authentication extension, acting in accordance with the code field in the reply. There are two rules:

1. If the mobile node and the foreign agent share a mobility security association, exactly one mobile-foreign authentication extension is required to be present in the registration reply, and the mobile node is required to check the authenticator

value in the extension. If no mobile-foreign authentication extension is found, or if more than one mobile-foreign authentication extension is found, or if the authenticator is invalid, the mobile node is required to discard the reply silently and should log the event as a security exception.

2. If the code field indicates that the home agent accepted or denied service, exactly one mobile-home authentication extension is required to be present in the registration reply, and the mobile node is required to check the authenticator value in the extension. If no mobile-home authentication extension is found, or if more than one mobile-home authentication extension is found, or if the authenticator is invalid, the mobile node is required to discard the reply silently and should log the event as a security exception.

If the code field indicates an authentication failure, either at the foreign agent or the home agent, then it is quite possible that any authenticators in the registration reply will also be in error. This could happen, for example, if the shared secret between the mobile node and home agent was erroneously configured. The mobile node should log such events as security exceptions.

Registration Request Accepted

If the code field indicates that the request has been accepted, the mobile node should configure its routing table appropriately for its current point of attachment (Section 5.9.1).

If the mobile node is returning to its home network and that network is one that implements ARP, the mobile node is required to follow the procedures described in Section 5.13 regarding gratuitous ARP.

If the mobile node has registered on a foreign network, it should reregister before the expiration of its registration lifetime. As described, for each pending registration request, the mobile node is required to maintain the remaining lifetime of this pending registration, as well as the original lifetime from the registration request. When the mobile node receives a valid registration reply, it is required to decrease the remaining registration lifetime by the amount, if any, by which the home agent decreased the originally requested lifetime.

This procedure is equivalent to the mobile node starting a timer for the granted lifetime at the time it sent the registration request, even though the granted lifetime is not known to the mobile node until the registration reply is received. The registration request is certainly sent before the home agent begins timing the registration lifetime. Therefore, this procedure ensures that the mobile node reregisters before the home agent expires and deletes the registration, regardless of any transmission delays for the registration messages that started the timing of the lifetime at the mobile node and its home agent.

Registration Request Denied

If the code field indicates that service is being denied, the mobile node should log the error. Before issuing future registration requests, the mobile node should adjust the parameters it uses to compute the identification field based on the corresponding field in the registration reply. Certain code values indicate that the mobile node may be able to "repair" the error. These include the following:

> **code 69: denied by foreign agent, lifetime too long**—In this case the lifetime field in the registration reply will contain the maximal lifetime value that that foreign agent is willing to accept in any registration request. The mobile node may attempt to register with this same agent using a registration lifetime in the request that is less than or equal to the value in the reply.

> **code 70: denied by foreign agent, poorly formed request**—Could be caused by an incomplete registration request or nonzero reserved bits.

> **code 133: denied by home agent, identification mismatch**—In this case the identification field in the registration reply will contain a value that allows the mobile node to synchronize with the home agent, based on the style of replay protection in effect (Section 4.9.6).

> **code 136: denied by home agent, unknown home agent address**—This code is returned by a home agent when the mobile node is performing dynamic home agent address resolution as described in the next section. In this case the home agent field within the reply will contain the unicast IP address of the home agent returning the reply. The mobile node may then attempt to register with this home agent in future registration requests.

4.6.3 Home Agent Discovery

Mobile nodes can use the directed broadcast address on their home network to find out the address of a real home agent. Registration requests using the directed broadcast address as the home agent's address will be received by every node on the mobile node's home network, including every home agent. Then, the home agents will reject the request returning a registration reply with a code of 136. However, the registration reply will contain the home agent's unicast address, so that the mobile node can reissue the registration request with the correct home agent address. Note that for this to work the mobile node must know the subnet prefix of its home address so that the directed broadcast address can be derived.

This method is obviously somewhat intrusive and should not be used except as a last resort. The broadcast registration will cause a lot of unnecessary processing by nodes on the home network that have nothing to do with mobility or the mobile node. The mobile node should normally not forget its home agent's address except in drastic cases of a disk crash or loss of nonvolatile memory. In such drastic cases the mobile node is likely to forget its own address along with its home agent's address. Perhaps the mobile node's home agent itself has crashed. In that case, however, typical home network administrative services should include providing backup for home agents so that there is always a machine serving a home agent's IP address, even if the particular machine identity changes as a result of a crash or scheduled maintenance.

4.6.4 Registration Retransmission

When no registration reply has been received within a reasonable amount of time, the mobile node may transmit another registration request. Handling replay protection for these requests is described in Section 4.9.6. The minimal value to wait before retransmission of registration requests (which is supposed to be at least one second) should be large enough to account for the size of the messages, twice the round-trip time for transmission to the home agent, and at least an additional 100 ms to allow for processing the messages before responding. The round-trip time for transmission to the home agent will be at least as large as the time required to transmit the messages at the link speed of the mobile node's current point of attachment. Some circuits add another 200 ms of satellite delay in the total round-trip time to the home agent.

The mobile node will be configured with some maximal value for retransmission waits—that is, when the link to the foreign agent seems live but the home agent is not responding. Each successive retransmission timeout period should be at least twice the previous period, as long as that is less than the configured maximum value. This maximum value is supposed to be at least one minute, but is not to be confused with the time between solicitations for new foreign agent service when the mobile node seems not to be within range of any foreign agent. If the home agent is not responding, but the foreign agent responds by reporting an ICMP error, then perhaps the home agent has crashed and registration procedures using the directed broadcast address should be employed.

4.7 Foreign Agent Registration Actions

The foreign agent plays a mostly passive role in Mobile IP registration. It relays registration requests between mobile nodes and home agents, and when it provides the care-of address, it decapsulates datagrams for delivery to the mobile node. It should also send periodic agent advertisement messages to advertise its presence if the mobile node cannot detect the foreign agent by link-layer means.

A foreign agent only sends Mobile IP registration messages on request by a mobile node or the mobile node's home agent. Otherwise, a foreign agent is not allowed to originate any registration messages. In particular, a foreign agent never creates a registration request or reply to indicate that a mobile node's registration lifetime has expired. A foreign agent also never originates a registration request message that asks for deregistration of a mobile node; however, it is required to relay valid deregistration requests originated by a mobile node.

4.7.1 Configuration and Registration Tables

Each foreign agent is required to be configured with a care-of address. In addition, for each pending or current registration, the foreign agent is required to maintain a *visitor list* entry containing the following information obtained from the mobile node's registration request:

- Link-layer source address of the mobile node
- IP source address (the mobile node's home address)
- IP destination address
- UDP source port
- Home agent address
- Identification field
- Requested registration lifetime
- Remaining lifetime of the pending or current registration

Any two nodes on the Internet may share mobility security associations; so, in particular, a foreign agent may share such an association with a mobile node or with a home agent. When relaying a registration request from a mobile node to its home agent, if the foreign agent shares a mobility security association with the home agent, it is required to add a foreign-home authentication extension to the request. The foreign agent must also check the required foreign-home authentication extension in the registration reply from the home agent. Similarly, when receiving a registration request from a mobile node, if the foreign agent shares a mobility security association with the mobile node, it is required to check the mobile-foreign authentication extension in the request and is required to add a mobile-foreign authentication extension to the registration reply to the mobile node.

4.7.2 Receiving Registration Requests

If the foreign agent accepts a registration request from a mobile node, it relays the request to the indicated home agent. Otherwise, if the foreign agent denies the request, it is required to send a registration reply to the mobile node with an appropriate denial code, except in cases when the foreign agent would be required to send out more than one such denial per second to the same mobile node. The following sections describe this behavior in more detail.

If a foreign agent receives a registration request from a mobile node in its visitor list, the existing visitor list entry for the mobile node should not be deleted or modified until the foreign agent receives a valid registration reply from the home agent with a code indicating success. The foreign agent is required to record the new pending request separately from the existing visitor list entry for the mobile node. If the mobile node requests deregistration, its existing visitor list entry should not be deleted until the foreign agent has received a successful registration reply. If the registration reply indicates that the new request (for registration or deregistration) was denied by the home agent, the existing visitor list entry for the mobile node is required to remain unchanged in spite of the unsuccessful registration reply. This behavior prevents malicious nodes from spoofing the foreign agent by sending erroneous registration requests that were not desired by the mobile node.

Validity Checks

Registration requests with an invalid, nonzero UDP checksum are required to be discarded silently.

Also, the authentication in the registration request has to be checked. If the foreign agent and the mobile node share a mobility security association, exactly one mobile-foreign authentication extension is required to be present in the registration request, and the foreign agent is required to check the authenticator value in the extension. If no mobile-foreign authentication extension is found, or if more than one mobile-foreign authentication extension is found, or if the authenticator is invalid, the foreign agent is required to discard the request and should log the event as a security exception. The foreign agent also should send a registration reply to the mobile node with code 67.

Forwarding a Valid Request to the Home Agent

If the foreign agent accepts the mobile node's registration request, it relays the request to the IP address in the home agent field of the registration request. The foreign agent is not allowed to modify any of the fields beginning with the fixed portion of the registration request up to and including the mobile-home authentication extension. Otherwise, an authentication failure is almost certain to occur at the home agent. In addition, the foreign agent must observe the following.

- It is required to process and remove any extensions following the mobile-home authentication extension.

- It may append any of its own nonauthentication extensions relevant to the home agent (for example, route optimization extensions as described in Chapter 6) if applicable.

- It is required to append the foreign-home authentication extension if the foreign agent shares a mobility security association with the home agent.

Fields within the IP header and the UDP header of the relayed registration request are required to be set as follows:

IP source address	The IP address of the interface from which the message will be sent
IP destination address	Same as the home agent field of the registration request
UDP source port	Variable
UDP destination port	434

After forwarding a valid registration request to the home agent, the foreign agent is required to begin timing the remaining lifetime of the pending registration based on the lifetime in the registration request. If this lifetime expires before receiving a valid registration reply, the foreign agent is required to delete its visitor list entry for this pending registration. If on relaying a registration request to a home agent the foreign agent receives an ICMP error message instead of a registration reply, then the foreign agent should deny the registration by sending (to the mobile node) a registration reply with an appropriate home agent unreachable failure code (within the range 80–95, inclusive).

4.7.3 Receiving Registration Replies

The foreign agent updates its visitor list when it receives a valid registration reply from a home agent. It then relays the registration reply to the mobile node.

Validity Checks

Registration replies with an invalid, nonzero UDP checksum are required to be discarded silently.

When a foreign agent receives a registration reply message it searches its visitor list for a pending registration request indexed by the mobile node home address indicated in the reply. If no pending request is found, the foreign agent discards the reply silently. The foreign agent is also required to discard the reply silently if the low-order 32 bits of the identification field in the reply do not match those in the request.

The authentication in the registration reply is required to be checked. If the foreign agent and the home agent share a mobility security association, exactly one foreign-home authentication extension is required to be present in the registration reply, and the foreign agent is required to check the authenticator value in the extension. If, in that case, no foreign-home authentication extension is found, or if more than one foreign-home authentication extension is found, or if the authenticator is invalid, the foreign agent is required to discard the reply silently and should log the event as a security exception. The foreign agent also is required to reject the mobile node's registration and should send a registration reply to the mobile node with rejection code 68.

Denying Invalid Requests

If the foreign agent denies the mobile node's registration request for any reason, it should send the mobile node a registration reply with a suitable denial code. In such a case, the home address, home agent, and identification fields within the registration reply are copied from the corresponding fields of the registration request.

If the reserved field is nonzero, the foreign agent is required to deny the request and should return a registration reply with status code 70 to the mobile node. If the request is being denied because the requested lifetime is too long, the foreign agent sets the lifetime in the reply to the maximal lifetime value it is willing to accept in any registration request, and sets the code field to 69. Otherwise, the lifetime should be copied from the lifetime field in the request.

Fields within the IP header and the UDP header of the registration reply are required to be set as follows:

IP source address	Copied from the IP destination address of the registration request, unless the all agents multicast address was used. In this case, the foreign agent's address (on the interface from which the message will be sent) is required to be used.
IP destination address	Copied from the IP source address of the registration request
UDP source port	434
UDP destination port	Copied from the UDP source port of the registration request

Forwarding Replies to the Mobile Node

A registration reply that satisfies the validity checks is relayed to the mobile node. The foreign agent also updates its visitor list entry for the mobile node to reflect the results of the registration request, as indicated by the code field in the reply. If the code indicates that the home agent has accepted the registration and the lifetime field is nonzero, the foreign agent is required to set the lifetime in the visitor list entry to the value in the lifetime field of the registration reply. If, instead, the lifetime field is 0, the foreign agent is required to delete its visitor list entry for the mobile node. Finally, if the code indicates that the registration was denied by the home agent, the foreign agent is required to delete its pending registration list entry, but not its visitor list entry, for the mobile node.

The foreign agent is not allowed to modify any of the fields beginning with the fixed portion of the registration reply up through and including the mobile-home authentication extension. Otherwise, an authentication failure is very likely to occur at the mobile node. In addition, the foreign agent must observe the following additional procedures.

- It must process and remove any extensions following the mobile-home authentication extension.

- It may append its own nonauthentication extensions relevant to the mobile node if applicable.

- It must append the mobile-foreign authentication extension if the foreign agent shares a mobility security association with the mobile node.

Relevant fields within the IP header and the UDP header of the relayed registration reply are set according to the rules presented in the previous section.

After forwarding a valid registration reply to the mobile node, the foreign agent is required to update its visitor list entry for this registration as follows. If the registration reply indicates that the registration was accepted by the home agent, the foreign agent resets the timer of the lifetime of the registration to the lifetime granted in the registration reply. Unlike the mobile node's timing of the registration lifetime, the foreign agent considers this lifetime to begin when it forwards the registration reply message, ensuring that the foreign agent will not expire the registration before the mobile node does. If the granted lifetime is 0, the visitor list entry is deleted.

4.8 Home Agent Processing for Registrations

Home agents play a reactive role in the registration process. The home agent receives registration requests from the mobile node (perhaps relayed by a foreign agent), updates its record of the mobility bindings for this mobile node, and issues a suitable registration reply in response to each.

A home agent is not allowed to transmit a registration reply except when replying to a registration request received from a mobile node. In particular, the home agent is not allowed to generate a registration reply to indicate that the lifetime has expired.

4.8.1 Configuration and Registration Tables

Each home agent is required to be configured with an IP address and with the prefix size for the home network. The home agent is required to be configured with the home address and mobility security association of each of its authorized mobile nodes. When the home agent accepts a valid registration request from a mobile node that it serves as a home agent, the home agent is required to create or modify the entry for this mobile node in its mobility binding list containing the

- Mobile node's care-of address
- Identification field from the registration reply
- Remaining lifetime of the registration

The home agent may also maintain mobility security associations with various foreign agents. When receiving a registration request from a foreign agent, if the home agent shares a mobility security association with the foreign agent, the home agent is required to check the authenticator in the required foreign-home authentication extension in the message, based on this mobility security association. Similarly, when sending a registration reply to a foreign agent, if the home agent shares a mobility security association with the foreign agent, the home agent is required to include a foreign-home authentication extension in the message, based on this mobility security association.

4.8.2 Receiving Registration Requests

If the home agent accepts an incoming registration request, it is required to update its record of the mobile node's mobility bindings and should send a registration reply with a suitable code. Otherwise, in cases when the home agent denies the request, it should send a registration reply with an appropriate code specifying the reason the request was denied.

Validity Checks

Registration requests with an invalid, nonzero UDP checksum are required to be discarded silently by the home agent. The authentication in the registration request must be checked. This involves the following three operations:

1. The home agent is required to check for the presence of a valid mobile-home authentication extension and perform the indicated authentication. Exactly one mobile-home authentication extension is required to be present in the registration request, and the home agent is required to check the authenticator value in the extension. If no mobile-home authentication extension is found, or if more than one mobile-home authentication extension is found, or if the authenticator is invalid, the home agent is required to reject the mobile node's registration and should send a registration reply to the mobile node with code 131. The home agent is required to then discard the request silently and should log the error as a security exception. Note that this includes the case when the mobile node is completely unknown to the home agent.

2. The home agent is required to check that the registration identification field is correct using the context selected by the SPI within the mobile-home authentication extension. See Section 4.9.6 for a description of how this is performed. If incorrect, the home agent is required to reject the request and should send a registration reply to the mobile node with code 133, including an identification field computed in accordance with the rules detailed in Section 4.9.6. The home agent is required to do no further processing with such a request, although it should log the error as a security exception.

3. If the home agent shares a mobility security association with the foreign agent, the home agent is required to check for the presence of a valid foreign-home authentication extension. Exactly one foreign-home authentication extension is required to be present in the registration request in this case, and the home agent is required to check the authenticator value in the extension. If no foreign-home authentication extension is found, or if more than one foreign-home authentication extension is found, or if the authenticator is invalid, the home agent is required to reject the mobile node's registration and should send a registration reply to the mobile node with code 132. The home agent is required to then discard the request silently and should log the error as a security exception.

In addition to checking the authentication in the registration request, home agents are required to deny registration requests that are sent to the subnet-directed broadcast address of the home network (as opposed to being unicast to the home agent). The home agent is required to discard the request and should return a registration reply with code 136. In this case the registration reply will contain the home agent's unicast address; hence, the mobile node can reissue the registration request with the correct home agent address (see Section 4.6.3).

Accepting a Valid Request

If the registration request satisfies the validity checks in the previous section, the home agent is required to update its mobility binding list for the requesting mobile node and is required to return a registration reply to the mobile node. In this case, the reply code will be either 0 (if the home agent supports simultaneous mobility bindings), or 1 (if it does not). See Section 4.8.3 for details on building the registration reply message.

The home agent updates its record of the mobile node's mobility bindings as follows, based on the fields in the registration request.

- If the lifetime is 0 and the care-of address equals the mobile node's home address, the home agent deletes all of the entries in the mobility binding list for the requesting mobile node. This is how a mobile node requests that its home agent cease providing mobility services.

- If the lifetime is 0 and the care-of address does not equal the mobile node's home address, the home agent deletes only the entry containing the care-of address from the mobility binding list for the requesting mobile node. Any other active entries containing other care-of addresses will remain active.

- If the lifetime is nonzero, the home agent adds an entry containing the requested care-of address to the mobility binding list for the mobile node. If the S bit is set and the home agent supports simultaneous mobility bindings, the previous mobility binding entries are retained. Otherwise, the home agent removes all previous entries in the mobility binding list for the mobile node.

In all cases the home agent is required to send a registration reply to the source of the registration request, which might indeed be a different foreign agent than the one with the care-of address that is being deregistered. If the home agent shares a mobility security association with the foreign agent with the care-of address that is being deregistered, and that foreign agent is different from the one that relayed the registration request, the home agent may also send a registration reply to the foreign agent with the care-of address that is being deregistered. The home agent is not allowed to send such a reply if it does not share a mobility security association with the foreign agent. If no reply is sent, the foreign agent's visitor list will expire naturally when the original lifetime expires.

The home agent is not allowed to increase the lifetime above that requested by the mobile node. However, it is not an error for the mobile node to request a lifetime longer than the home agent is willing to accept. In this case, the home agent simply reduces the lifetime to a permissible value and returns this value in the registration reply. The lifetime value in the registration reply informs the mobile node of the granted lifetime of the registration, indicating when it should reregister to maintain continued service. After the expiration of this registration lifetime, the home agent is required to delete its entry for this registration in its mobility binding list. The home agent might grant less than the requested lifetime, for example, if it has no stable storage and the mobile node requests a lifetime that is too long (or infinite).

If the registration request duplicates an accepted current registration request, the new lifetime is not allowed to extend beyond the lifetime originally granted. A registration request is a duplicate if the home address, care-of address, and identification fields all equal those of an accepted current registration.

In addition, if the home network implements ARP (Plummer 1982), and the registration request asks the home agent to create a mobility binding for a mobile node that previously had no binding (the mobile node was previously assumed to be at home), then the home agent is required to follow the procedures described in Section 5.13 with regard to ARP, proxy ARP, and gratuitous ARP. If the mobile node already had a previous mobility binding, the home agent is required to continue to follow the rules for proxy ARP described there.

Denying an Invalid Request

If the registration reply does not satisfy all of the required validity checks, the home agent should return a registration reply to the mobile node with a code that indicates the reason for the error. If a foreign agent was involved in relaying the request, the foreign agent can then delete its pending visitor list entry. Also, the mobile node can inspect the reason for the error, try to fix the error, and issue another request.

This section lists a number of reasons why the home agent might reject a request, and provides the code value it should use in each instance. Many reasons for rejecting a registration are administrative in nature. For example, a home agent may

- Limit the number of simultaneous registrations for a mobile node by rejecting any registrations that would cause its limit to be exceeded, and return a registration reply with error code 135

- Refuse to grant service to mobile nodes that have entered unauthorized service areas and indicate reply code 129

- Help the mobile node find a usable home agent by indicating code 136

- Help the mobile node resynchronize its replay protection by indicating code 133

The home agent is normally assumed to be configured with the necessary memory and processing resources needed to provide service to its mobile nodes; thus, the insufficient resources rejection code (130) is expected to be used rarely if at all by the home agent. If the reserved field is nonzero, the home agent is required to deny the request with a code of 134. See the next section for additional details on building the registration reply message.

4.8.3 Sending Registration Replies

If the home agent accepts a registration request, it then is required to update its record of the mobile node's mobility bindings and should send a registration reply with a suitable code. Otherwise, if the home agent has denied the request, it should send a registration reply with an appropriate code specifying the reason the request was denied. The following sections provide additional detail for the values the home agent supplies in the fields of registration reply messages. First, the home agent must pick values for the IP and UDP header fields of a registration reply.

IP/UDP Fields

IP source address	Copied from the IP destination address of a registration request, unless a multicast or broadcast address was used. If the IP destination address of the registration request was a broadcast or multicast address, then the home agent sets the IP source address of the registration reply to the unicast IP address by which it wishes to be known to the mobile node.
IP destination address	Copied from the IP source address of the request
UDP source port	Copied from the UDP destination port of the request
UDP destination port	Copied from the UDP source port of the request

When the mobile node returns home and sends a deregistration request, the IP destination address in the registration reply will be set to the mobile node's home address, as copied from the IP source address of the request. In this case, when transmitting the registration reply, the home agent is required to transmit the reply directly to the home network as if the mobile node were at home, bypassing any mobility binding list entry that may still exist at the home agent for the destination mobile node.

Suppose, instead, that a mobile node returned home after being registered with a care-of address and the home agent rejects its new registration request. The home agent's binding for the mobile node would still indicate that datagrams addressed to the mobile node should be tunneled to the mobile node's registered care-of address. The mobile node would thus not receive the rejection notice and would not be able to take corrective action. The effect of this special case is that when sending the registration reply indicating the rejection of the deregistration, the home agent has to ignore any existing binding for the mobile node and transmit the reply as if the mobile node were at home. This is analogous to the fact that home agents reject registration requests coming from a new care-of address to the new care-of address instead of the care-of address known from the existing and valid binding known to the home agent.

Registration Reply Fields

The code field of the registration reply is chosen in accordance with the rules detailed above. When accepting a registration, a home agent should send a reply with code 1 if it does not support simultaneous registrations.

The lifetime field is required to be copied from the corresponding field in the registration request unless the requested value is greater than the maximal length of time the home agent is willing to provide the requested service. In such a case the lifetime must be set to the maximal lifetime allowed by the home agent (for the particular mobile node and care-of address). The home agent may shorten registration lifetimes, especially when it cannot keep track of its mobile nodes' bindings on nonvolatile storage.

The home address field is required to be copied from the corresponding field in the registration request.

If the home agent field in the registration request contains a unicast address of the home agent, then that field is required to be copied into the home agent field of the registration reply. Otherwise, the home agent is required to set the home agent field in the registration reply to its unicast address. In this latter case the home agent is required to reject the registration with code 136 to prevent the mobile node from possibly being registered simultaneously with two or more home agents.

Extensions

The following order of Mobile IP extensions that a home agent appends to a registration reply is required to be followed: (1) the IP header, followed by the UDP header, followed by the fixed-length portion of the registration reply; (2) if present, any nonauthentication extensions used by the mobile node (which may or may not also be used by the foreign agent); (3) the mobile-home authentication extension; (4) if present, any non-authentication extensions used only by the foreign agent; and (5) the foreign-home authentication extension if present.

Note that items (1) and (3) are required to appear in every registration reply sent by the home agent. Items (2) and (4) are optional. Item (5) is only required to be included when the home agent and the foreign agent share a mobility security association.

4.9 Registering Securely

The mobile computing environment is potentially very different from the ordinary computing environment. In many cases mobile computers will be connected to the network via wireless links. Such links are particularly vulnerable to passive eavesdropping, active replay attacks, and other active attacks. Thus, security techniques assume added importance for wireless mobile network connections. Some of the relevant techniques are described in this section.

4.9.1 Message Authentication Codes

Home agents and mobile nodes are required to be able to perform authentication. The default algorithm is keyed MD5 (Rivest 1992), with a key size of 128 bits. The default mode of operation is to both precede and follow the data to be hashed by the 128-bit key; that is, MD5 is to be used in *prefix + suffix* mode. The foreign agent is also required to support authentication using keyed MD5 and key sizes of 128 bits or greater with manual key distribution. Other authentication algorithms, algorithm modes, key distribution methods, and key sizes may also be supported.

4.9.2 Areas of Security Concern in this Protocol

The Mobile IP registration protocol will result in a mobile node's traffic being tunneled to its care-of address. This tunneling feature could be a significant vulnerability if the registration were not authenticated. Such remote redirection (Section 1.9), for instance as performed by the mobile registration protocol, is widely understood to be a security problem in the current Internet if not authenticated (Bellovin 1989). Moreover, the ARP is not authenticated and potentially can be used to steal another host's traffic. The use of gratuitous ARP (Section 5.13) brings with it these risks associated with the use of ARP.

4.9.3 Key Management

Mobile IP needs a strong authentication mechanism (for instance, keyed MD5) to prevent potential attacks based on the registration protocol. However, network key management protocols are not widely deployed. Key distribution to hundreds (or thousands!) of network entities would be very time-consuming for system administrators. Therefore, Mobile IP messages with the foreign agent are not usually required to be authenticated. In a commercial environment it might be important to authenticate all messages between the foreign agent and the home agent so that billing is possible and service providers do not provide service to users that are not legitimate customers.

4.9.4 Picking Good Random Numbers

The strength of any authentication mechanism depends on several factors, including the innate strength of the authentication algorithm, the secrecy of the key used, the strength of the key used, and the quality of the particular implementation. To make keyed MD5 authentication (for which support is required) useful, the 128-bit key must be both pseudorandom and secret—that is, known only to authorized parties. If *nonces* are used in connection with replay protection, they must also be selected carefully. Eastlake et al. (1994) provide more information on generating pseudorandom numbers—in other words, numbers that satisfy the same tests for randomness as are satisfied by truly random numbers. It is known that many existing random number generators fail such tests.

4.9.5 Privacy

Users who have sensitive data should use mechanisms that do not conflict with Mobile IP to provide appropriate protection (such as encryption). Users concerned about traffic analysis should consider the appropriate use of link encryption. If absolute location privacy is desired, the mobile node can create a tunnel to its home agent (Montenegro 1997). Then, datagrams destined for correspondent nodes will appear to emanate from the home network, and it may be more difficult to pinpoint the location of the mobile node.

4.9.6 Replay Protection for Registration Requests

The identification field is used to let the home agent verify that a registration message has been freshly generated by the mobile node, and thus not replayed by an attacker from some previous registration. Two methods are described in this section: *timestamps* (mandatory) and *nonces* (optional). All mobile nodes and home agents are required to implement timestamp-based replay protection. These nodes may also implement nonce-based replay protection (Bird et al. 1993).

The style of replay protection in effect between a mobile node and its home agent is part of the mobility security association. A mobile node and its home agent need to agree on which method of replay protection they will use, because one method allows some leeway in the lower order bits of the identification field and the other method does not. The interpretation of the identification field depends on the method of replay protection.

Whatever method is used, the low-order 32 bits of the identification are required to be copied unchanged from the registration request to the reply. The foreign agent uses those bits (and the mobile node's home address) to match registration requests with corresponding replies. The mobile node is required to verify that the low-order 32 bits of any registration reply are identical to the bits it sent in the registration request.

The identification in a new registration request is not allowed to be the same as in other requests, and should not repeat while the same security context is being used between the mobile node and the home agent. Retransmission is also allowed. When timestamps are used, a new registration identification is chosen for each retransmission; thus it counts as a new registration. When nonces are used, the unanswered request is retransmitted unchanged; thus the retransmission does not count as a new registration. In this way a retransmission will not require the home agent to resynchronize with the mobile node by issuing another nonce in the case in which the original registration request (rather than its registration reply) was lost by the network.

Replay Protection Using Timestamps

The basic idea of timestamp replay protection is that the node generating a message inserts the current time of day, and the node receiving the message checks that this timestamp is sufficiently close to its own time of day. Obviously the two nodes must have adequately synchronized time-of-day clocks. As with other messages, time synchronization messages may detect tampering by an authentication mechanism determined by the security context between the two nodes.

If timestamps are used, the mobile node is required to set the identification field to a 64-bit value formatted as specified by the Network Time Protocol (*NTP*) (Mills 1992). The low-order 32 bits of the NTP format represent fractional seconds, and those bits that are not available from a time source should be generated from a good source of randomness. Note, however, that when using timestamps, the 64-bit identification used in a registration request from the mobile node is required to be greater than that used in any previous registration request, as the home agent also uses this field as a sequence number. Without such a sequence number, it would be possible for a delayed duplicate of an earlier registration request to arrive at the home agent (within the clock synchronization required by the home agent), and thus be applied out of order, mistakenly altering the mobile node's current, registered care-of address.

On receipt of a registration request with a valid mobile-home authentication extension, the home agent is required to check the identification field for validity. To be valid, the timestamp contained in the identification field is required to be close enough to the home agent's time-of-day clock, and the timestamp is required to be greater than all previously accepted timestamps for the requesting mobile node. Tolerances and resynchronization details are considered to be part of a particular mobility security association.

If the timestamp is valid, the home agent copies the entire identification field into the registration reply when it returns the reply to the mobile node. If the timestamp is not valid, the home agent copies only the low-order 32 bits into the registration reply and supplies the high-order 32 bits from its own time of day. In this latter case, the home agent is required to reject the registration by returning code 133 (identification mismatch) in the registration reply.

Before using the high-order bits for clock resynchronization, the mobile node is required to verify that the low-order 32 bits of the identification in the registration reply are identical to those in the rejected registration attempt.

Replay Protection Using Nonces

Implementors of this optional mechanism should examine Section 4.10.2 for a patent that may be applicable to nonce-based replay protection.

The basic idea of nonce replay protection is that node A includes a new random number in every message to node B, and checks that node B returns that same number in its next message to node A. Both messages use an authentication code to protect against alteration by an attacker. At the same time node B can send its own nonces in all messages to node A (to be echoed by node A), so that it too can verify that it is receiving fresh messages.

The home agent may be expected to have resources for computing pseudorandom numbers (Eastlake, Crocker, and Schiller 1994) useful as nonces or for other purposes. It inserts a new nonce as the high-order 32 bits of the identification field of every registration reply. The home agent copies the low-order 32 bits of the identification from the registration request message into the low-order 32 bits of the identification in the registration reply. When the mobile node receives an authenticated registration reply from the home agent, it saves the high-order 32 bits of the identification for use as the high-order 32 bits of its next registration request.

The mobile node is responsible for generating the low-order 32 bits of the identification in each registration request. Ideally it should generate its own random nonces. However it may use any expedient method, including duplication of the random value sent by the home agent. The method chosen is of concern only to the mobile node, because it is the node that checks for valid values in the registration reply. The high-order and low-order 32 bits of the identification chosen should both differ from their previous values. The home agent uses a new high-order value and the mobile node uses a new low-order value for each registration message. The foreign agent uses the low-order value (and the mobile host's home address) to match registration replies correctly with pending requests. This process is illustrated in Figure 4.6, in which the home agent, HA, establishes synchronization by sending the 32-bit number HA-nonce$_1$ in the high order bytes of the identification field of a registration reply message to the mobile host, MH. In its next registration request message, the mobile host sends HA-nonce$_1$ in the higher order bytes of the identification field and inserts MH-nonce$_1$ in the lower order four bytes of the field. The home agent inserts MH-nonce$_1$ in the low order 4 bytes of the identification in the registration reply, along with a new 32-bit nonce HA-nonce$_1$ in the high-order bytes, and so on.

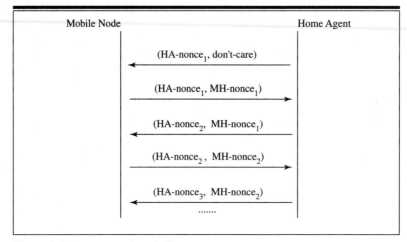

Figure 4.6 Nonce synchronization.

If a registration is rejected because of an invalid nonce, the registration reply message always provides the mobile node with a new nonce to be used in the next registration. Thus the nonce protocol is self-synchronizing.

4.10 Patent Issues

4.10.1 IBM Patent No. 5,159,592

The following notice has been published as part of the Mobile IP Internet draft development. As the sole inventor of the patent, I also feel honor bound to submit my opinion (not informed by legal counsel on the matter, nor by IBM corporate opinion) that the aforementioned patent is relevant to a wide range of technology involving the action of home agents assisting the routing of packets for mobile nodes addressed via a home network.

> Charles Perkins, editor of this draft, is sole inventor of U.S. Patent No. 5,159,592, assigned to IBM. In a letter dated May 30, 1995, IBM brought this patent to the attention of the IETF, stating that this patent "relates to the Mobile IP." We understand that IBM did not intend to assert that any particular implementation of Mobile IP would or would not infringe the patent, but rather that IBM was meeting what it viewed as a duty to disclose information that could be relevant to the process of adopting a standard.
>
> Based on a review of the claims of the patent, IETF believes that a system of registering an address obtained from a foreign agent, as described in the draft, would not necessarily infringe any of the claims of the patent; and that a system in which an address

is obtained elsewhere and then registered can be implemented without necessarily infringing any claims of the patent. Accordingly, our view is that the proposed protocol can be implemented without necessarily infringing the Perkins Patent.

Parties considering adopting this protocol must be aware that some specific implementations, or features added to otherwise non-infringing implementations, may raise an issue of infringement with respect to this patent or to some other patent.

This statement is for the IETF's assistance in its standard-setting procedure, and should not be relied on by any party as an opinion or guarantee that any implementation it might make or use would not be covered, or would not be asserted by IBM to be covered, by the Perkins Patent or any other patent.

4.10.2 IBM Patent No. 5,148,479

This patent, assigned to IBM, may be relevant to those who implement nonce-based replay protection as described in Section 4.9.6. Note that nonce-based replay protection is an optional feature of Mobile IP. Timestamp-based replay protection on the other hand (Section 4.9.6) must be supported by all implementations of Mobile IP.

4.11 Example Scenarios

This section presents examples for several common registration scenarios. Important values used in the examples are

Mobile node's home address	129.34.78.5
Mobile node's home agent	129.34.78.254
Foreign agent's wireless address	137.0.0.11
Foreign agent's care-of address	9.2.20.11
DHCP-allocated care-of address	9.2.43.94
Mobile node's source port	1094
Foreign agent's source port	1105
Care-of address registration lifetime	60,000 seconds
Home agent-granted lifetime	35,000 seconds

Other values are constants, with the values specified by the Mobile IP protocol.

4.11.1 Registering with a Foreign Agent Care-of Address

Figure 4.7 depicts a sequence of packets with values listed for some important fields. This example roughly corresponds to a sequence of events, as illustrated in Figure 4.1. The mobile node receives an agent advertisement over a wireless medium from a foreign agent and wishes to register with that agent using the advertised foreign agent care-of address. The mobile node wishes only IP-in-IP

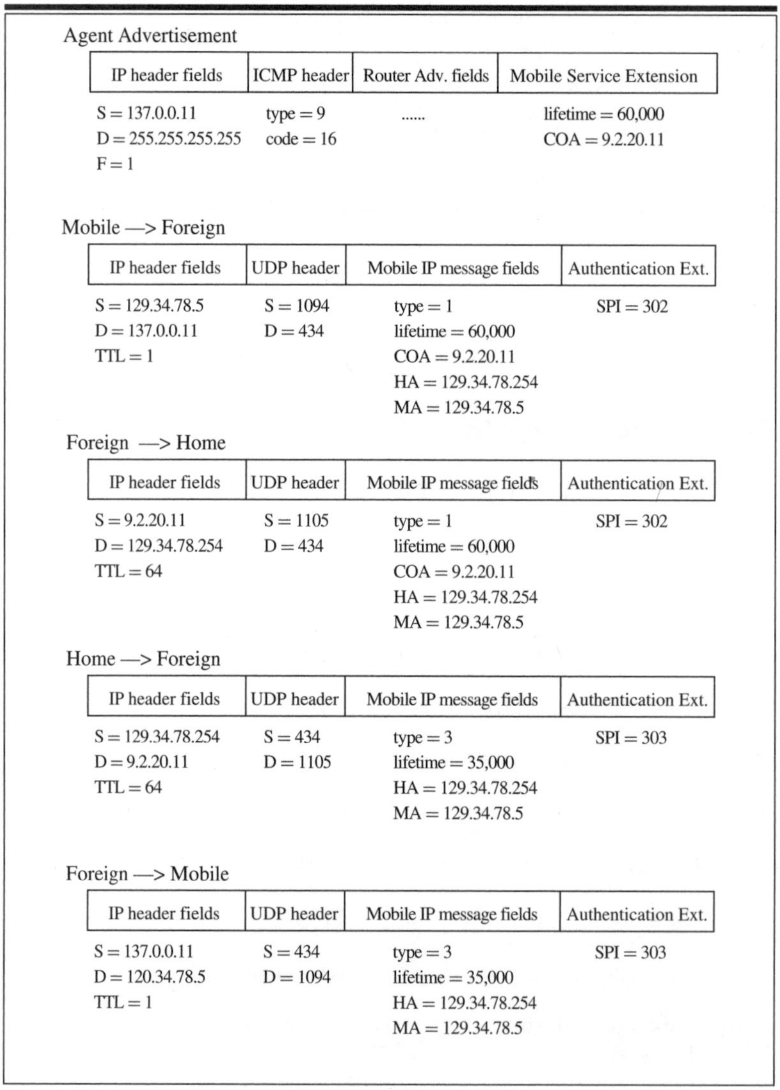

Agent Advertisement

IP header fields	ICMP header	Router Adv. fields	Mobile Service Extension
S = 137.0.0.11	type = 9	......	lifetime = 60,000
D = 255.255.255.255	code = 16		COA = 9.2.20.11
F = 1			

Mobile —> Foreign

IP header fields	UDP header	Mobile IP message fields	Authentication Ext.
S = 129.34.78.5	S = 1094	type = 1	SPI = 302
D = 137.0.0.11	D = 434	lifetime = 60,000	
TTL = 1		COA = 9.2.20.11	
		HA = 129.34.78.254	
		MA = 129.34.78.5	

Foreign —> Home

IP header fields	UDP header	Mobile IP message fields	Authentication Ext.
S = 9.2.20.11	S = 1105	type = 1	SPI = 302
D = 129.34.78.254	D = 434	lifetime = 60,000	
TTL = 64		COA = 9.2.20.11	
		HA = 129.34.78.254	
		MA = 129.34.78.5	

Home —> Foreign

IP header fields	UDP header	Mobile IP message fields	Authentication Ext.
S = 129.34.78.254	S = 434	type = 3	SPI = 303
D = 9.2.20.11	D = 1105	lifetime = 35,000	
TTL = 64		HA = 129.34.78.254	
		MA = 129.34.78.5	

Foreign —> Mobile

IP header fields	UDP header	Mobile IP message fields	Authentication Ext.
S = 137.0.0.11	S = 434	type = 3	SPI = 303
D = 120.34.78.5	D = 1094	lifetime = 35,000	
TTL = 1		HA = 129.34.78.254	
		MA = 129.34.78.5	

Figure 4.7 Registering via a foreign agent.

encapsulation, does not want broadcasts, and does not want simultaneous mobility bindings. The mobile node requests the maximal lifetime made available by the foreign agent (here, 60,000 seconds). The foreign agent takes note of the mobile node's address and UDP source port information, and substitutes the natural values into the registration request as it is relayed to the home agent. The home agent approves the request (after checking the message digest according to the algorithm indexed by SPI 302), but reduces the binding lifetime to 35,000 seconds.

4.11.2 Registering with a Colocated Care-of Address

In the second example, illustrated in Figure 4.8, the mobile node enters a foreign network that contains no foreign agents. The mobile node obtains an address from a DHCP server (Droms 1993) for use as a colocated care-of address. The mobile node supports minimal encapsulation and GRE, desires a copy of broadcast datagrams on the home network, and does not want simultaneous mobility bindings. The field values used for the registration request and reply are illustrated in Figure 4.8.

Mobile —> Home Registration Request			
IP header fields	UDP header	Mobile IP message fields	Authentication Ext.
S = 129.34.78.5	S = 1094	type = 1	SPI = 302
D = 129.34.78.254	D = 434	lifetime = 665,535	
TTL = 64		COA = 9.2.43.94	
		HA = 129.34.78.254	
		MA = 129.34.78.5	
		D, M, G, B, = 1,1,1,1	

Home —> Mobile Registration Reply			
IP header fields	UDP header	Mobile IP message fields	Authentication Ext.
S = 129.34.78.254	S = 434	type = 3	SPI = 303
D = 129.34.78.5	D = 1094	lifetime = 35,000	
TTL = 64		COA = 9.2.43.94	
		HA = 129.34.78.254	
		MA = 129.34.78.5	

Figure 4.8 Registering with a colocated care-of address.

4.11.3 Deregistration

In the third example, illustrated in Figure 4.9, the mobile node returns home and wishes to deregister all care-of addresses with its home agent. The care-of address fields are the same as the mobile node's home address, and the requested (and granted) lifetimes are 0.

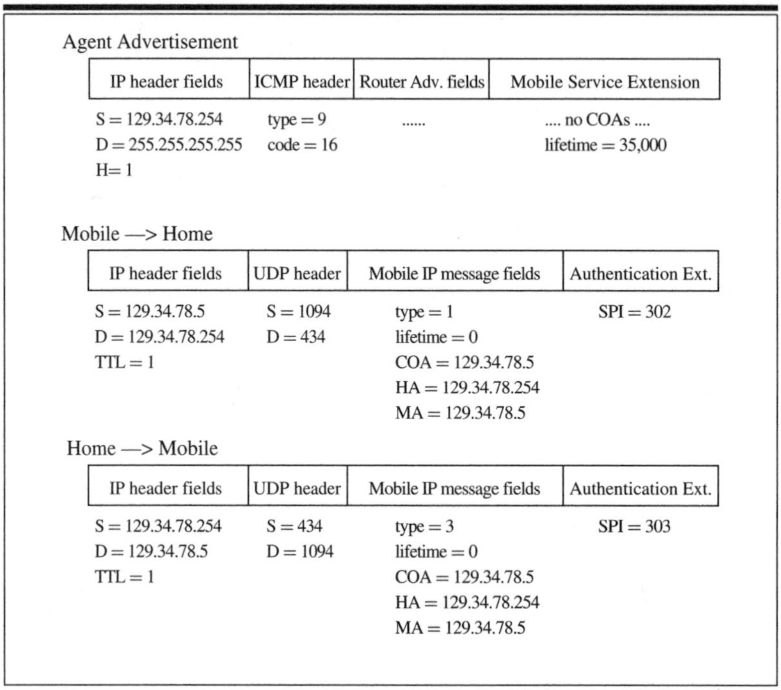

Agent Advertisement			
IP header fields	ICMP header	Router Adv. fields	Mobile Service Extension
S = 129.34.78.254 D = 255.255.255.255 H= 1	type = 9 code = 16	......	.... no COAs .... lifetime = 35,000

Mobile —> Home			
IP header fields	UDP header	Mobile IP message fields	Authentication Ext.
S = 129.34.78.5 D = 129.34.78.254 TTL = 1	S = 1094 D = 434	type = 1 lifetime = 0 COA = 129.34.78.5 HA = 129.34.78.254 MA = 129.34.78.5	SPI = 302

Home —> Mobile			
IP header fields	UDP header	Mobile IP message fields	Authentication Ext.
S = 129.34.78.254 D = 129.34.78.5 TTL = 1	S = 434 D = 1094	type = 3 lifetime = 0 COA = 129.34.78.5 HA = 129.34.78.254 MA = 129.34.78.5	SPI = 303

Figure 4.9 Deregistering when returning home.

4.12 Summary

This chapter discussed Mobile IP registration in depth. The mobile node uses the registration procedures to notify its home agent about its new or renewed association with a care-of address. When a foreign agent is involved at all, it plays a mostly passive role in the registration processes. The home agent uses the registration information provided by the mobile node to establish tunnels to the mobile node, as described in the next chapter. Since changing the care-of address has a crucial effect on the ability of the mobile node to get datagrams from the home agent to its current location, the messages used in the registration process have to be carefully authenticated. The mobile node and home agent are presumed to be configured with enough mutual trust and cryptographically sound key material to make the authentication reliable and possible.

The important procedures described in this chapter include issuing registration requests, issuing registration replies, discovering home agent addresses, verifying the authenticity and freshness of registration messages, and setting permissible values within the registration messages to enable selection of desired, optional features. The home agent discovery mechanism should substantially reduce the requirements for preconfiguration of the mobile node. Unfortunately, no relief is available yet for the difficult operation of preconfiguring mobile nodes with the mobility security associations that are needed to authenticate registration messages.

CHAPTER FIVE

Delivering Datagrams

Mobile IP requires the use of encapsulation to deliver datagrams from the home network to the current location of the mobile node (its care-of address). This chapter describes several methods of encapsulation (tunneling) that are available for use by the home agent on behalf of the mobile node:

- IP-in-IP encapsulation
- Minimal encapsulation
- GRE

In addition to tunneling, this chapter details other routing considerations that are relevant to mobility agents. The routing relationships between the mobile node and the foreign agent are described. Maintaining *tunnel soft state* to assist in the delivery and correct interpretation of ICMP error messages is specified in detail. The means for delivery of broadcast and multicast datagrams to the mobile node is explained, along with the existing standard and some proposed mechanisms for performing the necessary setup operations. The specialized uses of ARP by home agents and mobile nodes (proxy ARP and gratuitous ARP) are defined and described in detail. Some of the security problems associated with the use of encapsulation are pointed out. Lastly, a comparison is made between source routing and encapsulation that shows the reasons for preferring encapsulation instead of its theoretically equivalent alternative.

Encapsulation alters the normal IP routing for datagrams by delivering them to an intermediate destination that would otherwise not be selected based on the network part of the IP destination address field in the original IP header. Once the encapsulated datagram arrives at this intermediate destination node, it is decapsulated, yielding the original IP datagram, which is then delivered to the destination indicated by the original destination address field. This use of encapsulation and decapsulation of a datagram is frequently referred to as *tunneling* the datagram, and the encapsulator and decapsulator are then considered to be the endpoints of the tunnel.

Encapsulation may be desirable whenever the source (or an intermediate router) of an IP datagram must influence the route by which a datagram is to be delivered to its ultimate destination. Other possible applications of encapsulation include multicasting, preferential billing, choice of routes with selected security attributes, and general policy routing.

Much of the text of this chapter was drawn from the IETF Proposed Standard documents RFC 2003 (Perkins 1996a) and RFC 2004 (Perkins 1996c). Sections 5.9 and 5.11 on unicast and multicast routing were adapted from the Mobile IP standard document RFC 2002 (Perkins 1996b). The GRE encapsulation description in Section 5.4 was adapted from RFC 1701 (Hanks et al. 1994a) and RFC 1702 (Hanks et al. 1994b).

5.1 Tunneling Overview and Terminology

In the most general tunneling case, illustrated in Figure 5.1, the source, encapsulator, decapsulator, and destination are separate nodes. The encapsulator node is considered the *entry point* of the tunnel, and the decapsulator node is considered the *exit point* of the tunnel. Multiple source-destination pairs can use the same tunnel between the encapsulator and decapsulator. Today, IP encapsulation techniques are becoming generally useful for a variety of purposes within the Internet, including multicast and multiprotocol operation, security, and privacy. As described in Section 5.14, encapsulation is normally preferred to source routing for such operations.

Mobile IP requires each home agent and foreign agent to support tunneling datagrams using IP-in-IP encapsulation (Perkins 1996a). Any mobile node that uses a colocated care-of address is required to support receiving datagrams tunneled using

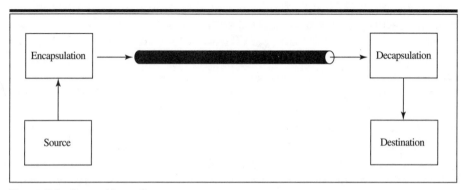

Figure 5.1 General tunneling.

IP-in-IP encapsulation. Minimal encapsulation (Perkins 1996a) and GRE encapsulation are alternate encapsulation methods that may optionally be supported by mobility agents and mobile nodes. The use of these alternative forms of encapsulation, when requested by the mobile node, is otherwise at the discretion of the home agent.

5.2 IP-in-IP Encapsulation

This section describes the method by which an IP datagram may be encapsulated (carried as payload; that is, data) within an IP datagram. To encapsulate an IP datagram using IP-in-IP encapsulation, an outer IP header (Postel 1981b) is inserted before the datagram's existing IP header, as shown in Figure 5.2. The shaded portion of the figure indicates that there may be other headers included between the inner header and the outer header of the encapsulated datagram. Such headers might, for instance, be included if there are security requirements to protect the original payload during tunneling.

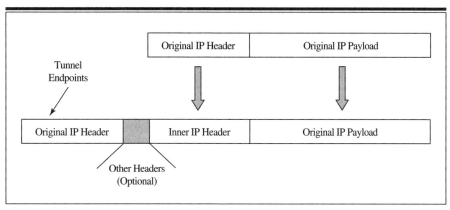

Figure 5.2 IP-in-IP encapsulation.

The outer IP header source address and destination address identify the endpoints of the tunnel. The inner IP header source address and destination address identify the original sender and recipient of the datagram respectively. The inner IP header is not changed by the encapsulator, except to decrement the TTL, and remains unchanged during its delivery to the tunnel exit point. No change to IP options in the inner header occurs during delivery of the encapsulated datagram through the tunnel. If need be, other protocol headers such as the IP *authentication header* (Kent 1997a) may be inserted between the outer IP header and the inner IP header. Note that the security options, if any, of the inner IP header may affect the choice of security options for the encapsulating (outer) IP header.

The fields in the outer IP header are set by the encapsulator as follows:

Version	4
IHL	The internet header length (*IHL*) is the length of the outer IP header measured in 32-bit words (Postel 1981b).
TOS	The type of service (*TOS*) is copied from the inner IP header.
Total length	The total length measures the length of the entire encapsulated IP datagram, including the outer IP header, the inner IP header, and its payload.
Identification, flags, fragment offset	These three fields are set as specified in RFC 791 (Postel 1981b). However, if the don't fragment (*DF*) bit is set in the inner IP header, it must also be set in the outer IP header. If the DF bit is not set in the inner IP header, it may nevertheless be set in the outer IP header, as described in Section 5.6.2.
TTL	The TTL field in the outer IP header is set to a value appropriate for delivery of the encapsulated datagram to the tunnel exit point.
Protocol	The protocol is set to 4, which is the protocol number for IP.
Header checksum	The header checksum (Postel 1981b) is the header checksum of the outer IP header.
Source address	The source address is the IP address of the encapsulator; that is, the tunnel entry point.
Destination address	The destination address is the IP address of the decapsulator; that is, the tunnel exit point.

Options	Any options present in the inner IP header are in general *not* copied to the outer IP header. However, new options specific to the tunnel path may be added.

When encapsulating a datagram, the TTL in the inner IP header is decremented by one if the tunneling is being done as part of forwarding the datagram; otherwise, the inner header TTL is not changed during encapsulation. If the resulting TTL in the inner IP header is 0, the datagram is discarded and an ICMP time exceeded message should be returned to the sender. An encapsulator never encapsulates a datagram with a TTL of 0.

The TTL in the inner IP header is not changed when decapsulating. If, after decapsulation, the inner datagram has a TTL of 0, the decapsulator is required to discard the datagram. If, after decapsulation, the decapsulator forwards the datagram to one of its network interfaces, it will decrement the TTL as a result of doing normal IP forwarding.

The encapsulator may use any existing IP mechanisms appropriate for the delivery of the encapsulated payload to the tunnel exit point. In particular, use of IP options is allowed, and use of fragmentation is allowed unless the DF bit is set in the inner IP header. This restriction on fragmentation is required so that nodes employing path maximum transfer unit (*MTU*) discovery (Mogul and Deering 1990) can obtain the information they seek. Path MTU (*PMTU*) discovery allows nodes to find out the largest size datagram (that is, the MTU) that can travel unfragmented between source and destination.

5.3 Minimal Encapsulation

5.3.1 Overview

Using IP headers to encapsulate IP datagrams requires the unnecessary duplication of several fields within the inner IP header. It is possible to save some additional space by creating another encapsulation mechanism to eliminate the duplication. This section describes a method by which an IP datagram may be encapsulated within an IP datagram, with less overhead than the default IP-in-IP encapsulation. The scheme outlined here is similar to that defined by Johnson (1994).

5.3.2 Specification

The minimal forwarding header described here can be used for datagrams that are not fragmented prior to encapsulation. Use of this encapsulating method is optional. Minimal encapsulation cannot be used when an original datagram is already fragmented, since there is no room in the minimal forwarding header to store fragmentation information.

To encapsulate an IP datagram using minimal encapsulation, the minimal forwarding header is inserted into the datagram, as shown in Figure 5.3.

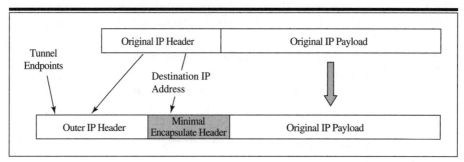

Figure 5.3 Minimal encapsulation.

The IP header of the original datagram is modified and the minimal forwarding header is inserted into the datagram after the IP header, followed by the unmodified IP payload of the original datagram (for example, transport header and transport data). No additional IP header is added to the datagram.

In encapsulating the datagram, the original IP header is modified as follows.

1. The protocol field in the IP header is replaced by protocol number 55, for the minimal encapsulation protocol.

2. The destination address field in the IP header is replaced by the IP address of the exit point of the tunnel.

3. If the encapsulator is not the original source of the datagram, the source address field in the IP header is replaced by the IP address of the encapsulator.

4. The total length field in the IP header is incremented by the size of the minimal forwarding header added to the datagram. This incremental size is either 12 or eight octets, depending on whether or not the original source address present (S) bit is set in the forwarding header.

5. The header checksum field in the IP header is recomputed or updated to account for the changes in the IP header described here for encapsulation.

The fields in the header format illustrated in figure 5.4 are defined as follows:

Protocol	Copied from the protocol field in the original IP header
S	The original source address present bit. If S is 0, the original source address field is not present and the length of the minimal tunneling header is eight octets. Otherwise, the original source address field is present and the length of the minimal tunneling header is 12 octets.
reserved	Sent as 0; ignored on reception
Header checksum	The 16-bit one's complement of the one's complement sum of all 16-bit words in the minimal forwarding header. For purposes of computing the checksum, the value of the checksum field is 0. The IP header and IP payload (after the minimal forwarding header) are not included in this checksum computation.
Original destination address	Copied from the destination address field in the original IP header
Original source address	Copied from the source address field in the original IP header. This field is present only if the original source address present, S, bit is set.

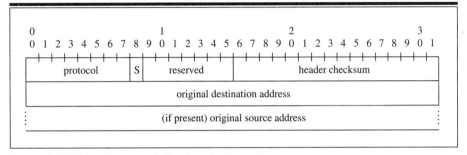

Figure 5.4 Minimal encapsulation header format.

When decapsulating a datagram, the following actions occur.

- The fields in the minimal forwarding header are restored to the IP header.

- The forwarding header is removed from the datagram.

- The total length field in the IP header is decremented by the size of the removed minimal forwarding header.

- The checksum field in the IP header is updated to reflect the new values in the fields of the IP header.

The encapsulator may use existing IP mechanisms appropriate for the delivery of the encapsulated payload to the tunnel exit point. In particular, use of IP options are allowed and use of fragmentation is allowed unless the DF bit is set in the IP header. This restriction on fragmentation is required so that nodes employing PMTU discovery (Mogul and Deering 1990) can obtain the information they seek.

5.4 Generic Record Encapsulation

GRE is more general than the other protocols described earlier. It can encapsulate numerous other protocols besides IP (Table 5.1). The entire encapsulated packet has the form presented in Figure 5.5.

Delivery Header	GRE Header	Packet Payload

Figure 5.5 GRE packet structure.

5.4.1 Packet header

The GRE packet header has the form illustrated in Figure 5.6. The GRE flags are encoded in the first two octets. Bit 0 is the most significant bit and bit 15 is the least significant bit. Bits 13 through 15 are reserved for the *ver* field. Bits 5 through 12 are reserved for future use and are required to be transmitted as 0.

The fields illustrated in Figure 5.6 have the following meaning:

C (bit 0)   If the C (checksum present) bit is set to 1, the checksum field is present and contains valid information.

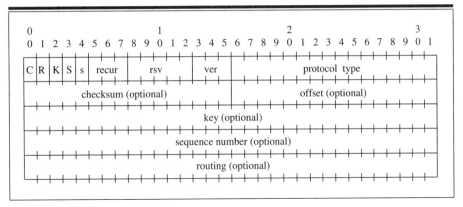

Figure 5.6 GRE packet header.

R (bit 1)	If the 'R' (routing present) bit is set to 1, it indicates that the offset and routing fields are present and contain valid information.
K (bit 2)	If the K (key present) bit is set to 1, it indicates that the key field is present in the GRE header. Otherwise, the key field is not present in the GRE header.
S (bit 3)	If the 'S' (sequence number present) bit is set to 1, it indicates that the sequence number field is present. Otherwise, the sequence number field is not present in the GRE header.
s (bit 4)	The meaning of the s (strict source route) bit is defined elsewhere. It is recommended that this bit only be set to 1 if all of the routing information consists of strict source routes.
Recur	Recur (recursion control) contains a three-bit unsigned integer that contains the number of additional encapsulations that are permissible. This *should* default to 0.
rsv	*Must* be zero. Ignored on reception.
Ver	Ver, the version number field, is required to contain the value 0. Other values, if any, are described elsewhere.
Protocol type	The protocol type field contains the protocol type of the payload packet. In general, the value will be the ethernet protocol type field for the packet. Currently defined protocol types are listed in Table 5.1.

Checksum

The checksum field contains the IP (one's complement) checksum of the GRE header and the payload packet. This field is present if the R or the C bit is set to 1, and contains valid information only if the C bit is set to 1.

Offset

The offset field indicates the octet offset from the start of the routing field to the first octet of the active source route entry to be examined. This field is present if the R or the C bit is set to 1, and contains valid information only if the R bit is set to 1.

Key

The key field contains a four-octet number that was inserted by the encapsulator. It may be used by the receiver to authenticate the source of the packet. The techniques for determining authenticity are not defined in the GRE specification. The key field is present only if the K bit is set to 1.

Sequence number

The sequence number field contains an unsigned 32-bit integer that is inserted by the encapsulator. It may be used by the receiver to establish the order in which packets have been transmitted from the encapsulator to the receiver. The exact algorithms for generating the sequence number and the semantics of their reception are not defined by the GRE specification.

Routing

The routing field is optional and present only if the R bit is set to 1. It has a variable length. The routing field is a list of source route entries (*SREs*), which are defined in the next section.

If either the C bit or the R bit is set, *both* the checksum and offset fields will be present in the GRE packet.

5.4.2 SRE Format

Each SRE has the format illustrated in Figure 5.7. The routing information field is terminated with a null SRE containing an address family of type 0x0000 and a length of 0.

The fields illustrated in Figure 5.7 have the following meaning:

Address Family

The address family field contains a two-octet value that indicates the syntax and semantics of the routing information field. The values for this field, and

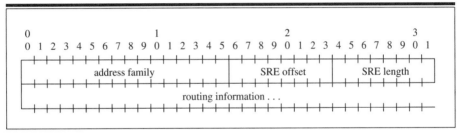

Figure 5.7 Source Route Entry format.

the corresponding syntax and semantics for routing information, are not defined as part of the GRE specification.

SRE offset   The SRE offset field indicates the offset (in octets) from the start of the routing information field to the first octet of the active entry in the SRE to be examined.

SRE Length   The SRE length field contains the number of octets in the SRE. If the SRE length is 0, this is the last SRE in the routing information field.

Routing information   The routing information field contains variable length data that may be used in routing this packet. The exact semantics of this field are not defined as part of the GRE specification.

Normally, a system that is forwarding delivery-layer packets will not differentiate GRE packets from other packets in any way. On the other hand, when a GRE packet is received by a system, the key, sequence number and checksum fields, if present (as indicated by the corresponding flags), may be checked. If the R bit is set to 1, the address family field should be checked to determine the semantics and use of the SRE length, SRE offset, and routing information fields. The way the SRE is processed depends on the particular address family.

Once all SREs have been processed, the source route is then complete, the GRE header should be removed, the payload's TTL is required to be decremented (if one exists), and the payload packet should be forwarded as a normal packet. The exact forwarding method depends on the protocol type field. The method for IP is described in the next section.

5.4.3 GRE over IP Networks

This section describes the use of GRE with IP (that is, IPv4, the current version of IP). It specifies how to use IP as the delivery protocol or the payload protocol and the special case of IP as both the delivery and payload. This section also describes using IP addresses and autonomous system (*AS*) numbers as part of a GRE source route.

IP as a Delivery Protocol

GRE packets encapsulated within IP will use IP protocol type 47.

IP as a Payload Protocol

IP packets will be encapsulated with an address family field of 0x800.

For the address family value of 0x800, the routing information field is an *IP address list* and indicates an IP source route. The first octet of the routing information field is the unsigned integer offset from the start of the SRE. The SRE offset indicates the first octet of the next IP address. The SRE length field consists of the total length of the IP address list in octets. The overall format is as illustrated in Figure 5.8.

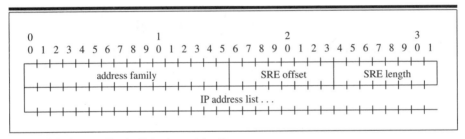

Figure 5.8 Source Route Entry format for IP.

For the address family value of 0xFFFE, the routing information field consists of a list of AS numbers and indicates an AS source route. The third octet of the routing information field contains an unsigned integer offset from the start of the SRE, called the *SRE offset*. The SRE offset indicates the first octet of the next AS number. The SRE length field consists of the total length of the AS number list in octets. The overall format is as illustrated in Figure 5.9.

IP as Both Delivery and Payload Protocol

When IP is encapsulated in IP, the TTL, TOS, and IP security options *may* be copied from the payload packet into the same fields in the delivery packet. The payload packet's TTL is required to be decremented when the packet is decapsulated to ensure that the packet cannot be forwarded indefinitely.

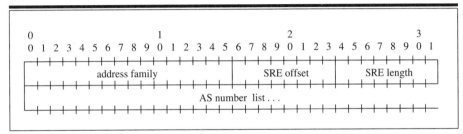

Figure 5.9 Source Route Entry Format for AS.

IP Source Routes

When a system is processing an SRE with an address family indicating an IP source route, it is required to use the SRE offset to determine the next destination IP address. If the next IP destination is this system, the SRE offset field should be increased by four (the size of an IP address). If the SRE offset is equal to the SRE length in this SRE, then the offset field in the GRE header should be adjusted to point to the next SRE (if any). This should be repeated until the next IP destination is not this system or until the entire SRE has been processed.

If the source route is incomplete, then the s (strict source route) bit is checked. If the source route is a strict source route and the next IP destination is *not* an adjacent system, the packet is required to be dropped; otherwise, the system should use the IP address indicated by the offset field to replace the destination address in the delivery header and forward the packet.

AS Source Routes

When a system is processing an SRE with an address family indicating an AS source route, it is required to use the SRE offset field to determine the next AS. If the next AS is the local AS, the SRE offset field should be increased by two (the size of an AS number). If the SRE offset is equal to the SRE length in this SRE, then the offset field in the GRE header should be adjusted to point to the next SRE (if any). This should be repeated until the next AS number is not equal to the local AS number or until the entire SRE has been processed.

If the source route is incomplete, then the s (strict source route) bit is checked. If the source route is a strict source route and the next AS is *not* an adjacent AS, the packet should be dropped. Otherwise, the system should use the AS number indicated by the SRE offset field to replace the destination address in the delivery header and forward the packet. The exact mechanism for determining the next delivery destination address given the AS number is not described in the GRE specification, but is found by consulting the Border Gateway Protocol (*BGP*) (Rekhter and Li 1995) routing tables.

5.4.4 Current List of Protocol Types

Currently assigned protocol types for GRE are shown in Table 5.1. Future protocol types must be taken from DIX ("DEC/Intel/Xerox") Ethernet encoding. For historical reasons, other values have been used for a number of protocols. See the IANA list of ether types for the complete list of these values, found at the following URL: ftp://ftp.isi.edu/in-notes/iana/assignments/ethernet-numbers.

Table 5.1 GRE Protocol Family Type Number Assignments.

Protocol Family	PTYPE (Protocol Type)
Reserved	0000
SNA	0004
OSI network layer	00FE
PUP	0200
XNS	0600
IP	0800
Chaos	0804
RFC 826 ARP	0806
Frame Relay ARP	0808
VINES	0BAD
VINES echo	0BAE
VINES loopback	0BAF
DECnet (phase IV)	6003
Transparent Ethernet bridging	6558
Raw frame relay	6559
Apollo domain	8019
Ethertalk (Appletalk)	809B
Novell IPX	8137
RFC 1144 TCP/IP compression	876B
IP autonomous systems	876C
Secure data	876D
Reserved	FFFF

5.5 Routing Failures and ICMP Messages

Routing loops within a tunnel are particularly dangerous when they cause datagrams to arrive again at the encapsulator. Suppose a datagram arrives at a router for forwarding and the router determines that the datagram has to be encapsulated before further delivery. Then, if the IP source address of the datagram matches the router's own IP address on any of its network interfaces, the router is not allowed to tunnel the datagram; instead, the datagram *should* be discarded. If the IP source address of the datagram matches the IP address of the tunnel destination (the tunnel that is typically chosen by the router based on the destination address in the datagram's IP header), the router is not allowed to tunnel the datagram; instead, the datagram *should* be discarded. Routing failures are often signaled by returning ICMP error messages to the encapsulating agent.

After an encapsulated datagram has been sent, the encapsulator may receive an ICMP message from any intermediate router within the tunnel. The action taken by the encapsulator depends on the type of ICMP message received. When the received message contains enough information, the encapsulator may use the incoming message to create a similar ICMP message, to be sent to the originator of the original unencapsulated IP datagram (the original sender). This process is referred to as *relaying* the ICMP message from the tunnel.

ICMP messages indicating an error in processing a datagram include a copy of (a portion of) the datagram causing the error. Relaying an ICMP message requires that the encapsulator strip off the outer IP header from this returned copy of the original datagram. In many typical cases the received ICMP message does not contain enough data to relay the message. There are additional mechanisms defined to handle these cases (Section 5.6). When relaying an ICMP message back to the originator of a datagram, host unreachable is preferable to network unreachable. Since the datagram was handled by the encapsulator, and the encapsulator is often considered to be on the same network as the destination address in the original unencapsulated datagram, then the datagram is considered to have reached the correct network, but not the correct destination node within that network.

5.5.1 Destination Unreachable (Type 3)

ICMP destination unreachable messages are handled by the encapsulator depending on their code field. The model suggested here represents the tunnel as extending a network to include nonlocal (for example, mobile) nodes. Thus, if the original destination in the unencapsulated datagram is on the same network as the encapsulator, certain destination unreachable code values may be modified to conform to the suggested model.

Network unreachable (code 0) An ICMP destination unreachable message *should* be returned to the original sender. If the original destination in the unencapsulated datagram is on the same network as the encapsulator, the newly generated destination unreachable message sent by the encapsulator may have code 1 (host unreachable), since presumably the datagram arrived at the correct network and the encapsulator is trying to create the appearance that the original destination is local to that network even if it is not. Otherwise, if the encapsulator returns a destination unreachable message, the code field is required to be set to 0 (network unreachable).

Host unreachable (code 1)   The encapsulator should relay host unreachable messages to the sender of the original unencapsulated datagram, if possible.

Protocol unreachable (code 2)   When the encapsulator receives an ICMP protocol unreachable message, it *should* send a destination unreachable message with code 0 or 1 (see the discussion for code 0) to the sender of the original unencapsulated datagram. Since the original sender did not use protocol 4 in sending the datagram, it would be meaningless to return code 2 to that sender.

Port unreachable (code 3)   This code should never be received by the encapsulator, since the outer IP header does not refer to any port number. It is not allowed to be relayed to the sender of the original unencapsulated datagram.

Datagram too big (code 4)   The encapsulator is required to relay ICMP datagram too big message to the sender of the original unencapsulated datagram.

Source route failed (code 5)   This code *should* be handled by the encapsulator itself and can never be relayed to the sender of the original unencapsulated datagram.

5.5.2 Source Quench (Type 4)

Instead of relaying ICMP source quench messages to the sender of the original unencapsulated datagram, the encapsulator *should* activate alternative congestion control mechanisms to help alleviate the congestion detected within the tunnel (Mankin and Ramakrishnan 1991).

5.5.3 Redirect (Type 5)

The encapsulator may handle the ICMP redirect messages itself, but can never relay the redirect to the sender of the original unencapsulated datagram.

5.5.4 Time Exceeded (Type 11)

ICMP time exceeded messages report (presumed) routing loops within the tunnel itself. The encapsulator must report time exceeded messages to the sender of the original unencapsulated datagram as host unreachable (type 3, code 1).

5.5.5 Parameter Problem (Type 12)

If the parameter problem message points to a field copied from the original unencapsulated datagram, the encapsulator may relay the ICMP message to the sender of the original unencapsulated datagram. Otherwise, if the problem occurs with an IP option inserted by the encapsulator, then the encapsulator is not allowed to relay the ICMP message to the original sender.

Note that an encapsulator following prevalent current practice will never insert any IP options into the encapsulated datagram, except possibly for security reasons. Therefore, usually ICMP parameter problems messages can be relayed back to the original sender.

5.5.6 Other ICMP Messages

Other ICMP messages are not related to the encapsulation operations described within this protocol specification and should be acted on by the encapsulator as specified by (Postel 1981a).

5.6 Tunnel Management

This section describes techniques to be used by the encapsulating agent (for example, a home agent) to overcome certain deficiencies related to error reporting from within tunnels.

5.6.1 Tunnel Soft State

Unfortunately, ICMP only requires IP routers to return eight octets (64 bits) of the datagram beyond the IP header. This is not enough to include a copy of the encapsulated (inner) IP header, so it is not always possible for the encapsulator to relay the ICMP message from the interior of a tunnel back to the original sender. Nevertheless, by carefully maintaining a soft state about tunnels into which it sends, the encapsulator can return accurate ICMP messages to the original sender in most cases. The encapsulator *should* maintain at least the following soft-state information about each tunnel:

- MTU of the tunnel (Section 5.6.2)
- TTL (path length) of the tunnel
- Ability to reach the end of the tunnel

The encapsulator uses the ICMP messages it receives from the interior of a tunnel to update the soft-state information for that tunnel. ICMP errors that could be received from one of the routers along the tunnel interior include

- Datagram too big

- Time exceeded

- Destination unreachable

- Source quench

When subsequent datagrams arrive that would transit the tunnel, the encapsulator checks the soft state for the tunnel. If the datagram would cause an ICMP error to be returned when it was encapsulated and sent through the tunnel (for example, if the TTL of the new datagram is less than the tunnel soft-state TTL), the encapsulator sends an ICMP error message back to the sender of the original datagram, but it also encapsulates the datagram and forwards it into the tunnel. The previous section explains how to return ICMP errors to the original sender.

Using this technique the ICMP error messages sent by the encapsulator will not always match up one to one with errors encountered within the tunnel, but they will accurately reflect the state of the network.

Tunnel soft state was originally developed for the IP address encapsulation (*IPAE*) specification (Gilligan, Nordmark, and Hinden 1994).

5.6.2 Tunnel MTU Discovery

When the (DF) bit is set by the originator and copied into the outer IP header, the proper MTU of the tunnel will be learned from ICMP datagram too big (type 3, code 4) messages reported to the encapsulator. To support sending nodes that use PMTU discovery (Knowles 1993, Mogul and Deering 1990), all encapsulator implementations are required to support PMTU discovery soft state within their tunnels. For Mobile IP (and many other applications of encapsulation), there are three primary advantages:

1. Any fragmentation that occurs because of the size of the encapsulation header is performed only once after encapsulation. This prevents multiple fragmentation of a single datagram, which improves the processing efficiency of the decapsulator and the routers within the tunnel.

2. If the source of the unencapsulated datagram is doing PMTU discovery, then it is helpful for the encapsulator to know the MTU of the tunnel. Any ICMP datagram too big messages from within the tunnel are returned to the encapsulator, and it is not always possible for the encapsulator to relay ICMP messages to the source of the original unencapsulated datagram. By maintaining a soft state

about the MTU of the tunnel, the encapsulator can return correct ICMP datagram too big messages to the original sender of the unencapsulated datagram to support its own PMTU discovery. In this case, the MTU that is conveyed to the original sender by the encapsulator *should* be the MTU of the tunnel minus the size of the encapsulating IP header. This will avoid fragmentation of the original IP datagram by the encapsulator.

3. If the source of the original unencapsulated datagram is not doing PMTU discovery, it is still desirable for the encapsulator to know the MTU of the tunnel. In particular, it is much better to fragment the original datagram when encapsulating, than to allow the encapsulated datagram to be fragmented. Fragmenting the original datagram can be done by the encapsulator without special buffer requirements and without the need to keep an IP reassembly state in the decapsulator. By contrast, if the encapsulated datagram is fragmented, then the decapsulator must reassemble the fragmented (encapsulated) datagram before decapsulating it, requiring a reassembly state and buffer space within the decapsulator.

Thus, the encapsulator *should* normally do PMTU discovery, requiring it to send all datagrams into the tunnel with the DF bit set in the outer IP header. However, there are problems with this approach. When the original sender sets the DF bit, the sender can react quickly to any returned ICMP datagram too big error message by retransmitting the original datagram. On the other hand, suppose that the encapsulator receives an ICMP datagram too big message from within the tunnel. In that case, if the original sender of the unencapsulated datagram had not set the DF bit, there may be nothing sensible that the encapsulator can do to let the original sender know of the error. The encapsulator may keep a copy of the sent datagram whenever it tries increasing the tunnel MTU, to allow it to fragment and resend the datagram if it gets a datagram too big response.

5.6.3 Congestion

An encapsulator might receive indications of congestion from the tunnel, for example, by receiving ICMP source quench messages from nodes within the tunnel. In addition, certain link layers and various protocols not related to the Internet suite of protocols might provide such indications in the form of a congestion experienced flag (Mankin and Ramakrishnan 1991). The encapsulator *should* reflect conditions of congestion in its soft state for the tunnel. Moreover, when subsequently forwarding datagrams into the tunnel, the encapsulator should use appropriate means for controlling congestion (Baker 1995). However, appropriate means do *not* include sending ICMP source quench messages to the original sender of the unencapsulated datagram.

5.7 Decapsulation by Routers

IP encapsulation potentially reduces the security of the Internet, and care needs to be taken in the implementation and deployment of IP encapsulation. For example, IP encapsulation makes it difficult for border routers to filter datagrams based on header fields. In particular, the original values of the source address, destination address, and protocol fields in the IP header, and the port numbers used in any transport header within the datagram, are not located in their normal positions within the datagram after encapsulation. Since any IP datagram can be encapsulated and passed through a tunnel, such filtering border routers need to examine all datagrams carefully. Such filtering should be integrated with IP authentication.

When IP authentication is used, encapsulated packets might be allowed to enter an organization when the encapsulating (outer) packet or the encapsulated (inner) packet is sent by an authenticated, trusted source. Encapsulated packets containing no such authentication represent a potentially large security risk.

IP datagrams that are encapsulated and encrypted (Kent 1997b) might also pose a problem for filtering routers. In this case, the router can pass the datagram only if it shares the security association used for the encryption. To allow this sort of encryption in environments in which all packets need to be filtered (or at least accounted for), a mechanism must be in place for the receiving node to communicate the security association securely to the border router. This might, more rarely, also apply to the security association used for outgoing datagrams.

5.8 Decapsulation by IP Nodes

Network nodes that are capable of receiving encapsulated IP datagrams *should* admit only those datagrams fitting into one or more of the following categories.

- The protocol is harmless. Source address-based authentication is not needed.

- The encapsulating (outer) datagram comes from an authentically identified, trusted source. The authenticity of the source could be established by relying on physical security in addition to border router configuration, but is more likely to come from use of the IP authentication header.

- The encapsulated (inner) datagram includes an IP authentication header.

- The encapsulated (inner) datagram is addressed to a network interface belonging to the decapsulator, or to a node with which the decapsulator has entered into a special relationship for delivering such encapsulated datagrams.

Some or all of this checking could be done in border routers rather than the receiving node, but it is better if border router checks are used as a backup, rather than being the only check.

5.9 Unicast Datagram Routing

This section describes rules for (1) forwarding datagrams and (2) selecting routes that are used by mobile nodes and mobility agents.

5.9.1 Route Selection by Mobile Nodes

When connected to its home network, a mobile node operates without the support of mobility services; that is, it operates in the same way as any other fixed host. A mobile node may rely on DHCP to indicate a default router when connected to its home network or when away from home and using a colocated care-of address; DHCP is further detailed in Chapter 9. ICMP router advertisement is another method for discovering routers, as described in Section 3.2.1.

When registered on a foreign network, the mobile node chooses a default router using the following two rules.

1. If the mobile node is registered using a foreign agent's care-of address, then the mobile node may use that care-of address as the address of a default router. The mobile node may also consider the IP source address of the agent advertisement as another possible choice for the IP address of a default router. In such cases the IP source address is treated as the worst choice (lowest preference) for a default router.

2. If the mobile node is registered directly with its home agent using a colocated care-of address, then the mobile node should choose its default router from among those advertised in any ICMP Router Advertisement message that it receives for which its colocated care-of address and the router address match under the network prefix. If the mobile node's colocated care-of address matches the IP source address of the agent advertisement under the network prefix, the mobile node may also consider that IP source address as another possible choice for the IP address of a default router, along with any router addresses that might be known from the ICMP Router Advertisement portion of the message. If so, the IP source address is treated as the worst choice (lowest preference) for a default router. The network prefix may be obtained from the prefix-length extension in the Router Advertisement, if present. It is also permissible for the prefix to be obtained through other mechanisms (for example, proprietary protocols).

Beyond these rules, the actual selection of the default router is made by the selection method specified for ICMP router discovery (see Section 3.2.1, among the router addresses determined in this section. In any case, a mobile node registered by way of a foreign agent may choose its foreign agent as a default router. The mobile node may not use broadcast ARP to determine the layer-2 address of a foreign agent or any other default router. This makes the use of other routers advertised in the ICMP router advertisement problematic until new mechanisms are established for use with Mobile IP. Further experience will determine whether or not such a feature is useful.

Van Jacobson header compression (Jacobson 1990) will not function properly unless all TCP datagrams to and from the mobile node pass, respectively, through the same first- and last-hop router. The mobile node, therefore, is required to select its foreign agent as its default router if it performs Van Jacobson header compression with its foreign agent.

5.9.2 Routing by Foreign Agents

On receipt of an encapsulated datagram sent to its advertised care-of address, a foreign agent is required to compare the inner destination address to those entries in its visitor list. When the destination matches the address of any mobile node currently in the visitor list, the foreign agent forwards the decapsulated datagram to the mobile node. Otherwise, the foreign agent cannot forward the datagram without modifications to the original IP header; and a routing loop is likely to result. Note that if the foreign agent uses the techniques of route optimization (Chapter 6), better results can be obtained. Otherwise, the datagram should be discarded silently. ICMP destination unreachable is not allowed to be sent when a foreign agent is unable to forward an incoming tunneled datagram.

The foreign agent is not allowed to advertise the presence of any mobile node or router (Section 5.12) to other routers in its routing domain, nor to any other mobile node.

The foreign agent is required to route datagrams it receives from registered mobile nodes. At a minimum, this means that the foreign agent must verify the IP header checksum, decrement the IP TTL, recompute the IP header checksum, and forward such datagrams to a default router.

5.9.3 Routing by the Home Agent

The home agent is required to be able to intercept any datagrams on the home network addressed to the mobile node while the mobile node is registered away from home. Proxy and gratuitous ARP may be used in enabling this operation, as discussed in Section 5.13.

The home agent must compare the IP destination address of all arriving datagrams against the home address of any of its mobile nodes registered away from home. If it matches, the home agent tunnels the datagram to the mobile node's currently registered care-of address or addresses. If the home agent supports the optional capability of multiple simultaneous mobility bindings, it tunnels a copy to each care-of address in the mobile node's mobility binding list. If the mobile node has no current mobility bindings, the home agent is not allowed to attempt to intercept datagrams destined for the mobile node. Thus, in the configuration shown in Figure 2.2A, the home agent will not receive such datagrams. However, if the home agent is also a router handling common IP traffic, as in Figure 2.2B, it is possible that it will receive such datagrams for forwarding to the home network. In this case, the home agent is required to assume the mobile node is at home and simply forward the datagram directly to the home network.

Earlier sections in this chapter are concerned with methods of encapsulation that may be used for tunneling. Nodes implementing tunneling *should* also implement the tunnel soft-state mechanism (described in Section 5.6.1), which allows ICMP error messages returned from the tunnel to be reflected back correctly to the original senders of the tunneled datagrams.

Home agents should be able to decapsulate, and subsequently deliver, tunneled packets for which they are the tunnel endpoint. Such packets may be sent to the home agent by a mobile node for the purpose of maintaining location privacy, as mentioned in Section 4.9.5, or from its care-of address to coexist with ingress-filtering border routes (Section 7.2).

If the lifetime for a given mobility binding expires before the home agent has received another valid registration request for that mobile node, then that binding is deleted from the mobility binding list. The home agent is not allowed to send any registration reply message simply because the mobile node's binding has expired. The entry in the visitor list of the mobile node's current foreign agent will expire naturally, probably at the same time as the binding expires at the home agent. When a mobility binding's lifetime expires, the home agent is required to delete the binding, but it is required to retain any other (nonexpired) simultaneous mobility bindings that it holds for the mobile node.

When a home agent receives a datagram, intercepted for one of its mobile nodes registered away from home, the home agent examines the datagram to check if it is already encapsulated. If so, two special rules apply to the forwarding of that datagram to the mobile node.

1. If the inner (encapsulated) destination address is the same as the outer destination address (the mobile node's home address), then the home agent is also required to examine the outer source address of the encapsulated datagram (the source address of the tunnel). If this outer source address is the same as the mobile node's current care-of address, the home agent is required to discard that datagram silently to prevent a likely routing loop. If, instead, the outer source address is not the same as the mobile node's current care-of address, then the home agent should forward the datagram to the mobile node. To forward the datagram in this case, the home agent may simply alter the outer destination

address to the care-of address, rather than reencapsulate the datagram.

2. If the inner destination address is not the same as the outer destination address, the home agent should reencapsulate the datagram (recursive encapsulation), with the new outer destination address set equal to the mobile node's care-of address. That is, the home agent forwards the entire datagram to the mobile node in the same way as any other datagram (encapsulated or not).

5.10 Broadcast Datagrams

When a home agent receives a broadcast datagram, it only forwards the datagram to mobile nodes in its list that have requested forwarding of broadcast datagrams. A mobile node may request forwarding of broadcast datagrams by setting the B bit in its registration request message (Section 4.3). It is a matter of configuration at the home agent as to which specific categories of broadcast datagrams will be forwarded to such mobile nodes. One proposal to allow the mobile node to request a particular configuration is detailed in Section 7.3.1. The home agent should never forward ARP broadcast packets to the mobile node.

If the D bit was set in the mobile node's registration request message, indicating that the mobile node is using a colocated care-of address, the home agent simply tunnels appropriate broadcast IP datagrams to the mobile node's care-of address. The mobile node detunnels the received datagram in the same way as any other datagram tunneled directly to it. The home agent will send broadcast datagrams with only a single encapsulating header, as illustrated in Figure 5.10.

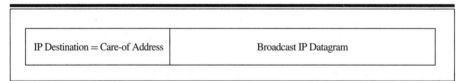

| IP Destination = Care-of Address | Broadcast IP Datagram |

Figure 5.10 Sending broadcast packets to a colocated care-of address.

If the D bit is not set, then the mobile node has indicated that it is using a foreign agent care-of address, and the foreign agent will thus decapsulate arriving datagrams before forwarding them to the mobile node. In this case, to forward such a received broadcast datagram to the mobile node, the home agent is first required to encapsulate the broadcast datagram in a unicast datagram addressed to the mobile node's home address, and then is required to tunnel this resulting datagram to the mobile node's care-of address. This extra level of encapsulation is required so that the foreign agent can determine which mobile node should receive the datagram after it is decapsulated.

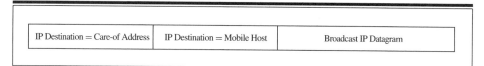

Figure 5.11 Sending broadcast packets to a foreign agent care-of address.

When decapsulated by the foreign agent, the inner datagram will thus be a unicast IP datagram addressed to the mobile node, identifying to the foreign agent the intended destination of the encapsulated broadcast datagram, and will be delivered to the mobile node in the same way as any tunneled datagram arriving for the mobile node. The foreign agent is not allowed to decapsulate the encapsulated broadcast datagram and cannot use a local network broadcast to transmit it to the mobile node.

In either case, the mobile node must decapsulate the datagram it receives to recover the original broadcast datagram.

5.11 Multicast Datagram Routing

As mentioned previously, a mobile node that is connected to its home network functions in the same way as any other fixed host or router. Thus, when it is at home, a mobile node functions identically to other multicast senders and receivers. This section describes the behavior of a mobile node that is visiting a foreign network.

To receive multicasts a mobile node is required to join the multicast group in one of two ways. First, a mobile node may join the group via a local multicast router on the visited subnet. This option assumes that there is a multicast router present on the visited subnet. If the mobile node is using a colocated care-of address, it should use this address as the source IP address of its Internet Group Membership Protocol (*IGMP*) (Deering 1989) messages; otherwise, it is required to use its home address.

Alternatively, a mobile node that wishes to receive multicasts may join groups via a bidirectional tunnel to its home agent, assuming that its home agent is a multicast router. The mobile node tunnels IGMP messages to its home agent and the home agent forwards multicast datagrams down the tunnel to the mobile node. The rules for multicast datagram delivery to mobile nodes in this case are identical to those for broadcast datagrams. Namely, if the mobile node is using a colocated care-of address (and the D bit was set in the mobile node's registration request), then the home agent should tunnel the datagram to its care-of address. Otherwise, the home agent is first required to encapsulate the datagram in a unicast datagram addressed to the mobile node's home address and then is required to tunnel the resulting datagram (recursive tunneling) to the mobile node's care-of address.

A mobile node that wishes to send datagrams to a multicast group also has two options: (1) send directly on the visited network or (2) send via a tunnel to its home agent. Because multicast routing in general depends on the IP source address, a mobile node that sends multicast datagrams directly on the visited network is required to use a colocated care-of address as the IP source address. In contrast, a mobile node that tunnels a multicast datagram to its home agent is required to use its home address as the IP source address in the (inner) multicast datagram. This second method is used only when the home agent is a multicast router.

5.12 Mobile Routers

A mobile node can be a router that is responsible for the mobility of one or more entire networks moving together, perhaps on an airplane, a ship, a train, an automobile, a bicycle, or a kayak. The nodes connected to a network served by the mobile router may themselves be fixed nodes or mobile nodes or routers. In this book, such networks are called *mobile networks*.

A mobile router may act as a foreign agent and provide a foreign agent care-of address to mobile nodes connected to the mobile network. Typical routing to a mobile node via a mobile router in this case is illustrated by the following example.

1. A laptop computer is disconnected from its home network and later attached to a network port in the seat back of an aircraft. The laptop computer uses Mobile IP to register on this foreign network, using a care-of address discovered through the aircraft's agent advertisement.

2. The aircraft network is itself mobile. Suppose the node serving as the foreign agent on the aircraft also serves as the default router that connects the aircraft network to the rest of the Internet. When the aircraft is at home, this router is attached to some fixed network at the airline's headquarters, which is the router's home network. While the aircraft is in flight, this router registers from time to time over its radio link with a series of foreign agents below it on the ground. This router's home agent is a node on the fixed network at the airline's headquarters.

3. Some correspondent node sends a datagram to the laptop computer, addressing the datagram to the laptop's home address. This datagram is initially routed to the laptop's home network.

4. The laptop's home agent intercepts the datagram on the home network and tunnels it to the laptop's care-of address, which in this example is an address of the node serving as router and foreign agent on the aircraft. Normal IP routing will route the datagram to the fixed network at the airline's headquarters.

5. The aircraft router's home agent there intercepts the datagram and tunnels it to its current care-of address, which in this example is served by some agent on the ground underneath the aircraft. The original datagram from the correspondent

node has now been encapsulated twice: once by the laptop's home agent and again by the aircraft's home agent.

6. The agent on the ground decapsulates the datagram, yielding a datagram still encapsulated by the laptop's home agent, with a destination address of the laptop's care-of address. The ground agent sends the resulting datagram over its radio link to the aircraft.

7. The foreign agent on the aircraft decapsulates the datagram, yielding the original datagram from the correspondent node with a destination address of the laptop's home address. The aircraft foreign agent delivers the datagram over the aircraft network to the laptop's link-layer address.

This example illustrates the case in which a mobile node is attached to a mobile network. That is, the mobile node is mobile with respect to the network, which itself is also mobile (here with respect to the ground). If, instead, the node is fixed with respect to the mobile network (the mobile network is the fixed node's home network), then either of two methods may be used to cause datagrams from correspondent nodes to be routed to the fixed node.

A home agent may be configured to have a permanent registration for the fixed node, that indicates the mobile router's address as the fixed host's care-of address. The mobile router's home agent will usually be used for this purpose. The home agent is then responsible for advertising connectivity using normal routing protocols to the fixed node. Any datagram sent to the fixed node will thus use recursive tunneling (that it, more than one level of encapsulation) during part of its travel to the fixed node.

Alternatively, the mobile router may advertise connectivity to the entire mobile network using normal IP routing protocols through a bidirectional tunnel to its own home agent. This method avoids the need for recursive tunneling of datagrams, but introduces the need for additional protocol operations.

5.13 ARP, Proxy ARP, and Gratuitous ARP

This section describes how home agents and mobile nodes manipulate ARP cache handling by other nodes on the home network. Because of difficulties with ARP, a mobile node is effectively barred from using it anywhere else but on the home network.

The use of ARP (Plummer 1982) requires special rules for correct operation when wireless or mobile nodes are involved. The requirements specified in this section apply to all home networks in which ARP is used for address resolution.

In addition to the normal use of ARP for resolving a target node's link-layer address from its IP address, there are two distinguished uses of ARP.

1. A *proxy ARP* (Postel 1984) is an ARP reply sent by one node on behalf of another node that is either unable or unwilling to answer its own ARP requests. The sender of a proxy ARP reverses the sender and target protocol address fields as described by (Plummer 1982), but supplies some configured link-layer address (generally, its own) in the sender hardware address field. The node receiving the reply will then associate this link-layer address with the IP address of the original target node, causing it to transmit future datagrams for this target node to the node with that link-layer address.

2. A *gratuitous ARP* (Stevens 1994) is an ARP packet sent by a node to update other nodes' ARP caches. A gratuitous ARP may use either an ARP request or an ARP reply packet. In either case, the ARP sender protocol address and ARP target protocol address are both set to the IP address of the cache entry to be updated, and the ARP sender hardware address is set to the link-layer address to which this cache entry should be updated. When using an ARP reply packet, the target hardware address is also set to the link-layer address to which this cache entry should be updated. (This field is not used in an ARP request packet.) The gratuitous ARP packet is required to be transmitted as a local broadcast packet on the local link. According to (Plummer 1982), any node receiving any ARP packet (request or reply) is required to update its local ARP cache with the sender protocol and hardware addresses in the ARP packet if the receiving node has an entry for that IP address already in its ARP cache. This requirement in the ARP protocol applies even for ARP request packets and for ARP reply packets that do not match any ARP request transmitted by the receiving node (Plummer 1982).

Figure 5.12 illustrates the operation of gratuitous ARP. In Figure 5.12(a), mobile node Z is attached to its home network and naturally answers ARP requests. The router, home agent, and nodes X and Y all associate Z's IP address with Z's *MAC address* Z_MAC. In Figure 5.12(b), mobile node Z is roaming and the home agent has broadcast an ARP reply indicating that Z's MAC address is HA_MAC. Until Z returns home, the home agent will continue to *proxy ARP* for Z.

While a mobile node is registered on a foreign network, its home agent uses proxy ARP (Postel 1984) to reply to ARP requests it receives that seek the mobile node's link-layer address, as follows. When receiving an ARP request, the home agent is required to examine the target IP address of the request. If this IP address matches the home address of any mobile node for which it has a registered mobility binding, the home agent is required to transmit an ARP reply on behalf of the mobile node. After exchanging the sender and target addresses in the packet (as required by the proxy ARP specification (Postel 1984)), the home agent sets the sender link-layer address field of the ARP reply to be its own link-layer address from the interface over which the reply will be sent.

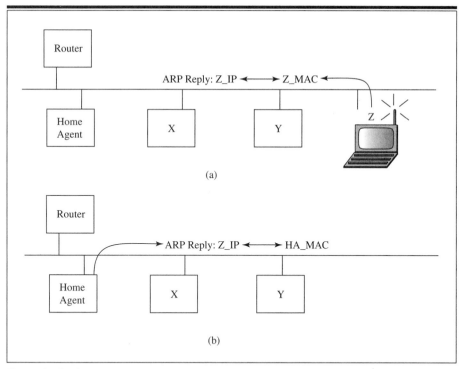

Figure 5.12 Gratuitous ARP by the home agent.

When a mobile node leaves its home network and registers a binding on a foreign network, its home agent uses gratuitous ARP to update the ARP caches of nodes on the home network. This causes such nodes to associate the link-layer address of the home agent with the mobile node's home (IP) address. When registering a binding for a mobile node for which the home agent previously had no binding (the mobile node was assumed to be at home), the home agent is required to broadcast a gratuitous ARP on behalf of the mobile node on the link on which the mobile node's home address is located. Since broadcasts on the local link (such as Ethernet) are typically not guaranteed to be reliable, the gratuitous ARP packet should be retransmitted a small number of times to increase its reliability.

When a mobile node returns to its home network, all nodes on the mobile node's home network must once again learn to associate the mobile node's own link-layer address with the mobile node's home (IP) address. The mobile node and its home agent again use gratuitous ARP for this purpose, with the mobile node's link-layer address in the ARP reply message. The mobile node is required to broadcast this gratuitous ARP on its home network before sending its deregistration request message to its home agent. The gratuitous ARP packet should be retransmitted a small number of times (typically three) to increase its reliability, but these retransmissions should proceed in parallel with the transmission and processing of its deregistration request.

When the mobile node's home agent receives and accepts this deregistration request, the home agent is also required to broadcast a gratuitous ARP on the mobile node's home network. This gratuitous ARP is also used to associate the mobile node's home address with the mobile node's own link-layer address. In the case of wireless network interfaces, the area within transmission range of the mobile node will likely differ from that within range of its home agent. Therefore, a gratuitous ARP is transmitted by both the mobile node and its home agent. The ARP packet from the home agent is required to be transmitted as a local broadcast on the mobile node's home link, and should be retransmitted a small number of times to increase its reliability. These retransmissions, however, should proceed in parallel with the transmission and processing of its deregistration reply.

While the mobile node is away from home, it is not allowed to transmit any broadcast ARP request or ARP reply messages. Moreover, while the mobile node is away from home, it is not allowed to reply to ARP requests in which the target IP address is its own home address, unless the ARP request is sent by a foreign agent with which the mobile node is attempting to register or a foreign agent with which the mobile node has an unexpired registration. Such ARP packets must never be sent to a broadcast address. In the latter case, the mobile node is required to use a unicast ARP reply to respond to the foreign agent. Note that if the mobile node is using a colocated care-of address and receives an ARP request in which the target IP address is its care-of address, then the mobile node should reply to this ARP request. Note also that when transmitting a registration request on a foreign network, a mobile node discovers the link-layer address of a foreign agent by storing the address as it is received from the agent advertisement from that foreign agent. The mobile node is *not* permitted to obtain this information by transmitting a broadcast ARP message on the foreign network.

The specific order in which each of the requirements for the use of ARP, proxy ARP, and gratuitous ARP are applied, relative to the transmission and processing of the mobile node's registration request and registration reply messages when leaving or returning home, are important to the correct operation of the protocol. When a mobile node leaves its home network, the following steps (in this order) are required to be performed.

1. The mobile node decides to register away from home, perhaps because it has received an agent advertisement from a foreign agent and has not recently received one from its home agent.

2. Before transmitting the registration request, the mobile node disables its own future processing of any ARP requests it may subsequently receive requesting the link-layer address corresponding to its home address, except insofar as necessary to communicate with foreign agents on visited networks.

3. The mobile node transmits its registration request.

4. When the mobile node's home agent receives and accepts the registration request, it performs a gratuitous ARP on behalf of the mobile node and begins using proxy ARP to reply to ARP requests that it receives requesting the mobile node's link-layer address. If, instead, the home agent rejects the registration request, no change ARP processing (gratuitous or proxy) is performed by the home agent.

When a mobile node later returns to its home network, the following steps (in this order) are required to be performed.

1. The mobile node decides to deregister all care-of addresses, perhaps because it has received an agent advertisement from its home agent.

2. Before transmitting the registration request, the mobile node reenables its own future processing of any ARP requests it may subsequently receive requesting its link-layer address.

3. The mobile node performs a gratuitous ARP for itself.

4. The mobile node transmits its registration request.

5. When the mobile node's home agent receives and accepts the registration request, it stops using proxy ARP to reply to ARP requests that it receives requesting the mobile node's link-layer address. It then performs gratuitous ARP on behalf of the mobile node. If, instead, the home agent rejects the registration request, no change in ARP processing (gratuitous or proxy) is performed by the home agent.

Notice also that use of gratuitous ARP carries with it all of the security risks already present with the general use of ARP.

5.14 Source Routing Alternatives

It is generally true that encapsulation and the IP *LSR* option (Section 1.5.3) can be used in similar ways to affect the routing of a datagram. In fact, some of the first approaches to Mobile IP were based on the observation that a datagram addressed to a home network can nevertheless reach a mobile node away from home if the datagram includes the IP LSR option.

Those initial approaches failed, however. There are several technical reasons to prefer encapsulation:

- There are unsolved security problems associated with the use of the IP source-routing options.

- Current Internet routers exhibit performance problems when forwarding datagrams that contain IP options, including the IP source-routing options.

- Many current Internet nodes process IP source-routing options incorrectly.

- Firewalls may exclude IP source-routed datagrams.

- Insertion of an IP source-routing option may complicate the processing of authentication information by the source and/or destination of a datagram, depending on how the authentication is specified to be performed.

- It is considered impolite for intermediate routers to make modifications to datagrams they did not originate, whereas encapsulation is considered acceptable.

These technical advantages must be weighed against the disadvantages posed by the use of encapsulation.

- Encapsulated datagrams typically are larger than source-routed datagrams.

- Encapsulation cannot be used unless it is known in advance that the node at the tunnel exit point can decapsulate the datagram.

Since the majority of Internet nodes today do not perform well when IP LSR options are used, the second technical disadvantage of encapsulation is not as serious as it might at first seem.

5.15 Summary

The discussion of encapsulation techniques and other routing considerations in this chapter concludes the description of the base Mobile IP specification. The techniques described are the last required piece of the puzzle. Once a mobile node finds a care-of address and informs the home agent of that care-of address, encapsulation to the care-of address is all that is needed for the home agent to get datagrams to the mobile node. Having three separate ways to perform the encapsulation should provide sufficient flexibility for this crucial feature of the protocol. GRE can even be used with mobile IP to provide mobility for mobile nodes using network-layer protocols other than IP. Recent discussion, however, has indicated a possible need to allow the use of newer encapsulation protocols, such as PPTP or LZTP.

Since tunneling is effectively an extension of the Internet routing paths, ICMP messages become important to agents using the tunnels. Presenting to the rest of the Internet the model of a contiguous home network requires special handling of the ICMP messages by the tunnel entry point. This requires maintaining a soft state by the home agent and attending to detailed rules about relaying ICMP messages to correspondent nodes. Another part of maintaining the model of the home network involves correct maintenance of the ARP caches of the nodes attached to the home network. This is done by the home agent and mobile node by using the techniques of proxy ARP and gratuitous ARP.

Unfortunately, in the base protocol, the home agent is saddled with the responsibility of tunneling each and every datagram to the care-of address. This has the effect of inserting the home agent as a single point of failure in many communication paths that might otherwise be scalably distributed around the routing fabric of the Internet. The next chapter shows techniques for alleviating this problem.

CHAPTER SIX

Route Optimization

This chapter presents the draft protocol definition for route optimization, which means the elimination of *triangle routing* (see Figure 6.1) whenever the correspondent node is able to perform the necessary protocol operations. The route optimization protocol definition is largely concerned with three areas:

1. Supplying a *binding update* to any correspondent node that needs one (and has some realistic chance to process it correctly)

2. Providing the means to create the needed authentication and replay protection so that the recipient of a binding update message can believe it

3. Allowing for the mobile node and foreign agent to create a *registration key* for later use in making a smooth transition to a new point of attachment

The ways provided for the mobile node and foreign agent to obtain a registration key are as follows:

- Use the mobility security association they share if it exists, or can be established using ISAKMP (Maughan 1997) or SKIP (Aziz 1996)

- Use the mobile node's public key if it exists

- Use the foreign agent's public key, if it exists, to enable the home agent to create public keys for both entities

- Use the security association between the foreign agent and home agent, if it exists, to enable the home agent to create the registration keys for both entities

- Use the Diffie-Hellman key exchange algorithm

Lastly, the use of *special tunnels* is detailed, so that foreign agents that lose track of one of their visiting mobile nodes can still forward datagrams to the home agent for another try at delivery.

The base Mobile IP protocol (as described in Chapters 3 through 5 of this book) allows any mobile node to move about, changing its point of attachment to the Internet, while continuing to be identified by its home IP address. Correspondent nodes sending IP datagrams to a mobile node send them to the mobile node's home address in the same way as with any other destination. This scheme allows transparent interoperation between mobile nodes and their correspondent nodes, but forces all datagrams for a mobile node to be routed through its home agent. Thus, datagrams to the mobile node are often routed along paths that are significantly longer than optimal. For example, if a mobile node is visiting some subnet, even datagrams from a correspondent node on the same subnet must be routed through the Internet to the mobile node's home agent (on its home network), only then to be tunneled back to the original subnet for final delivery. This indirect routing can significantly delay the delivery of the datagrams to mobile nodes, and it places an unnecessary burden on the networks and routers along its path through the Internet.

This chapter defines extensions to the operation of the base Mobile IP protocol to allow for better routing, so that datagrams can be routed from a correspondent node to a mobile node without going to the home agent first. These extensions are collectively known as *route optimization*.

Route optimization extensions provide a means for nodes that implement them to cache the binding of a mobile node and to then tunnel their own datagrams directly to the care-of address indicated in that binding, bypassing the possibly lengthy route to and from that mobile node's home agent. Extensions are also provided to allow datagrams in flight when a mobile node moves and datagrams sent based on an out-of-date cached binding to be forwarded directly to the mobile node's new care-of address.

Since route optimization affects the routing of IP datagrams to the mobile node, it can be authenticated using the same type of mechanisms used in the base Mobile IP protocol. This authentication generally relies on a mobility security association established in advance between the sender and receiver of such messages.

6.1 Route Optimization Overview

This section provides an overview of the protocols and operations of route optimization. These can be divided into four main parts:

1. Updating *binding caches*

2. Managing smooth handoffs between foreign agents

3. Acquiring registration keys for smooth handoffs

4. Using special tunnels

6.1.1 Binding Caches

Route optimization provides a means for any node to maintain a binding cache containing the care-of address of one or more mobile nodes. When sending an IP datagram to a mobile node, if the sender has a binding cache entry for the destination mobile node, it may tunnel the datagram directly to the care-of address indicated in the cached mobility binding.

In the absence of any binding cache entry, datagrams destined for a mobile node will be routed to the mobile node's home network in the same way as any other IP datagram, and then tunneled to the mobile node's current care-of address by the mobile node's home agent. This is the only routing mechanism supported by the base Mobile IP protocol. As a side effect of this indirect routing of a datagram to a mobile node, it would be nice if the original sender of the datagram were informed of the mobile node's current mobility binding, giving the sender an opportunity to cache the binding. In Figure 6.1, the Internet host is going to have to route each datagram for the mobile node *indirectly*, through its home agent. If the internet host had a binding cache entry for the mobile node, it would be able to send packets *directly* back to the mobile node without the services of the home agent.

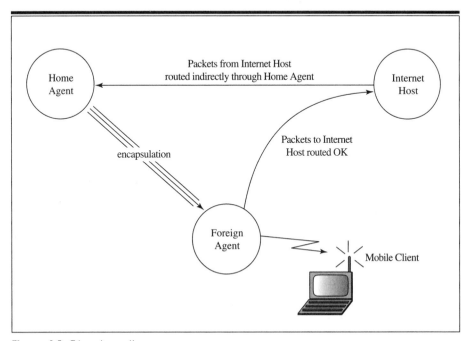

Figure 6.1 Triangle routing.

Any node may maintain a binding cache to optimize its own communication with mobile nodes. A node may create or update a binding cache entry for a mobile node only when it has received and authenticated the mobile node's mobility binding. As before, each binding in the binding cache also has an associated lifetime, specified in the binding update message in which the node obtained the binding. After the expiration of this time period, the binding is to be deleted from the cache. In addition, a node cache may use any reasonable strategy for managing the space within the binding cache. When a new entry needs to be added to the binding cache, the node may choose to drop any entry already in the cache, if needed, to make space for the new entry. For example, a least recently used (*LRU*) strategy for cache entry replacement is likely to work well.

When a mobile node's home agent intercepts a datagram from the home network and tunnels it to the mobile node, the home agent may deduce that the original source of the datagram has no binding cache entry for the destination mobile node. The home agent should then send a binding update message to the original source node, informing it of the mobile node's current mobility binding. No acknowledgment for such a binding update message is needed, because additional, future datagrams from this source node intercepted by the home agent for the mobile node will cause transmission of another binding update. For a binding update to be authenticated by the original source node, the source node and the home agent must have established a mobility security association.

Similarly, when any node (for example, a foreign agent) receives a tunneled datagram, if it has a binding cache entry for the destination mobile node (and thus has no visitor list entry for this mobile node), the node receiving this tunneled datagram may deduce that the tunneling node has an out-of-date binding cache entry for this mobile node. In this case the receiving node should send a binding warning message to the mobile node's home agent, advising it to send a binding update message to the node that tunneled this datagram. The mobile node's home agent can be determined from the binding cache entry; often the home agent address is learned from the binding update that established this cache entry. The address of the node that tunneled this datagram can be determined from the datagram's header, because the address of the node tunneling this datagram is the outer source address of the encapsulated datagram. As in the case of a binding update sent by the mobile node's home agent, no acknowledgment of this binding warning is needed, because additional, future datagrams for the mobile node tunneled by the same node will cause the transmission of another binding warning. However, unlike the binding update message, no authentication of the binding warning message is necessary, because it does not directly affect the routing of IP datagrams to the mobile node.

When sending an IP datagram, if the sending node has a binding cache entry for the destination node, it should tunnel the datagram to the mobile node's care-of address using the encapsulation techniques used by home agents (described in Chapter 5).

6.1.2 Foreign Agent Smooth Handoff

When a mobile node moves and registers with a new foreign agent, the base Mobile IP protocol does not notify the mobile node's previous foreign agent. IP datagrams intercepted by the home agent after the new registration are tunneled to the mobile node's new care-of address. On the other hand, datagrams in flight that had already been intercepted by the home agent and tunneled to the old care-of address when the mobile node moved are lost and are assumed to be retransmitted by higher level protocols if needed. The old foreign agent eventually deletes its registration for the mobile node after the expiration of the registration lifetime.

Route optimization provides a means for the mobile node's previous foreign agent to be reliably notified of the mobile node's new mobility binding, allowing datagrams in flight to the mobile node's previous foreign agent to be forwarded to its new care-of address. This notification also allows any datagrams tunneled to the mobile node's previous foreign agent, from correspondent nodes with out-of-date binding cache entries for the mobile node, to be forwarded to its new care-of address. Finally, this notification allows any resources consumed by the mobile node at the previous foreign agent (such as radio channel reservations) to be released immediately, rather than waiting for its registration lifetime to expire.

As part of the registration procedure, the mobile node may request that its new foreign agent attempt to notify its previous foreign agent on its behalf, by including a previous foreign agent notification extension in its registration request message sent to the new foreign agent. The new foreign agent then builds a binding update message and transmits it to the mobile node's previous foreign agent as part of registration, requesting an acknowledgment from the previous foreign agent. The extension includes only those values needed to construct the binding update message that are not already contained in the registration request message. The authenticator for the binding update message is computed by the mobile node using the registration key shared with its previous foreign agent. This notification will typically include the mobile node's new care-of address, allowing the previous foreign agent to create a binding cache entry for the mobile node to serve as a *forwarding pointer* (Johnson 1994) to its new location. Any tunneled datagrams for the mobile node that arrive at its previous foreign agent after the forwarding pointer has been created will then be retunneled by that foreign agent to the mobile node's new care-of address.

For this smooth handoff to be secure, during registration with a new foreign agent, the mobile node and the foreign agent usually need to establish a new shared secret key called a *registration key*. The registration key is used to authenticate the notification sent to the previous foreign agent. Other uses of the registration key are possible, such as an encryption key for providing privacy over a wireless link between the mobile node and its foreign agent; however, such uses (Cheswick and Bellovin 1994) are beyond the scope of this book. Once established, the registration key for a mobile node can be stored by the foreign agent with the mobile node's visitor list entry. The following Section (6.1.3) gives an overview of the methods for establishing a registration key. The mobile service extension of the agent advertisement message is revised under route optimization to include a bit indicating that the foreign agent sending the advertisement supports smooth handoffs. If this bit is not set in the agent advertisement from the foreign agent, the mobile node should not request a registration key in its registration request message.

The mobile node is responsible for occasionally retransmitting a binding update message to its previous foreign agent until the matching binding acknowledge message is received or until the mobile node can be sure that the foreign agent has expired its binding. The mobile node is likely to select a small timeout value for the remaining registration lifetime available to such bindings sent to previous foreign agents. Also note that the current and previous foreign agents are likely to be very close to each other. Thus, the notification mechanism prepared here will be much more effective than a method involving the home agent.

6.1.3 Establishing Registration Keys

Foreign agents are expected to become inexpensive and widely available as Mobile IP becomes fully deployed. Mobile nodes will likely find it difficult to manage long-term security relationships with so many foreign agents. To perform securely the operations needed for smooth handoffs from one foreign agent to the next, however, any careful foreign agent should require assurance that it is getting authentic handoff information, and not arranging to forward in-flight datagrams to a bogus destination. The biggest complication in the route optimization protocol involves the creation of sufficient trust between the mobile node and foreign agent when none existed beforehand, while preferring the use of security associations between foreign agents and mobile nodes whenever they do exist.

Note that the mobile node can only rarely verify the identity of the foreign agent in any absolute terms. It can only act on the presumption that the foreign agent is performing its duties by correct adherence to protocol. Again, foreign agents are mostly passive devices. Any entity that is willing to perform the services would be accepted by the mobile node, even if the foreign agent were somehow malicious "on the side." For instance, neither the mobile node nor any home agent would be likely to determine if a foreign agent duplicated the mobile node's traffic stream, shared the mobile node's data with some adversary, or replayed mobile node data after the expiration of the mobile node's binding at that care-of address. If the foreign agent were to perform more active attacks, such as dropping datagrams intentionally or modifying the datagrams according to some dark purpose, the mobile node would not necessarily know where the problem was originating. However, all of these same points are true for existing infrastructure routers, so the situation is no worse than what already exists now.

In short, knowing the exact identity of the foreign agent is not crucial to the process of establishing a registration key. Only an agreement to follow protocol can be expected or enforced. If the mobile node has a way to obtain a certified public key for the foreign agent, then the identity may be established in a firmer fashion; however, the required public key infrastructure seems to be at least five years distant. Therefore, methods are proposed in this chapter by which an *anonymous foreign agent* (that is, one whose identity cannot be ascertained) can create a registration key with a mobile node during the registration process. In this chapter, the following methods for establishing a registration key are proposed, in order of declining preference. Other methods of establishing keys may become available in the future.

1. If the foreign agent and mobile node share a security association, or can establish such an association using ISAKMP or SKIP, the foreign agent can choose the new registration key.

2. If the home agent and the foreign agent share a security association, the home agent can choose the new registration key.

3. If the foreign agent has a public key, it can again use the home agent to supply a registration key.

4. If the mobile node includes its public key in its registration request, the foreign agent can choose the new registration key.

5. The mobile node and its foreign agent can execute a Diffie-Hellman key exchange protocol (Diffie and Hellman 1976) as part of the registration protocol.

Once the registration key is established, the method for performing smooth handoff seems natural. The following sections give a brief overview of each of the methods for establishing the registration key. Once the key is established and able to be used by way of a (possibly newly created) SPI, the smooth handoff involves simply sending a binding update to the previous foreign agent at the right time.

The Home Agent as a Key Distribution Center (KDC)

Crucial to methods 2 and 3 listed in the previous section is that the home agent and mobile node are already known to share a mobility security association, which can be used to encode the registration key for delivery to the mobile node. Thus, if the home agent can securely deliver the key to the foreign agent, it can be used as a *KDC* for the mobile node and its new foreign agent. The mobile node requests this by including a registration key request extension in its registration request message. When the home agent chooses the registration key, it sends it back in two different extensions to the registration reply. One extension has the encrypted key for the foreign agent and the other extension has the same key encrypted differently for the mobile node.

For the registration key to be established using this method, the home agent must be able to transmit securely an encrypted copy of the registration key to the foreign agent. This is straightforward if the foreign agent already has a mobility security association with the home agent. Frequent visitors from some home network should probably create such a mobility security association between the foreign agent on the visited network and the home agent serving their home network. Note that MD5 can be used here for the purpose of transmitting registration keys, secure against eavesdroppers. The expression

$$expr_1 = \text{MD5}(\text{secret} \parallel regrep \parallel \text{secret}) \oplus (key)$$
where *regrep* is the registration reply message payload and $\oplus$ is exclusive-or

can be included in the appropriate registration reply extension and encodes the key in a way that allows recovery only by the recipient. It is secure against replay because of the identification field in the registration reply message. The recipient recovers the key by computing

$$expr_2 = \text{MD5}(\text{secret} \parallel regrep \parallel \text{secret})$$

which then yields

$$key = expr_1 \oplus expr_2$$

Use of MD5 avoids entanglements with the legal issues surrounding the export of encryption technology and reduces the computational power needed to secure the password against eavesdroppers.

If no such mobility security association exists, but the foreign agent has a public key available, it can still ask the home agent to use it to pick a registration key. This is preferable to asking the mobile node to pick a good registration key, because doing so may depend on using resources not available to all mobile nodes. Simply selecting pseudorandom numbers is by itself a significant computational burden. Moreover, allowing the home agent to pick the key fits well into the existing registration procedures. On the other hand, it is possible that a mobile node could do with less than perfect pseudorandom numbers as long as the registration key were to be used in the restricted fashion envisioned for smooth handoffs.

Using the Foreign Agent as a KDC

When the foreign agent and mobile node share a mobility security association, there is no need to pick a registration key. The mobile node can secure its binding update to the foreign agent whenever it needs to by using the existing security association. This is the most desirable case.

Otherwise, the mobile node can include its public key (such as *RSA* [which stands for Rivest, Shamir, and Adleman, the inventors of the RSA cryptosystem] [Schneier 1994]) if available in its registration request to the foreign agent, using a mobile node public key extension. The foreign agent chooses the new registration key and returns a copy of it encrypted with the mobile node's public key, using a foreign-mobile registration key reply extension.

6.1.4 Using Diffie-Hellman with the Foreign Agent

The Diffie-Hellman key exchange algorithm (Diffie and Hellman 1976) can be used. Diffie-Hellman is a public key cryptosystem that allows two parties to establish a shared secret key, such that the shared secret key cannot be determined by other parties overhearing the messages exchanged during the algorithm. It is already used, for example, in other protocols that require a key exchange, such as in the CDPD system (CDPD Consortium 1993).

This technique, which has greatly advanced the state of modern cryptography, is nevertheless known to suffer from a man-in-the-middle attack. In other words, a malicious agent *could* pretend to be the foreign agent to the mobile node, pretend to be the mobile node to the foreign agent, and then participate as an unwanted third member in the key exchange. Armed with the information, the malicious agent *could* at a later time disrupt the smooth handoff or initiate the handoff prematurely. To prevent this attack, each registration key produced using the technology in this chapter is effectively authenticated by the home agent.

Even so, if Diffie-Hellman were not so expensive computationally, it could likely serve the needs of many mobile nodes. The man-in-the-middle attack is no worse than a malicious agent pretending to be a foreign agent in any other circumstance. Moreover, the mobile node and/or the foreign agent are presumably in direct contact, so the malicious man-in-the-middle would be detectable with high probability if either of the nodes notices the reception of duplicate packets. Nevertheless, the home agent, as the KDC, encrypts Diffie-Hellman results to avoid such attacks. However, the algorithm itself uses exponentiations involving numbers with hundreds of digits. It may take a long time for some mobile nodes to compute, time that could come at the expense of interactivity or convenient operation of user application programs. For this reason, Diffie-Hellman is considered the least desirable alternative for establishing registration keys. Even so, since it requires no other configuration, it should be required in all implementations of foreign agents that advertise support for smooth handoffs.

Briefly, the Diffie-Hellman algorithm involves the use of two large public numbers: a prime number (p) and a generator (g) The prime number and the generator must be known by both parties involved in the algorithm, but need not be kept secret; these values may be the same or different for each execution of the algorithm and are not used once the algorithm completes. Each party

1. chooses a private random number;

2. produces a computed value based on this random number, the prime and the generator; and

3. sends the computed value in a message to the other party.

The computed value is the number g^x mod p, where x is the private random number, p is the prime which is sent as part of the transaction, and g is the generator.

Each party then computes the (same) shared secret key using its own private random number, the computed value received from the other party, and the prime and generator values. The shared secret is the number c^y mod p, where $c = g^x$ is the computed value which uses the other party's private number, p is the same as before, and y is the receiver's private number. Since $(g^x)^y = (g^y)^x = g^{xy}$, and since knowing the computed values mod p does not enable passive listeners to determine the private values, the algorithm does successfully allow the two parties to agree on an otherwise undetectable secret.

To use this algorithm during registration with a foreign agent, the mobile node includes a Registration Key Request extension in its Registration Request message, that contains its nonzero values for the prime and generator, along with the computed value from its own private random number. If no other strategy is available, the foreign agent then chooses its own private random number and includes a Diffie-Hellman Registration Key Reply extension in its Registration Request to the Home Agent; the extension includes the foreign agent's own computed value based on its chosen random number and the supplied prime and generator values from the mobile node. The mobile node and the foreign agent each independently form the same shared secret key from their own chosen random number, the computed value supplied by the other party, and the prime and generator values.

The Diffie-Hellman algorithm itself has been covered by a patent (Hellman, Diffie, and Merkle 1980) in the United States that finally expired on April 27, 1997. An implementation of the Diffie-Hellman key exchange algorithm is available in the free RSAREF toolkit from RSA Laboratories (1994).

Establishing a registration key using Diffie-Hellman is computationally more expensive than most methods described in Section 6.1.3. The use of Diffie-Hellman described here is designed to allow the Diffie-Hellman computations to be overlapped with other activities. The mobile node may choose (or be manually configured with) the prime and generator values at any time, or it may use the same two values for a number of registrations. The mobile node may also choose its private random number and calculate its computed value at any time. For example, after completing one registration, the mobile node may choose the private random number for its next registration and begin the computation of its new computed value based on this random number, such that it has completed this computation before it is needed in its next registration. Even more simply, the mobile node may use the same private random number and computed value for any number of registrations. The foreign agent may choose its private random number and begin computation of its computed value based on this number as soon as it receives the mobile node's registration request message, and it need only complete this computation before it sends the matching registration reply message for the mobile node's registration.

This could be extended to support other similar key exchange algorithms either by adding a new request and reply extension for each, or by adding a field in the extensions to indicate which algorithm is to be used. Currently, Diffie-Hellman seems the only obvious choice.

6.1.5 Special Tunnels

Suppose a foreign agent receives a tunneled datagram but it doesn't have a visitor list entry for the mobile node. Moreover, suppose the foreign agent has no binding cache entry for the destination mobile node. To attempt delivery of the datagram in this case, the node must encapsulate the datagram as a special tunnel datagram (Section 6.7) destined to the mobile node. Using a special tunnel allows the home agent to avoid a possible routing loop when a foreign agent has forgotten that it is serving as the mobile node's foreign agent, perhaps because the foreign agent has crashed and lost its visitor list state. The special tunnel allows the home agent to see the address of the node that tunneled the datagram and to avoid tunneling the datagram back to the same node.

6.2 Route Optimization Message Formats

Route optimization defines four message types used for management of binding cache entries. Each of these messages begins with a one-octet field indicating the type of the message, and the type numbers fit in the numbering space of RFC 2002 (Perkins 1996b) for UDP messages to port 434.

The following type codes are defined in this chapter:

16 Binding warning message

17 Binding request message

18 Binding update message

19 Binding acknowledge message

Route optimization also requires one minor change to existing Mobile IP messages: A new flag bit must be added to the registration request message, replacing a previously unused, reserved bit in the message. This section describes each of the new route optimization messages and the change to the registration request message.

6.2.1 Binding Warning Message

A binding warning message is used to advise a mobile node's home agent that another node appears to have either no binding cache entry or an out-of-date binding cache entry for some mobile node. When any node detunnels a datagram, if it is not the current foreign agent for the destination mobile node it should send a binding warning message to the mobile node's home agent.

The format of the binding warning message is illustrated in Figure 6.2 and contains the following fields:

Type	16
Reserved	Sent as 0; ignored on reception
Mobile node home address	The home address of the mobile node to which the binding warning message refers
Target node address	The address of the node tunneling the datagram that caused the binding warning message; the target of the binding update message sent by the home agent

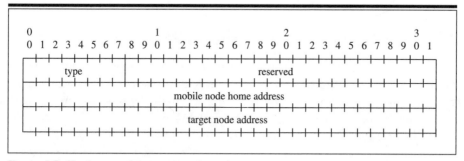

Figure 6.2 Binding warning message format.

A home agent will receive a binding warning message if a node maintaining a stale binding cache entry for one of the home agent's mobile nodes uses the out-of-date entry. When a home agent receives a binding warning message, it should send a binding update message to the target node address identified in the binding warning, containing the care-of address for the mobile node identified in the mobile node home address.

6.2.2 Binding Request Message

A binding request message is used by a node to request a mobile node's current mobility binding from the mobile node's home agent.

The format of the binding request message is illustrated in Figure 6.3, and contains the following fields:

Type	17
Reserved	Sent as 0; ignored on reception
Mobile node home address	The home address of the mobile node to which the binding request refers
Identification	A 64-bit sequence number assigned by the node sending the binding request message; used to assist in matching requests with replies and used to protect against replay attacks

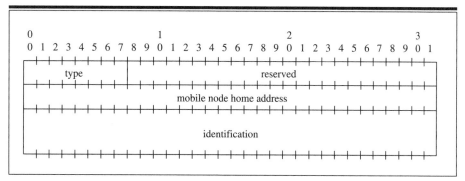

Figure 6.3 Binding request message format.

When the home agent receives a binding request message it consults its home list and determines the correct binding information to be sent to the requesting node. Before satisfying the request, the home agent is required to check whether or not the mobile node has allowed (see Section 6.2.6) the information to be disseminated. If the mobile node specified the private (P) bit in its registration request message, then the home agent must make no further attempt to satisfy binding requests on behalf of that mobile node. In this case the home agent should return a binding update in which both the care-of address is set equal to the mobile node's home address and the lifetime is set to 0. Such a binding update message indicates that the binding cache entry for the specified mobile node should be deleted.

6.2.3 Binding Update Message

The binding update message is used to send a notification about a mobile node's current mobility binding. It should be sent by the mobile node's home agent in response to a binding request message or a binding warning message. It should also be sent by a mobile node or by the foreign agent with which the mobile node is registering when notifying the mobile node's previous foreign agent that the mobile node has moved.

The format of the binding update message is illustrated in Figure 6.4, and contains the following fields:

Type	18
A	The A (acknowledge) bit is set by the node sending the binding update message to request that a binding acknowledge message be returned.
I	The I (identification present) bit is set by the node sending the binding update message if the identification field is present in the message.
M	If the M (minimal encapsulation) bit is set, datagrams may be tunneled to the mobile node using the minimal encapsulation protocol (Section 5.3).
G	If the G (GRE) bit is set, datagrams may be tunneled to the mobile node using GRE (Section 5.4).
Reserved	Sent as 0; ignored on reception
Lifetime	The number of seconds remaining before the binding cache entry must be considered expired. A value of all ones indicates infinity. A value of 0 indicates that no binding cache entry for the mobile node should be created and that any existing binding cache entry (and visitor list entry, in the case of a mobile node's previous foreign agent) for the mobile node should be deleted. The lifetime is typically equal to the remaining lifetime of the mobile node's registration.
Mobile node home address	The home address of the mobile node to which the binding update message refers

Care-of address	The current care-of address of the mobile node. When set equal to the home address of the mobile node, the binding update message indicates that no binding cache entry for the mobile node should be created and any existing binding cache entry (and visitor list entry, in the case of a mobile node's previous foreign agent) for the mobile node should be deleted.
Identification	If present, the identification field contains a 64-bit number assigned by the node sending the binding request message, used to assist in matching requests with replies and to protect against replay attacks.

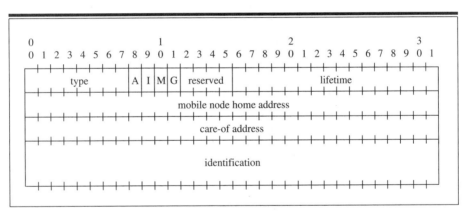

Figure 6.4 Binding update message format.

Each binding update message indicates the binding's maximal lifetime. When sending the binding update message, the home agent should set this lifetime to the remaining registration lifetime. A node wanting to provide continued service with a particular binding cache entry may attempt to reconfirm that mobility binding before the expiration of the registration lifetime. Such reconfirmation of a binding cache entry may be appropriate when the node has indications that the binding cache entry is still needed (such as an open transport-level connection to the mobile node). This reconfirmation is performed by the node sending a binding request message to the mobile node's home agent, requesting it to reply with the mobile node's current mobility binding in a new binding update message. Note that the node maintaining the binding should also keep track of the home agent's address to be able to fill in the destination IP address of future binding requests.

When a node receives a binding update message, it is required to verify the authentication in the message using the mobility security association it shares with the mobile node's home agent. The authentication data is found in the route optimization authentication extension (Section 6.2.5), which is required. If the authentication succeeds, then a binding cache entry should be updated for use in future transmissions of data to the mobile node. Otherwise, an authentication exception should be raised.

6.2.4 Binding Acknowledge Message

A binding acknowledge message is used to acknowledge receipt of a binding update message. It should be sent by a node receiving the binding update message if the acknowledge (A) bit is set in the binding update message.

The format of the binding acknowledgment message is illustrated in Figure 6.5 and contains the following fields:

Type	19
N	If the N (negative acknowledge) bit is set, the acknowledgment is negative. For instance, if the binding update was not accepted but the incoming datagram has the acknowledge (A) flag set, then the N bit should be set in this binding acknowledge message.
Reserved	Sent as 0; ignored on reception
Mobile node home address	Copied from the binding update message being acknowledged

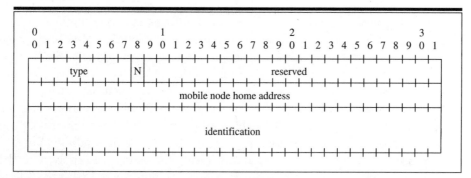

Figure 6.5 Binding acknowledgment message format.

Identification copied from the binding update message being acknowledged, if present

If the binding acknowledgement is sent in response to a previous foreign agent notification (Section 6.3.1) it must be tunneled to the mobile node at the new care-of address.

6.2.5 Route Optimization Authentication Extension

The route optimization authentication extension is used to authenticate binding cache optimization management messages. It has the same format (illustrated in Figure 6.5) as the three other authentication extensions defined for base Mobile IP (Section 6.5), but is distinguished by the type field of the extension, which is 35. The authenticator value is computed, as before, from the stream of bytes including the shared secret, the UDP payload (the binding cache management message), all prior extensions in their entirety, and the type and length of this extension, but not including the authenticator field itself or the UDP header. This extension is required to be used in any binding update message.

6.2.6 Modified Registration Request Message

One bit is added to the flag bits in the registration request message to indicate that the mobile node would like its home agent to keep its mobility binding private. Normally the home agent sends binding update messages to correspondent nodes as needed to allow them to cache the mobile node's binding. If the mobile node sets the private (P) bit in the registration request message, the home agent is not permitted to send the mobile node's binding in binding update messages. Instead, each binding update message should give the mobile node's care-of address equal to its home address, and should give a lifetime value of 0.

Thus, the registration request message under route optimization begins as shown in Figure 6.6.

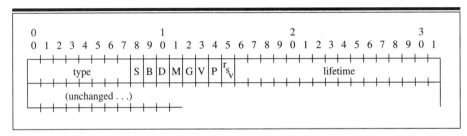

Figure 6.6 Requesting privacy.

P   The private (*P*) bit is set by the node sending the binding update message to indicate that the home agent should keep its mobility binding private. In any binding update message sent by the mobile node's home agent, the care-of address should be set equal to the mobile node's home address and the lifetime should be set equal to 0.

6.3 Format of Smooth Handoff Extensions

This section describes the format details for messages that are used to enable a smooth handoff from the previous foreign agent to the new foreign agent when a mobile node initiates a new registration.

6.3.1 Previous Foreign Agent Notification Extension

The previous foreign agent notification extension may be included in a registration request message sent to a foreign agent. It asks the new foreign agent to send a binding update message to the mobile node's previous foreign agent on behalf of the mobile node. The previous foreign agent may then delete the mobile node's visitor list entry and, if a new care-of address is included in the binding update message, create a binding cache entry for the mobile node. The previous foreign agent notification extension contains only those values not otherwise contained in the registration request message that are needed for the new foreign agent to construct the binding update message.

The fields of the message, illustrated in Figure 6.7, are as follows:

Type	96
Length	10 plus the length of the authenticator
Cache lifetime	The number of seconds remaining before the binding cache entry created by the previous foreign agent must be considered expired. A value of all ones indicates infinity. A value of 0 indicates that the previous foreign agent should not create a binding cache entry for the mobile node once it has deleted the mobile node's visitor list entry. The cache lifetime value is copied to the lifetime field of the binding update message.
Previous foreign agent address	The IP address of the mobile node's previous foreign agent to which the new foreign agent should send a binding update message on behalf of the mobile node

New care-of address   The care-of address for the new foreign agent to send to the previous foreign agent in the constructed binding update message. This should be either the care-of address being registered in this new registration (that is, to cause IP datagrams from the previous foreign agent to be tunneled to the new foreign agent) or the mobile node's home address (that is, to cause the previous foreign agent to delete its visitor list entry only for the mobile node, but not forward datagrams for it).

SPI   Four bytes; an opaque identifier. The SPI is copied to the route optimization authentication extension by the new foreign agent.

Authenticator   The authenticator value to be used in the route optimization authentication extension in the binding update message sent by the new foreign agent to the mobile node's previous foreign agent. This authenticator is calculated only over the binding update message body.

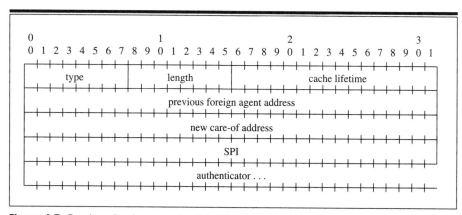

Figure 6.7 Previous foreign agent notification format.

The binding cache entry created at the mobile node's previous foreign agent is treated in the same way as any other binding cache entry.

6.3.2 Modified Mobile Service Extension

Performing smooth handoffs requires one minor change to the existing Mobile IP mobility agent advertisement extension (Section 3.3.1). A new flag bit, the S bit, replaces a previously unused reserved bit in the extension to indicate that the foreign agent supports smooth handoffs, and thus registration key establishment. By default, every foreign agent that supports smooth handoffs is supposed to support at least the establishment of a registration key by using Diffie-Hellman key exchange.

Thus, the proposed modification to the mobile service extension, illustrated in Figure 6.8, keeps the advertisement almost the same as described in Section 3.3.1, except for adding the following bit:

S   The S (*smooth handoff*) bit is set by the foreign agent sending the agent advertisement message to indicate that it supports smooth handoffs and registration key establishment, and thus the Diffie-Hellman registration key request and Diffie-Hellman registration key reply extensions.

More detailed information about the use of this extension by foreign agents is given in Section 6.9.1.

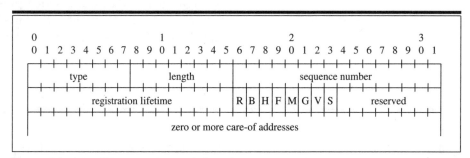

Figure 6.8 Advertising smooth handoff service.

6.4 Extensions Requesting a Registration Key

The following extensions may be used by mobile nodes or foreign agents to request the establishment of a registration key. See Sections 6.7, 6.8.5, and 6.9 for appropriate algorithms that allow each node to tailor the use of these extensions to fit most closely its configured requirements.

113   Foreign agent key request extension

114   Mobile node public key extension

115   Foreign agent public key extension

116   Registration key request extension

6.4.1 Foreign Agent Key Request Extension

If the foreign agent receives a registration key request from a mobile node and it has a security association with the home agent, it may append the foreign agent key request extension to the registration request after the mobile-home authentication extension. The home agent will use the SPI specified in the key request extension to encode the registration key in the subsequent registration reply message. The format of the foreign agent key request extension is illustrated in Figure 6.9 and the fields are as follows:

Type   113

Length   4

SPI   Four bytes; an opaque identifier

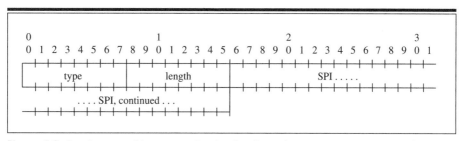

Figure 6.9 Foreign agent key request extension format.

6.4.2 Mobile Node Public Key Extension

If the mobile node has a public key, it can ask its prospective foreign agent to choose a registration key and use the mobile node's public key to encode the chosen registration key. No eavesdropper will be able to decode the registration key, even if it is broadcast to all entities with access to the network medium used by the mobile node. If using the public key, the foreign agent should still include the selected key in the registration request before it goes to the home agent. Then, the home agent can authenticate the selected encoded registration key as part of the registration reply message. The format of the mobile node public key extension is illustrated in

Figure 6.10 and has the following fields:

Type	114
Length	The length (typically quite large) of the mobile node's public key
Mobile node public key	(variable length)

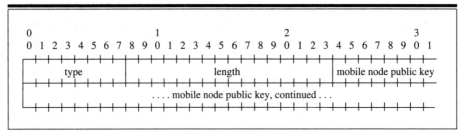

Figure 6.10   Mobile node public key extension format.

6.4.3   Foreign Agent Public Key Extension

If the foreign agent has a public key, it can ask the home agent to choose a registration key and to use the foreign agent's public key to encode the chosen registration key. Then, the home agent can authenticate the selected encoded registration key as part of the registration reply message. The format of the foreign agent public key extension is illustrated in Figure 6.11 and has the following fields:

Type	115
Length	Four, plus the length (typically quite large) of the foreign agent's public key

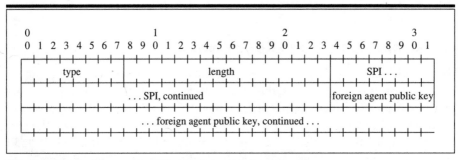

Figure 6.11   Foreign agent public key extension format.

SPI   Four bytes; an opaque identifier.

Foreign agent's public key   Variable length

The SPI is provided for the home agent to transcribe into the eventual foreign agent public key reply extension to the registration reply message.

6.4.4 Registration Key Request Extension

The registration key request extension, illustrated in Figure 6.12, may be included in a registration request message sent to a foreign agent. If the lengths of all the parameters in the key request extension are zero, then the mobile node is asking the foreign agent to supply a key by any means it has available except Diffie-Hellman.

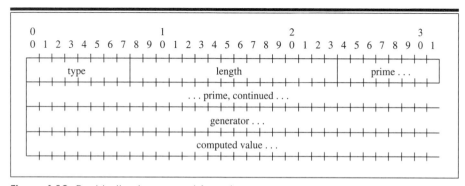

Figure 6.12 Registration key request format.

If the lengths are nonzero, then the mobile node is enabling the foreign agent to perform the Diffie-Hellman key exchange algorithm (as described in Section 6.1.4) if the other possible key establishment methods are not available. The foreign agent should then select a good pseudorandom registration key, and include a Diffie-Hellman registration key reply extension in the registration request message sent to the home agent to complete the key exchange. The home agent will also include the same extension in the registration reply sent to the mobile node, and then it will be authenticated as part of the reply message. The format of the registration key request extension contains the following fields:

Type   116

Length   Three times the length of each of the prime, generator, and computed value. The prime, generator, and computed value must all be the same length, which must be a multiple of eight bits.

Prime	One of the two public numbers involved in the Diffie-Hellman key exchange algorithm. The prime should be a large prime number.
Generator	One of the two public numbers involved in the Diffie-Hellman key exchange algorithm. If p is the value of the prime used for this Diffie-Hellman exchange, the generator should be both less than p and a primitive root of p.
Computed value	The public computed value from the mobile node for this Diffie-Hellman exchange. The mobile node chooses a large random number, x. If g is the value of the generator and p is the value of the prime, the computed value in the extension is $g^x \; mod \; p$.

When using nonces for replay protection, the identification field in the binding update message is used differently to allow replay protection even though the binding update is not being sent in reply to a request directly from the target node. In this case the home agent is required to set the high-order 32 bits of the identification field to the value of the nonce that will be used by the home agent in the next binding update message sent to this node. The low-order 32 bits of the identification field are required to be set to the value of the nonce being used for this message.

Thus, on each binding update message, the home agent communicates to the target node the value of the nonce that will be used next time. If no binding updates are lost in the network, the home agent and the target node can remain synchronized with respect to the nonces being used. If, however, the target node receives a binding update with what it believes to be an incorrect nonce, it may resynchronize with the home agent by using a binding request message.

6.5 Extensions to Supply a Registration Key

The following extensions are used to supply a registration key to a requesting entity, either a foreign agent or a mobile node, and are the counterparts to the corresponding extensions used to request registration keys that were described in the previous section.

120	Home-mobile key reply extension
121	Foreign agent key reply extension
122	Mobile node public key reply extension
123	Foreign agent public key reply extension
124	Diffie-Hellman key reply extension

6.5.1 Home-Mobile Key Reply Extension

The home-mobile key reply extension may be used in registration reply messages to send a registration key from the mobile node's home agent to the mobile node. When used, the home agent is also required to include a key reply extension in the registration reply message, which gives a copy of the same key to the mobile node's new foreign agent. The home-mobile key reply extension, illustrated in Figure 6.13, is authenticated along with the rest of the registration reply message, and thus no additional authenticator is included in the extension. The SPI used to encode the registration key may be different than the SPI used to authenticate the registration reply message. The home-mobile key reply format has the following fields:

Type	120
Length	Four, plus the length of the encrypted key for the mobile node
SPI	Four bytes; an opaque identifier
Mobile node encrypted key	Variable length. The mobile node encrypted key is the registration key chosen by the home agent and encrypted under the mobility security association between the home agent and the mobile node. The same key must be sent in the same registration reply message and encrypted for the foreign agent in a foreign agent registration key extension.

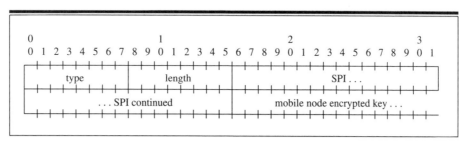

Figure 6.13 Home-mobile key reply format.

6.5.2 Foreign Agent Key Reply Extension

The home-foreign registration key reply extension may be used in registration reply messages to send a registration key from the mobile node's home agent to the mobile node's new foreign agent. When used, the home agent is also required to include a home-mobile registration key reply extension in the registration reply message, which gives a copy of the same key to the mobile node. The home-foreign registration key reply extension, illustrated in Figure 6.14, is authenticated by including an authenticator in the extension that is computed based on the mobility security association (and SPI) shared between the home agent and the foreign agent. For this extension to be used, the home agent is required to share a mobility security association with the foreign agent. The fields of the extension are as follows:

Type	121
Length	Four, plus the length of the encrypted foreign agent's key plus the length of the authenticator
SPI	Four bytes; an opaque identifier
Foreign agent encrypted key	Variable length; the registration key chosen by the home agent and encrypted under the mobility security association between the home agent and the foreign agent
Authenticator	Variable length; a value computed from a stream of bytes including the shared secret and the fields in this extension other than the authenticator field itself

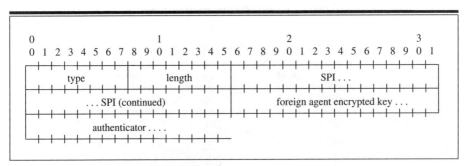

Figure 6.14 Home-foreign key reply format.

The key that is sent in this extension must also be sent by the home agent to the mobile node and encoded for the mobile node in a mobile node registration key extension in the same registration reply message.

6.5.3 Mobile Node Public Key Reply Extension

When the mobile node sends a mobile node public key request to its prospective foreign agent, the foreign agent can immediately select a registration key. The foreign agent inserts this registration key into the mobile node public key reply extension to the registration request, along with an SPI for future reference. The home agent subsequently transcribes the extension without change into the registration reply message. This procedure allows the mobile node to be protected against common man-in-the-middle attacks.

The mobile node public key reply extension is illustrated in Figure 6.15. The fields of the extension are as follows:

Type	122
Length	The length (in bytes) of the computed value
SPI	Four bytes; an opaque identifier
Mobile node's encoded key	The foreign agent chooses a suitable key, possibly a pseudorandom number, and encodes it using the mobile node's public key.

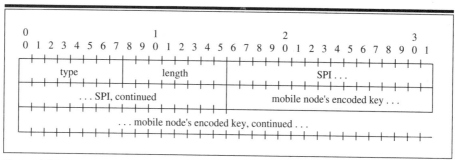

Figure 6.15 Mobile node public key reply format.

6.5.4 Foreign Agent Public Key Reply Extension

In response to a foreign agent public key request extension the home agent will select a registration key and encode it twice into two separate key reply extensions of the registration reply message. The foreign agent public key reply extension contains the registration key encoded with the public key of the foreign agent.

The foreign agent public key reply message is illustrated in Figure 6.16 and contains the following fields:

Type   123

Length   Four, plus the length (in bytes) of the foreign agent encoded key

SPI   Four bytes; an opaque identifier

Foreign agent's encoded key   The foreign agent chooses a suitable pseudo-random number and encodes it using the mobile node's public key.

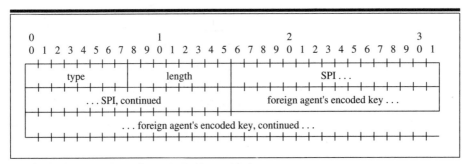

Figure 6.16 Foreign agent public key reply format.

The SPI, provided by the foreign agent for transcribing into this extension, is ultimately targeted for use by the mobile node.

6.5.5 Diffie-Hellman Key Reply Extension

When the mobile node has included a registration key request extension in its registration request message to the foreign agent, and the foreign agent has no public key or security association with the home agent, the last resort is to perform the Diffie-Hellman key exchange. If the mobile node wishes to enable this computation, it should include prime, generator, and computed value entries with nonzero length in its request. After performing the necessary computation, the foreign agent should include the Diffie-Hellman registration key reply extension included in the registration request message sent to the home agent. The extension, which is illustrated in Figure 6.17, has the following fields:

Type   125

Length   Four, plus the length (in bytes) of the computed value

SPI	Four bytes; an opaque identifier
Computed value	The foreign agent chooses a large random number, y. If g is the value of the generator and p is the value of the prime, the computed value in the extension is $g^y \bmod p$. The values of the generator and prime are found in the Diffie-Hellman registration key request extension from the mobile node's registration request message.

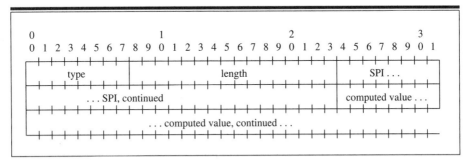

Figure 6.17 Diffie-Hellman registration key reply format.

The foreign agent supplies a new SPI along with the new registration key so that the new key will be useful in the same way as keys created by any other method. The extension is sent to the home agent, which transcribes it to the authenticated registration reply.

6.6 Using Special Tunnels

Whenever any node receives a tunneled datagram for which it has no visitor list entry for the datagram's destination, the node is not serving the mobile node as a foreign agent. Thus, the care-of address used by the tunnel originator is surely incorrect, and the tunneling node has an out-of-date binding cache entry for the destination mobile node. If the node receiving the tunneled datagram has a binding cache entry for the destination, it should retunnel the datagram to the care-of address indicated in its binding cache entry.

If a foreign agent receiving the tunneled datagram has no binding cache entry for the destination, it cannot retunnel the node to its destination. Instead, the foreign agent should forward the datagram to the destination mobile node's home agent using a special form of tunneling called a *special tunnel*. To tunnel the datagram using a special tunnel, the new IP header's destination address is set equal to the destination address in the tunneled datagram. Thus, both the inner *and* outer destination addresses are set to the home address of the mobile node. The tunneled datagram will thus be routed to the mobile node's home network, where it will be intercepted by the mobile node's home agent in the same way as other datagrams addressed to the mobile node.

6.6.1 Home Agent Handling of Special Tunnels

When the home agent receives the special tunnel datagram, it is addressed to the mobile node. The home agent should then decapsulate and tunnel the datagram to the current care-of address for the mobile node. However, the home agent may not tunnel the datagram to the current care-of address if the special tunnel of the datagram originated at that care-of address, as indicated by the outer source address of the special tunnel. The use of the special tunnel format allows the home agent to identify the node that tunneled the datagram to it (as well as the original sender of the datagram). If the home agent believes that the current care-of address for the mobile node is the same as the source of the special tunnel, then the home agent should discard the datagram. When that happens, the foreign agent serving the mobile node appears to have lost its entry for the mobile node in its visitor list. For example, the foreign agent may have crashed and rebooted.

Otherwise, after tunneling the datagram to the current care-of address for the mobile node, the home agent should notify the source of the special tunnel of the mobile node's current binding by sending it a binding update message. The home agent should also send a binding update message to the sender of the original datagram (the inner source address of the tunneled datagram) if it shares a mobility security association with this node.

6.6.2 Foreign Agents and Special Tunnels

When a foreign agent is the endpoint of a tunneled datagram, it examines its visitor list for an entry for the destination mobile node, as in the base Mobile IP protocol. If no visitor list entry is found, the foreign agent examines its binding cache for a cache entry for the destination mobile node. If one is found, the foreign agent retunnels the new care-of address indicated in the binding cache entry. In this case the foreign agent may also infer that the sender of the datagram has an out-of-date binding cache entry for this mobile node, since it otherwise would have tunneled the datagram directly to the correct, new care-of address. The foreign agent *should* then send a binding warning message to the mobile node's home agent. The foreign agent probably learned the address of the home agent in the registration reply message for the mobile node, or in a later binding update message from which the binding cache entry was created.

If a foreign agent receives a tunneled datagram for a mobile node for which it has no visitor list entry or binding cache entry, the foreign agent should forward the datagram to the mobile node's home agent by sending it as a special tunnel.

The home agent will intercept the special tunnel datagram addressed to the mobile node in the same way that it intercepts any datagram for the mobile node while it is away from home.

6.7 Mobile Node Key Requests

If the mobile node detects that its new foreign agent supports smooth handoffs, it may begin a smooth handoff from its previous foreign agent, as well as ask its new foreign agent to aid in supplying a registration key for the new registration. The following code fragment illustrates a good algorithm for the mobile node to follow during registration to allow maximal flexibility in selecting the new registration key. Any particular mobile node may be configured to use one, none, or any subset of the key establishment procedures made available as part of the route optimization protocol.

```
if (got 'S' bit) {
        if (have registration key with previous FA) {
                /* append previous foreign agent notification */
        }

        /* Set up registration key */
        if (have security association with current FA) {
                ;           /* Don't need to create a registration key */
        }
        else if (have a public key) {
                /* append MN Public Key request */
        }
        else if (want D-H exchange) {
                /* compute a value for prime p and generator g */
                /* use it when appending MN Key request */
        }
        else
                /* append MN key request with null
                   computed value, etc */
}
```

6.8 Miscellaneous Home Agent Operations

6.8.1 Home Agent Rate Limiting

A home agent is required to provide some mechanism to limit the rate at which it sends binding update messages to the same node about any given mobility binding. This rate limiting is especially important because it is expected that, within the short term, most Internet nodes will not support maintenance of a binding cache. In this case, continual transmissions of binding update messages to such a correspondent node will only add unnecessary overhead to the home agent and correspondent node, and along the Internet path between these nodes.

6.8.2 Receiving Registration Key Requests

When the home agent receives a registration request message, an extension requesting a registration key (Section 6.4) may be present in the message, requesting the home agent to provide a registration key to the mobile node and its foreign agent, as described in Section 6.1.2. In that event, the home agent employs a good algorithm for producing random keys (Eastlake et al. 1994) and encrypts the result separately for use by the foreign agent and the mobile node. The chosen key is encrypted under the mobility security association shared between the home agent and the mobile node, and the encrypted key is placed in a home-mobile registration key reply extension (Section 6.5.1) in the registration reply message. The same key is also encrypted under the mobility security association shared between the home agent and the foreign agent, and the encrypted key is placed in a home-foreign registration key reply extension (Section 6.5.2) in the registration reply message. When the home agent transmits the registration reply message containing reply extensions to the foreign agent, the message has the overall structure illustrated in Figure 6.18. The mobile node gets the registration key, typically encoded using an algorithm. The encoding of the foreign agent's copy of the key depends on the particular key request made by the foreign agent, and may also depend on the SPI if one is specified along with the encoded key.

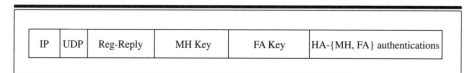

Figure 6.18 Structure of registration key reply extensions.

If the home agent cannot satisfy a request to select a registration key, it *may* still satisfy the registration attempt. In this case, the home agent returns a registration reply message indicating success, but does not include any key reply extension.

6.8.3 Mobility Security Association Management

One of the most difficult aspects of route optimization for Mobile IP in the Internet today is that of providing authentication for all messages that affect the routing of datagrams to a mobile node. In the base Mobile IP protocol, only the home agent is aware of the mobile node's mobility binding and only the home agent tunnels datagrams to the mobile node. Thus, all routing of datagrams to the mobile node while away from its home network is controlled by the home agent. Authentication is currently based on a manually established mobility security association between the home agent and the mobile node. Since the home agent and the mobile node are both owned by the same organization (both are assigned IP addresses within the same IP subnet), this manual configuration is manageable and, for example, can be performed while the mobile node is at home.

However with route optimization, authentication is more difficult to manage, since a binding update may need to be sent to any node in the Internet. Since no general authentication or key distribution protocol is available in the Internet today, the route optimization procedures defined in this chapter make use of the same type of manual key distribution used in the base Mobile IP protocol. For use with route optimization, a mobility security association held by a correspondent node or a foreign agent must include the same parameters as required by base Mobile IP (Section 4.9).

For a correspondent node to be able to create a binding cache entry for a mobile node, the correspondent node and the mobile node's home agent are required to have established a mobility security association. This mobility security association, however, may be used in creating and updating binding cache entries at this correspondent node for all mobile nodes served by this home agent. Doing so places the correspondent node in a fairly natural relationship with respect to the mobile nodes served by this home agent. For example, these mobile nodes may represent different people affiliated with the same organization owning the home agent and these mobile nodes, with which the user of the correspondent node often collaborates. As another example, the correspondent node may be a server set up for use by many mobile nodes. The effort of establishing the necessary mobility security association with the home agent may be more easily justified than the effort of doing so with each mobile node. It is similarly possible for a home agent to have a manually established mobility security association with the foreign agents often used by its mobile nodes, or for a particular mobile node to have a manually established mobility security association with the foreign agents serving the foreign networks that it often visits.

In general, if the movement and communication patterns of a mobile node or the group of mobile nodes served by the same home agent are sufficient to justify establishing a mobility security association with the mobile node's home agent, users or network administrators are likely to do so. Without establishing a mobility security association, nodes will not currently be able to use the route optimization extensions but can use the base Mobile IP protocol.

6.8.4 Using a Master Key at the Home Agent

Rather than storing each mobility security association that it has established with many different correspondent nodes and foreign agents, a home agent may manage its mobility security associations so that each of them can be generated from a single master key. With the master key, the home agent could build a key for any given other node by computing the node-specific key as

```
MD5(node-address || master-key || node-address)
```

where node-address is the IP address of the particular node for which the home agent is building a key, and master-key is the single master key held by the home agent for all mobility security associations it has established with correspondent nodes. The node-specific key is built by computing an MD5 hash over a string consisting of the master key with the node-address concatenated as a prefix and as a suffix.

Using this scheme, when establishing each mobility security association the network administrator managing the home agent computes the node-specific key and communicates this key to the network administrator of the other node through some communications device not susceptible to network snooping, such as over the telephone. The mobility security association is configured at this other node in the same way as any mobility security association. At the home agent, however, no record need be kept that this key has been given out. The home agent need only be configured to know that this scheme is in use for all of its mobility security associations (perhaps only for a specific set of its mobile nodes).

When the home agent needs a mobility security association as part of route optimization, it builds the node-specific key based on the master key and the IP address of the other node with which it is attempting to authenticate. If the other node knows the correct node-specific key, the authentication will succeed; otherwise, it will fail as it should.

6.8.5 Home Agent Supplying Registration Keys

When the home agent receives a registration request message with registration key extensions, it usually performs one of two operations: It either selects and encodes a registration key for both the mobile node and the foreign agent or it transcribes the registration key already selected by the foreign agent into the appropriate extension to the registration reply message. Both operations enable the mobile node to be sure that it is dealing with the same foreign agent with which the home agent is dealing.

When building the registration reply, the home agent should follow an algorithm such as the following to be as useful as possible for all the registration key establishment scenarios that use the current route optimization protocol.

```
/* Set up registration key */
if (foreign agent key request) { /* then have security assn. */
        /* append MN Key Reply to registration reply */
        /* append FA key reply to registration reply */
}
```

```
        else if (have foreign agent public key) {
                /* append MN Key Reply to registration reply */
                /* append FA Public Key reply to registration reply */
        }
        else if (have FA public key reply) {
                /* append MN Key Reply to registration reply */
                /* append FA Public Key reply to registration reply */
        }
        else {
                /* fail */
                /* append key request failure to reply */
        }
        /* append mobile-home authentication extension at end */
```

6.9 Miscellaneous Foreign Agent Operations

This section details various operational considerations important for foreign agents wishing to support smooth handoffs. This includes

- Processing previous foreign agent notification messages

- Maintaining up-to-date binding cache entries

- FA algorithm to establish registration keys

- Using special tunnels

6.9.1 Previous Foreign Agent Notification

When a foreign agent receives a previous foreign agent notification message, it creates a binding update for the previous foreign agent using the specified SPI and precomputed authenticator sent to it by the mobile node. The binding update message is also required to set the A bit so that the previous foreign agent will know to send a binding acknowledgment message back to the mobile node.

During the time the mobile node visited the previous foreign agent, it requested a registration key and, if the request was successful, has a mobility security association and SPI with the previous foreign agent. When the previous foreign agent receives the binding update, it can authenticate the message using that mobility security association and SPI. If the message authentication is correct, the visitor list entry for this mobile node at the previous foreign agent will be deleted and a binding acknowledge message returned to the sender. In addition, if a new care-of address was included in the binding update message, the previous foreign agent will create a binding cache entry for the mobile node. The previous foreign agent can then tunnel datagrams to the mobile node's new care-of address using that binding cache, just as any node maintaining a binding cache. The previous foreign agent is also expected to return a binding acknowledgment message to the mobile node.

Note that this binding acknowledgment is addressed to the mobile node. Thus, it needs to be tunneled using the new binding cache entry. The tunneled acknowledgment should then be delivered directly to the new foreign agent, without having to go to the home network. This creates an interesting problem for the new foreign agent when it receives the acknowledgment before the registration reply from the home agent. It is suggested that the new foreign agent deliver the acknowledgment to the mobile node anyway, even though the mobile node is technically unregistered. If there is concern that this provides a loophole for unauthorized traffic to the mobile node, the new foreign agent could limit the number of datagrams delivered to the unregistered mobile node to this single instance. Alternatively, a new extension to the registration reply message can be defined to carry along the acknowledgment from the previous foreign agent. This latter approach would have the benefit that fewer datagrams would be transmitted over bandwidth-constrained wireless media during registration.

When the binding acknowledgment message from the previous foreign agent is received by the new foreign agent it decapsulates it and sends it to the mobile node. In this way the mobile node can discover that its previous foreign agent has received the binding update message. This is important because otherwise the previous foreign agent could become a "black hole" for datagrams destined for the mobile node based on out-of-date binding cache entries at other nodes. The new foreign agent has no further responsibility for helping to update the binding cache at the previous foreign agent and does not retransmit the message even if no acknowledgment is received.

If the acknowledgment has not been received after sufficient time, the mobile node is responsible for retransmitting another binding update message to its previous foreign agent. Although the previous foreign agent may have already received and processed the binding update message (the binding acknowledge message may have been lost in transit to the new foreign agent), the mobile node should continue to retransmit its binding update message until the previous foreign agent responds with a binding acknowledgment.

The registration key established with this previous foreign agent is typically destroyed as part of the processing of this binding update message, or soon afterward. Since the previous foreign agent deletes the visitor list entry for the mobile node, it also deletes its record of the registration key. A registration key is thus useful only for notification to the previous foreign agent after moving to a new care-of address. When no subsequent use of this registration key is expected, no reply protection is necessary for the binding update message used for the notification. Some foreign agents may choose to retain the key for a short time in case the mobile node does not receive the acknowledgment and resends the binding update later.

6.9.2 Maintaining Binding Caches

It is possible that the binding cache entry taken by the previous foreign agent from the information in the extension will be deleted from its cache at any time. In this case, the previous foreign agent will be unable to retunnel subsequently arriving tunneled datagrams for the mobile node, and would resort to using a *special tunnel*. Mobile nodes should assign small lifetimes to such bindings so that they will not take up space in the foreign agent's binding cache for very long.

6.9.3 Rate Limiting

A foreign agent is required to provide some mechanism to limit the rate at which it sends binding warning messages to the same node about any given mobility binding. This rate limiting is especially important because it is expected that, within the short term, many Internet nodes will not support maintenance of a binding cache. In this case, continual transmissions of binding warning messages to such a correspondent node will only add unnecessary overhead at the foreign agent and correspondent node, and along the Internet path between these nodes.

6.9.4 FA Algorithm to Establish Registration Keys

The foreign agent, when it receives a request from a mobile node for a registration key, is faced with a variety of possible actions. The action selected by the foreign agent depends on the resources it has available. The foreign agent typically attempts to reduce as much as possible the computational burden placed on the mobile node, but it relies on the security association with the greatest cryptographic strength to encode the registration key. Furthermore, if the foreign agent performs the key selection, it still supplies the encoded key in an extension to the registration request message, so that the process of registration will also have the effect of authenticating its choice of registration key to the mobile node. This strategy reduces the opportunity for interlopers to mount man-in-the-middle attacks.

The following code fragment, executed when the foreign agent receives a key request of some variety, exhibits an algorithm that may be useful for implementors of foreign agents. The algorithm is supposed to use the strongest security association available, ask the home agent to help create one, or use Diffie-Hellman to establish a registration key as a last resort.

```
if (previous foreign agent notification) {
        /* build the binding update and authentication extension */
}

/* Set up registration key */
if (have security association with HA) {
        /* Append FA key request to registration request */
}
```

```
else if (have a public key) {
        /* append FA Public Key request to registration request */
}
else if (have mobile node's public key) {
        /* pick a good key */
        /* append FA public key reply to registration request */
}
else if (want D-H exchange) {
        /* start the computation, put result into the registration reply */
        /* eventually append it to the registration key request */
else {
        /* do nothing */
}
```

6.9.5 Using Special Tunnels

If a foreign agent receives a tunneled packet to a mobile node that is not on its visitor's list, the base Mobile IP specification allows the foreign agent to discard the packet. Unfortunately, discarding packets is bad for the performance of any TCP sessions on mobile nodes that had formerly used the care-of address of the foreign agent. To counteract this problem, the foreign agent *may* reencapsulate the undeliverable packet and deliver the encapsulated result back to the mobile node's home network. This is accomplished by using the care-of address as the source address of the outer IP header, and the mobile node's home address as the destination address. Then the home agent or mobile node will intercept the tunneled packet when it returns to the home network. Moreover, the recipient will be sure not to return the tunneled packet back to the same care-of address, by inspecting the source address of the encapsulated header.

6.10 Summary

Correspondent nodes can bypass the home agent if they are given current information regarding the mobile node's care-of address. Route optimization enables correspondent nodes to obtain that information by defining the protocol operations needed to deliver binding updates to the correspondent nodes. The information contained within the binding update is comparable with that contained in the registration requests that a mobile node sends to its home agent: both contain the care-of address and additional control information specifying features made available by the foreign agent.

Binding updates sent to a mobile node's previous foreign agent allow the mobile node to make smoother transitions as it moves from one point of attachment to the next. Each foreign agent that can handle such binding updates can then forward packets in flight to the mobile node's new care-of address. Such smooth hand-offs may be quite valuable to counteract the unwanted effects of dropped packets, especially given TCP's current assumptions about the network causes of dropped packets.

The main difficulty with enabling foreign agents to perform the smooth handoffs is that the foreign agent may often be unlikely to have any security association with the mobile node. With no security association, the foreign agent could not accept binding updates for the mobile node. On the other hand, all the security assocation needs to do is to make the foreign agent confident that the mobile node is the same as the mobile node that it had in its visitor list recently, and this much trust can be established by using the registration key request extensions available for route optimization. Various kinds of keys may be obtained, some with the help of the home agent acting as a KDC. As a last resort, the foreign agent and mobile node can establish a registration key using the Diffie-Hellman key exchange.

As one further refinement to avoid dropped packets, foreign agents may choose to return undeliverable packets to the home agent by way of a *special tunnel*. Such tunneled packets get one more chance for successful delivery, after having been delayed by a round-trip time to the wrong care-of address. This delay is often sufficient for the home agent to receive the current care-of address for the mobile node that was unknown to the tunneling foreign agent.

CHAPTER SEVEN

Miscellaneous Topics

This chapter presents several miscellaneous topics pertinent to Mobile IP that are experimental or do not fit naturally within the subject matter of the previous chapters.

First, some of the effects of firewall protection and filtering by border routers are described. As possible antidotes to the problems, some initial proposals are put forth to allow harmonious coexistence of mobile computers and firewalls. Following that, protocols are described by which mobile nodes may select broadcast and multicast datagrams that are to be sent to the mobile node's care-of address so that unnecessary traffic does not have to clog the tunnel.

Several algorithms are discussed by which mobile nodes can detect that they have moved from one point of attachment to another within the Internet. The standard methods rely on characteristics of the agent advertisements broadcast by foreign agents in the neighborhood. For cases when there are no foreign agents, some initial ideas are offered to allow the mobile node to detect when it needs to acquire another colocated care-of address.

As with many Proposed Standard protocols, Mobile IP is required to specify a collection of *managed objects* for use with the Simple Network Management Protocol (*SNMP*). While the collection is not detailed in this book, Section 7.6 presents enough information so that diligent implementors will be able understand the objects specified for managing Mobile IP.

Lastly, regional registration is proposed to allow mobile nodes to localize the effect of their motion by cooperating with local foreign agents forming a registration and tunneling hierarchy. This method allows the home agent to remain unaware of the exact care-of address in use by the mobile node, as long as the mobile node stays within the same hierarchy. This technique appears to have important applications in solving security problems.

7.1 Firewalls

The existence of *firewalls* (Cheswick and Bellovin 1994) is an unfortunate reality in today's Internet. Firewalls perform the function of discriminating against IP datagrams transiting the enterprise's border routers to protect the computing assets of the enterprise against attack by the millions of Internet computers not associated with the enterprise. The most basic mechanism used by firewalls is filtering out any datagrams that do not meet strict criteria. For instance, a firewall might discard any datagrams not addressed to a set of nodes with particular internal Internet addresses and/or ports.

Border routers can be configured to discard incoming datagrams that seem to emanate from internal computers. The philosophy here is to prevent computers in the external Internet from spoofing internal computers. The value of this technique may be less than first imagined, given that the external source of such incoming datagrams would not be able to get responses from the target of the spoof. Nevertheless such filtering operation is in place today.

Consider the communication between a mobile node and a correspondent node. Figure 7.1 illustrates three relevant placements for firewalls between various administrative domains:

- Protecting the *home domain*

- Protecting the *correspondent domain*; that is, the administrative domain where the correspondent node resides

- Protecting the *foreign domain*

This chapter shows how the three placements affect the operation of Mobile IP.

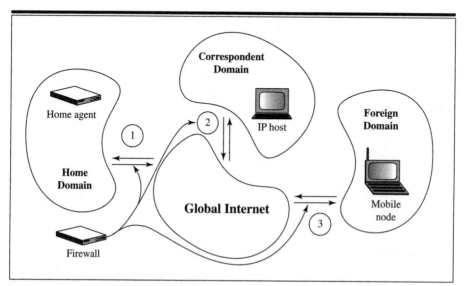

Figure 7.1 Three firewall placements.

7.1.1 Ingress Filtering

It has recently been proposed (Ferguson 1996) that border routers at the periphery of an administrative domain (for instance, supporting an Internet Service Provider [*ISP*]) carefully discard datagrams that seem to emanate from an address external to the administrative domain. This feature is called *ingress filtering*. Eliminating such exceptionally addressed datagrams reduces, to some degree, the opportunity for malicious Internet users to mount attacks that use datagrams carrying fictitious IP source addresses. Attacks that use the attacker's IP source address would, of course, be amenable to quick resolution by at least the simple expedient of denying service to that source address, if not taking legal action.

7.2 Reverse Tunneling

Such security operations as ingress filtering and use of firewalls spell trouble for the elegantly simple protocol operations previously outlined for Mobile IP. Ingress filtering, as just described, often makes it impossible for a mobile node to address a datagram to a correspondent node directly using its home address as the source IP address of the datagram. And firewalls that discard incoming datagrams addressed from internal addresses make it difficult for mobile nodes to send datagrams addressed (for instance) to neighbors on their home network.

Unfortunately, given the operation of today's routers and firewalls, all known solutions to these problems have various defects that make them unattractive. New features are needed in firewalls and mobility agents to provide truly acceptable support for mobile networking.

The first and simplest step toward a solution is to allow all datagrams from a mobile node registered away from its home network to be *reverse tunneled*, or tunneled back to the home agent from its care-of address (Cheshire and Baker 1996, Montenegro 1997). This has the obvious drawback that an additional and possibly lengthy routing path across the Internet is required for all transmissions between a mobile node and a correspondent node. Thus, what was before able to be called *triangle routing* would be degraded to *quadrilateral routing*, with the attendant performance degradation and susceptibility to network partition and congestion sharply increased. Note that the mobile node cannot tunnel datagrams to its correspondent nodes. There is no way to know that the correspondent node can perform decapsulation, and most Internet nodes today do not have this feature.

The advantage of reverse tunneling is, essentially, that as far as the rest of the Internet is concerned, all datagrams from the mobile node seem to emanate from its home network. Thus, disregarding the significant routing delays, the exceptional placement of the mobile node and its IP source address is not visible to the firewalls and routers. Reverse tunneling can be implemented in one of two ways, both of which require that the care-of address be used as the source address of the tunnel IP header.

1. The foreign agent can keep track of the home agent with which the mobile node is registered and tunnel *all* datagrams from the mobile node to the home agent.

2. The mobile node can perform the needed encapsulation.

   The problem with the first method is that foreign agents are not absolutely required to support encapsulation, only decapsulation. This is changing, however, given discussion in the Mobile IP Working Group. The problem with the second method is that the mobile node is then seen as emanating a datagram from an IP source address that does not correspond to any IP address associated with its own network interfaces.
   However, the second method does offer the opportunity for additional flexibility, because it is possible that the mobile node will be disposed to make a sharper determination about when reverse tunneling is needed than the foreign agent would make.

7.2.1 Firewall Traversal Discovery

Once reverse tunneling is known to be supported, the next steps involve making a determination about whether it is needed. This part of the puzzle remains to be solved, and efforts are currently under way within the IETF Mobile IP Working Group to devise protocols. One reasonable outcome would be extending the foreign agent (or DHCP) to provide the necessary information that can be acted on by the mobile node. For now there are some simple but not very satisfactory methods that can be put in place for use by the mobile node:

- Manual configuration
- Isolating the mobile nodes into administratively provided foreign domains called *pockets*

   The first two firewall traversal configurations (illustrated in Figure 7.1) are of more interest to mobile users. The third firewall position doesn't really have much effect one way or the other on the way Mobile IP operates, because the mobile node would have the same difficulty communicating with the correspondent node whether it was at home or away. The first traversal involves getting past the firewall protecting the home domain. This is needed because mobile nodes issue datagrams with their home address as the source IP address. Home firewalls typically filter out such datagrams to protect computers in the home domain from impersonation by computers outside the home domain.

The second general traversal problem involves getting datagrams from within a foreign domain to traverse the border routers or firewalls protecting that foreign domain. The ingress filtering problem described in Section 7.1.1 presents substantially more difficulty here, because the nomadic user can be presumed to have much less trust established with any visited domain than with the home domain. The level of trust that can be established is the essential factor determining the nomadic ability to create and use security associations with the security entities (for example, firewalls and border routers) involved.

Once the mobile node has the necessary information to contact firewalls, it could probably proceed to set up the necessary security associations with those firewalls, although the protocol operations to do so are currently not specified. Again, it is likely that (in the absence of defined protocols) many mobile nodes will have to rely on manually configured security associations in the near term. In real life this means that a nomadic user may have to contact a system administrator before being able to traverse the domain firewalls at the visited site. Given the necessary security associations, the mobile node would probably be required to authenticate (and possibly even encrypt) at least some (if not all) datagrams reverse tunneled through the firewalls that are to be traversed.

7.2.2 Manual Configuration

Until protocol support has been designed, standardized, and deployed, probably the best hope for firewall traversal lies in the ability of nomadic users to make specific arrangements for traversal of the firewalls. This might mean that nomadic users would have to contact their home administrator, and the administrator of any site they might visit, to get special permission (probably for a limited time) at the firewall. Setting up special permissions at the home firewall could likely be a much longer term arrangement. Even so, occasional revalidation and resetting of security associations would be required.

7.2.3 Isolating Mobile Nodes

Suppose that when a nomadic user visits a foreign domain the user is limited to operating Mobile IP within a restricted set of networks. Suppose further that all such foreign networks are administered in such a way that they are completely isolated from contact with other networks within the visited domain, but allowed relatively free transmission with networks outside the visited domain. Here such restricted foreign networks are called *pockets*, as presented in Figure 7.2. When the mobile node is used in a pocket, the nomadic user is (for all practical purposes) operating outside the visited domain and should not be faced with any difficulties arising from traversing the border of the visited domain.

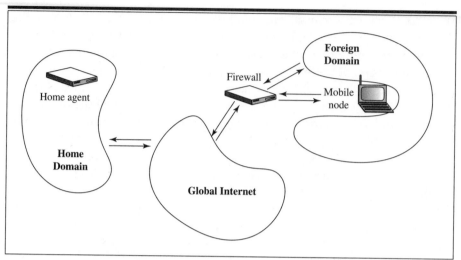

Figure 7.2 Isolating mobile nodes in foreign domains.

Of course, communication with nodes within the visited domain will become correspondingly more difficult with this arrangement. However, specific targets protected within the firewall could be allowed to receive datagrams from the pocket router, even though they were not allowed such access from general Internet routers or from the other border routers. Likewise, the pocket router would be allowed to send datagrams from the pocket out onto the global Internet without undue restriction.

7.2.4 Topology Advertisement

One method that, while possible, is *not* likely to progress very far is *topology advertisement*. Using this scheme a foreign agent would presumably advertise information about its firewall configuration for use by the mobile node. It is reasonable to expect that foreign agents might be configured with the necessary information. However, discussions with system administrators indicate that it is not very likely that any such topological information about internal firewall configuration would be publicly disseminated. Security agent advertisements, modeled on the mobility agent advertisements of Chapter 3, would be more acceptable as long as sensitive topology information is not divulged.

7.3 Broadcast Preference Extension

Assuming that the mobile node is not currently attached to its home network, unicast datagrams destined for the mobile node's home address will be sent to it by the home agent at its care-of address. The mobile node is unlikely to wish to receive all the broadcast packets that it would normally receive on its home network. For instance, when the mobile node is not attached to its home network it would not have any use for handling ARP packets (Plummer 1982). However, there are many cases when the mobile node would find certain IP broadcast datagrams useful.

Mobile IP allows the home agent to transmit IP broadcast datagrams to the mobile node. However, in the base protocol it is assumed that the home network administrator will configure the mobile node's home agent so that only the desired broadcast datagrams are transmitted from the home agent to the mobile node.

As an alternative, this section describes a proposed extension to the Mobile IP registration request message, that allows the mobile node to specify which broadcast datagrams it wishes to receive while it is away from its home network. The mobile node would use this extension during its registration process at its current point of attachment. *The message format in this section is not yet standardized.*

7.3.1 Broadcast Preference Extension Format

The broadcast preference extension (Patel and Perkins 1996) allows a mobile node to specify, at the time it registers its current care-of address, those IP broadcast datagrams that it wants to receive from its home network (via its home agent). The broadcast preference extension may be included several times within a single registration request. Each preference selects a particular kind of broadcast that the mobile node wants to receive. If the mobile node wishes to receive several kinds of broadcast datagrams, it includes several preference extensions. Each preference extension specifies conditions on the protocol number and the port number, which must both be satisfied by a broadcast datagram before the home agent should forward the broadcast to the mobile node. Figure 7.3 illustrates the extension, which contains the following fields:

Type	40
Length	4
C	If the C (clean) flag is set, the home agent is instructed to eliminate any retained specifications for broadcasts that the mobile node had included in any previous broadcast preference extensions.
P	If the P (permanent) flag is set, the home agent is instructed to keep the following broadcast specification active until the mobile node registers again using the C flag.
A	If the A (additional) flag is set, the home agent is instructed to include this preference for receiving broadcasts along with other preferences previously specified by the mobile node.

X   If the X (exclude) flag is set, the home agent is instructed to exclude this preference for receiving broadcasts from other preferences previously specified by the mobile node.

Rsvd   0

Protocol Broadcasts selected by this broadcast preference extension must have the specified value in the protocol field of the IP header of the IP broadcast datagram. If the protocol field of the broadcast preference extension is 0, then no restriction is placed on that field in the IP header.

Port   Broadcasts selected by this broadcast preference extension must have the specified value in the appropriate field in the upper level protocol header, which follows the IP header of the IP broadcast datagram. If the port field of the broadcast preference extension is 0, then no restriction is placed on that field in the upper level protocol header.

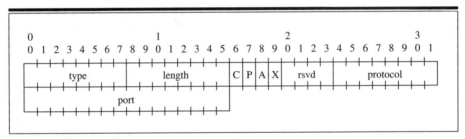

Figure 7.3 Broadcast preference extension format.

If the port field is nonzero, then the protocol field must also be nonzero. Also, when the port field is nonzero and the protocol value is 255, the broadcast preference is applied to both TCP and UDP. This special value is reserved otherwise, and used in this way it will make the common case more convenient when the same port number is used for TCP and for UDP for the same application. Note that the port field is included for convenience and technically represents a layering violation.

If the mobile node wishes to clear *all* of its preferences, it sends a broadcast preference extension with the C bit set, and both the port and protocol fields set to 0.

7.3.2 Home Agent Processing

If the home agent cannot satisfy the request, it is required to reject the registration request by issuing a registration reply using a new proposed status code, 144, indicating no support for the broadcast preference extension.

When a mobile node is attached to its home network, a home agent is not allowed to forward broadcasts to the mobile node. When a mobile node includes the P flag in the broadcast preference extension to a registration request, the home agent is required to keep track of the requested broadcast preferences for the mobile node until the mobile node clears the information with a new broadcast preference extension containing the C flag. In this way the mobile node may be relieved of the requirement to send in the same list of broadcast preference extensions every time it registers at a new care-of address.

Extensions with both the C bit and the X bit set are interpreted with a special meaning. When such a message is received by the home agent, the home agent begins sending *all* broadcast datagrams to the mobile node except the ones that are specified by the protocol and port fields. Subsequent extensions without the C bit set may exclude further broadcasts by not including the C bit.

If the home agent does not implement the protocol specified in the protocol field of the broadcast preference extension, it can still approve the mobile node's request as long as the mobile node did not also specify the port field. When the port field is 0, the home agent sends *all* broadcasts with the specified protocol (or excludes all such broadcasts if the X bit is set) to the mobile node. When there is a nonzero port specified and the home agent does not implement the requested protocol, the home agent is required to reject the registration request with status code 144.

7.3.3 Future Work

Should the broadcast preference extension provide any means to request that non-IP broadcast packets be forwarded to the mobile node?

Should the home agent be able to report the status on each broadcast preference extension individually, instead of accepting the registration request only if every extension is acceptable? An alternative would be to have another extension for use with registration reply messages, enabling the home agent to tell the mobile node exactly which broadcast preference extension was unacceptable to the home agent.

What other constraints on the transmission of broadcast datagrams should be considered, besides protocol and port numbers?

7.4 Multicast Preference Extension

This section describes another extension to the Mobile IP registration request message to allow the mobile node to specify its options in sending and receiving multicast datagrams for each multicast address individually. The mobile node appends the new extension to the registration request it sends from its current point of attachment. The multicast preference extension (Bhattacharya, Patel, and Perkins 1996) allows the mobile node to select the particular IP multicasts that the home agent or foreign agent should forward to the mobile node when it attaches to the Internet at a care-of address not on its home network. The protocol described in this section should be considered experimental at best and is *not* yet a proposed standard.

A mobile node on a foreign network may need to send and receive multicast packets either directly from the foreign network or from its home network via its home agent. Depending on the application and the multicast address, a mobile node may wish to have different options. While the Mobile IP specification specifies relevant details about the transmission and reception of multicast datagrams from its home network, it does not specify how a mobile node can choose these options in a foreign network. Notice that this extension in some sense allows the home agent to act as an IGMP proxy.

7.4.1 Multicast Preference Extension Format

The multicast preference extension allows a mobile node to specify, at the time it registers its current care-of address, options for sending and receiving at various multicast addresses. The multicast preference extension, illustrated in Figure 7.4, may be included several times within a single registration request, once for every multicast address.

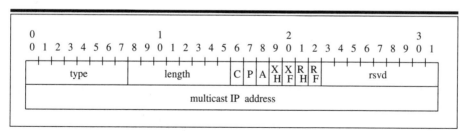

Figure 7.4 Multicast preference extension format.

The fields of the extension are as follows:

Type	41
Length	2 + (4 * number of multicast IP addresses included)
C	If the C (clean) flag is set, the mobility agent is instructed to eliminate any retained specifications for multicast datagrams that the mobile node had included in any previous multicast preference extensions.

P	If the P (permanent) flag is set, the mobility agent is instructed to keep the following multicast datagram specification active until the mobile node registers again using the C flag.
A	If the A (additional) flag is set, the mobility agent is instructed to include this preference for receiving multicasts along with other preferences previously specified by the mobile node. If the A flag is not set (0), the mobility agent is instructed to delete all nonpermanent preferences previously specified by the mobile node before storing this preference. If the P flag is set, the A flag is ignored.
XH	If the XH (transmit at home) flag is set, then the mobile node wishes to transmit packets destined to the address specified in the multicast IP address field in the mobile node's home network.
XF	If the XF (transmit in foreign) flag is set, then the mobile node wishes to transmit packets destined to the address specified in the multicast IP address field, in the mobile node's foreign network.
RH	If the RH (receive from home) flag is set, then the mobile node wishes to receive packets destined to the address specified in the multicast IP address field, from the mobile node's home network.
RF	If the RF (receive from foreign) flag is set, then the mobile node wishes to receive packets destined to the address specified in the multicast IP address field, in the mobile node's foreign network.
Rsvd	0
Multicast IP addresses	Flags and options specified by this multicast preference extension apply to the multicast IP addresses listed in this field.

The number of multicast IP addresses listed will determine the length of the multicast preference extension. If the mobile node wishes to clear *all* of its multicast preferences, it sends a multicast preference extension with the C bit set and zero multicast IP addresses listed.

7.4.2 Home Agent Considerations

If the home agent cannot satisfy the request, it is required to reject the registration request by issuing a registration reply using the new proposed status code, 145, indicating no support for the multicast preference extension.

When a mobile node is attached to its home network, a home agent is not allowed to forward multicasts to the mobile node, unless it is acting normally as a multicast router. When a mobile node is away from home, the following actions are required to be taken by the home agent.

- If the XH flag is set, then the home agent should transmit the packets received from the mobile node, on the local network.

- If the XF flag is set, no special actions are required from the home agent.

- If the RH flag is set, the home agent is required to respond to the IGMP membership queries (Deering 1989, Fenner 1996) by including the multicast address in its reports. The home agent *may* optionally tunnel the IGMP membership queries to the mobile host. Also, the home agent is required to tunnel the multicast packets to the mobile host for the specified multicast address.

- If the RF flag is set, no special actions are required from the home agent.

When a mobile node includes the P flag in the multicast preference extension to a registration request, the home agent is required to keep track of the requested multicast preferences for the mobile node until the mobile node clears the information with a new multicast preference extension containing the C flag. In this way, the mobile node may be relieved of the requirement to send the same list of multicast preference extensions every time it registers at a new care-of address.

7.4.3 Foreign Agent Considerations

If the XH flag is set, then the foreign agent is required to tunnel packets from the specified multicast address received from the mobile node to the home agent.

If the XF flag is set, and the foreign agent receives an IP-in-IP datagram from the mobile node, then the foreign agent is required to decapsulate the datagram and replace the source address in the multicast datagram with the care-of address, and then submit the datagram for IP processing.

If both the XH and XF flags are set, both of the preceding actions are required to be performed.

If the RH flag is set, then the foreign agent is required to process the tunneled multicast datagrams in one of the following ways:

- Transmit the multicast datagram from the interface sharing a link with the mobile node, with TTL set to 1

- Encapsulate the multicast datagram within a unicast IP datagram addressed to the mobile node's home address, and submit it for IP processing

If the RF flag is set, and the foreign agent is acting as the default router for the mobile node, the foreign agent transmits multicast datagrams with the specified multicast address to the mobile node.

7.4.4 Mobile Node Considerations

If the mobile host is attached to its home network, no special action is required by the mobile host.

If the mobile host is attached to a foreign network, and the registration request with the appended multicast preference extension is accepted by its home agent (and, if applicable, the foreign agent advertising the care-of address used in the registration), the following actions are required.

If the XH flag is set, the mobile host is required to encapsulate datagrams with the specified multicast address within a unicast IP datagram addressed to the home agent.

If the XF flag is set, it is required to do one of the following:

- Encapsulate every multicast datagram within a unicast IP datagram addressed to the foreign agent

- Transmit every multicast datagram with the source address set to the care-of address

If the RH flag is set, the mobile host has to be able to decapsulate IP-in-IP packets. Likewise, if the RF flag is set, the mobile host has to be able to respond to IGMP (Fenner 1996) membership queries.

Consider the following for future work: Is this a reasonable way to offload processing from the foreign agent? Should the preference extension contain another flag to distinguish the two modes of operation?

7.5 Movement Detection

Three primary mechanisms are provided for mobile nodes to detect when they have moved from one subnet to another. Other mechanisms may also be used. When the mobile node detects that it has moved, it should register with a suitable care-of address on the new foreign network. However, the mobile node is not allowed to register more frequently than once per second on average.

7.5.1 Lazy Cell Switching (*LCS*)

The first method of movement detection is based on the lifetime field within the main body of the ICMP Router Advertisement portion of the agent advertisement. A mobile node should, effectively, expire each advertisement at the end of its lifetime. If the mobile node fails to receive another advertisement from the same agent within the specified lifetime, it should assume that it has lost contact with that agent. If the mobile node has previously received an agent advertisement from another agent for which the lifetime has not yet expired, the mobile node may immediately attempt registration with that other agent. Otherwise, the mobile node should attempt to discover a new agent with which to register, perhaps by broadcasting an agent solicitation. Note that a mobile node should usually try to receive two more advertisements before expiring any advertisement.

7.5.2 Prefix Matching

The second method uses network prefixes. The prefix-length extension (Section 3.3.2) may be used in some cases by a mobile node to determine whether a newly received agent advertisement was received on the same subnet as the mobile node's current care-of address. If the prefixes differ, the mobile node may assume that it has moved. If a mobile node is currently using a foreign agent care-of address, the mobile node should not use this method of movement detection unless both the current agent and the new agent include the prefix-length extension in their respective agent advertisements. Similarly, if a mobile node is using a colocated care-of address, it should not use this method of movement detection unless the new agent includes the prefix-length extension in its advertisement and the mobile node knows the network prefix of its current colocated care-of address. If the prefix-matching method shows that the mobile node has moved, then a mobile node may choose instead to register with a foreign agent advertising a different network prefix, rather than reregister with its current care-of address. The agent advertisement on which the new registration is based must still be fresh according to its advertisement lifetime field.

Caution is indicated with the use of the prefix-length extension over wireless links, due to the irregular coverage areas provided by wireless transmitters. Without sufficient care, it is possible that two foreign agents advertising the same prefix might indeed provide different connectivity to prospective mobile nodes. The prefix-length extension should not be included in the advertisements sent by agents in such a configuration.

Foreign agents using different wireless interfaces would have to cooperate using special protocols to provide identical coverage in space, and thus be able to claim to have wireless interfaces situated on the same subnetwork. In the case of wired interfaces, a mobile node disconnecting and subsequently connecting to a new point of attachment may well send in a new registration request whether or not the new advertisement is on the same medium as the last recorded advertisement. Finally, in areas with dense populations of foreign agents it would seem unwise to require the propagation via routing protocols of the subnet prefixes associated with each individual wireless foreign agent. Such a strategy could lead to quick depletion of available space for routing tables, unwarranted increases in the time required for processing routing updates, and longer decision times for route selection if routes (which are almost always unnecessary) are stored for the numerous wireless "subnets."

7.5.3 Eager Cell Switching (*ECS*)

This last method of movement detection often improves somewhat on the first method in cases when the mobile node can detect beacons from multiple foreign agents simultaneously. There is also a basic assumption about the mobility patterns of nomadic users. Movement is considered most likely to proceed along trajectories with minimal second derivatives. In other words, the inertia usually associated with moving entities usually has the effect of keeping them moving along fairly straight lines. It takes more effort to stop moving or to begin moving in a drastically different direction.

Given such a simple yet realistic model of movement, it seems likely that a mobile computer, once it first enters a new wireless cell, will usually continue to proceed further into that new cell and, by implication, further along the way out of its previous cell. When this is true, it makes sense for the mobile computer to switch right away to any new care-of address that might be available within the new cell. With some care, this method makes it possible for mobile nodes to switch to new care-of addresses without any interruption in connectivity to the Internet. At all times the care-of address known to the home agent will belong either to the old foreign agent (likely still in range of the mobile node) or the new foreign agent (so much more so).

The only point requiring care is maintaining a list of current foreign agents (actually, a list of current care-of addresses). If a mobile node actually resides within range of two different foreign agents and is receiving beacons from both of them, the mobile node has to remember which was the most recently detected foreign agent and remain attached to that most recent one. Switching back and forth constantly from one foreign agent to another is to be avoided at all costs. Correct operation can be implemented by keeping track of which foreign agents are currently detectable, and not performing any new registration with foreign agents on that list. Once a foreign agent becomes unavailable, the next foreign agent on the list can be selected for registration. Straightforward modifications are needed to handle a combination of foreign agents and colocated care-of addresses.

7.5.4 Movement Detection without Foreign Agents

The previously described methods depend on the foreign agent advertisements in an essential way. However, many mobile nodes are configured to operate without the services of foreign agents, by obtaining colocated care-of addresses. Such mobile nodes still must detect that they have moved to a new point of attachment to the Internet before they initiate new registration procedures to report their colocated care-of address.

One might first ask how the mobile client can remain confident that its colocated care-of address is still valid. For instance, suppose a computer with a wireless attachment could move within range of some attachment point and get a valid IP address from DHCP, just as could any other computer. Then, when the wireless computer moves out of range, there is no DHCP-related protocol operation to inform the computer that its IP address is no longer valid.

Unfortunately, there does not exist a very good solution for that problem. After all, when there is no physical path for packets, the only detectable sign is the lack of traffic, which does not always indicate a break in connectivity. In cases when the wireless-attached node is using the services of a default router, it can ping the router occasionally, say once per second. Alternatively, the node might operate in a more promiscuous node, but this would consume an unnecessarily large amount of power, and that is usually a poor design choice in battery-operated mobile nodes.

7.6 Management Information Bases (*MIBs*)

This section introduces the MIB definitions for use with SNMP (McCloghrie and Rose 1991, SNMPv2 Working Group et al. 1996, Rose 1991). RFC 1902 (SNMPv2 Working Group et al. 1996) defines a simple management interface (*SMI*), which provides the mechanisms used for describing and naming objects associated with the management of network entities. As of the time of this writing, the MIBs specified for use with Mobile IP (Cong, Hamlen, and Perkins 1996) have not been implemented in any commercial product to the knowledge of the author. On the other hand, implementation of the MIB may be viewed as a requirement for advancement of Mobile IP to draft standard, so that work in this area is indicated. The text in this section follows closely the text in RFC 2006 (Cong, Hamlen, and Perkins 1996), but the particular MIP objects (managed objects) are not recited here in the interest of saving space and out of consideration for the reader.

7.6.1 Managed Object Definitions

Managed objects are accessed via a virtual information store called a *MIB*. Objects in the MIB are defined using the subset of Abstract Syntax Notation One (*ASN.1*) (CCITT 1988) defined in the SMI. In particular, each object type is named by an object identifier (*OID*)—an administratively assigned name. The object type together with an object instance serves to identify a specific instance of the object. The OID is denoted by a textual string of numbers separated by dots, termed the *descriptor*, to refer to the object type. So, for instance, the OID for the Internet is 1.3.6.1—in other words, the Internet subtree of object identifiers starts with the prefix 1.3.6.1. This string really means that the Internet is the first naming subtree under the Department of Defense (DOD), and DOD is the sixth naming subtree under "org," the subtree belonging to the identified organizations recognized by the International Organization Standardization and International Electrotechnical Committee (ISO/IEC). Such organizations form the third subtree from ISO, which is to say the ISO/IEC. Mobile IP objects are all named under the forty-fourth subtree of MIB-2 OID space, which is 1.3.6.1.2.1, so that Mobile IP OIDs all start with 1.3.6.1.2.1.44. Of course, no one ever remembers this in real life, and most would never bother to find out. The important points are that the name space for objects is suitably huge, hierarchically organized, and simple to navigate.

7.6.2 Object Selection Criteria for Mobile IP

To be consistent with Internet Architecture Board (*IAB*) directives and good engineering practice, the authors of the MIB specification do the following to identify and specify managed objects for Mobile IP:

- Partition management functionality among the mobile node, home agent, and foreign agent according to the architectural model used in Mobile IP

- Require that objects be essential for either fault or configuration management

- Limit the total number of objects

- Exclude objects that are simply derivable from others in this or other MIBs

- Exclude objects that are useful only for managing encapsulation protocols.

The Mobile IP objects are organized into various *groups*. Based on the first bulleted item, the MIB specification document is accordingly organized into major groups for mobile node objects, home agent objects, and foreign agent objects. In addition, there are some objects common to all three functional entities having to do with security, and those objects are organized into groups not specifically associated with a mobile node or mobility agent. For each entity, there are groups for two major protocol actions important for Mobile IP: advertisement and registration.

RFC 2006 does not define managed objects for the tunneling operations. Tunneling is used for purposes outside the domain of specification of Mobile IP and it was decided that an entirely separate Mobile IP specification should be created for managing tunnels. Unfortunately, this separate specification has not been produced yet. RFC 2006 also does not define managed objects for route optimization, or any of the other nonstandard protocols described in this book.

7.6.3 Security of SNMP

Using the SNMP interface, a network manager would be able to gather configuration information for the home agents, foreign agents, and mobile nodes within the administered domain of authority. In fact, most of the interesting configuration items for those entities could be set using the SNMP interface. For instance, a network manager could configure foreign agents to offer or not offer various tunneling protocols (minimal encapsulation or GRE). These configuration operations, as is typical with SNMP, can in theory completely determine the nature of the operation of the managed entities. Therefore, very strict security must attend the use of these SNMP operations. The exact nature of the security is outside the scope of this book; one experimental model is outlined in RFC 1910 (Waters 1996).

7.6.4 Mobile IP Managed Objects

With the preceding concepts in mind, and with a firm understanding of the base Mobile IP protocol, one can read RFC 2006 and create a fully functional SNMP MIB for managing Mobile IP nodes and agents. As promised, the objects themselves will not be enumerated in this book, but perhaps a look at one such object from RFC 2006 will be of some value.

```
mnState OBJECT-TYPE
    SYNTAX      INTEGER {
                    home(1),
                    registered(2),
                    pending(3),
                    isolated(4),
                    unknown(5)
                }
    MAX-ACCESS  read-only
    STATUS      current
    DESCRIPTION
            "Indicates mobile node's state of Mobile IP:
                home,
                    -- MN is connected to home network.
                registered,
                    -- MN has registered on foreign network
                pending,
                    -- MN has sent registration request and is
                       waiting for the reply
```

```
                     isolated,
                        -- MN is isolated from network
                     unknown
                        -- MN can not determine its state."
        ::= { mnSystem 1 }
```

The object `mnState` is object 1 in the object subtree `mnSystem`, and has OID 1.3.6.1.2.1.44.1.3.1.1. If you have been following this discussion, you should now be able to guess the OID for `mnSystem`. `mnState` has `OBJECT-TYPE INTEGER`, and has five defined states:

1. Home

2. Registered

3. Pending

4. Isolated

5. Unknown

It is not explained how one might expect to obtain any management information from a mobile node with an mnState that has the values 4 or 5.

7.7 Localizing Registrations

Mobile IP allows mobile computers to move freely between various points of attachment to the Internet. However, each time the mobile computer moves, a registration request message has to be approved by the mobile node's home agent. In cases when the home agent is far away, it may become too expensive or (in the cases of network partition) even impossible to complete these frequent registrations. Compared with the analogous situation for roaming mobile telephone subscribers, Mobile IP has much less of a problem because there is less data that has to be transacted with every registration, and no circuit-switched routes to be set up and torn down for the phone call. Nevertheless, the problem is sufficiently compelling to merit work toward a solution.

7.7.1 Overview

In this section a new variety of registration is proposed using a regional registration request and regional registration reply that is no longer always required to be transacted with the home agent. Bear in mind that this proposal is not at all standardized, and it is only one of possibly several suitable protocol techniques that might reduce the need for home agents to track closely the movements of their mobile nodes. Other approaches are described in an article by Katz (1994).

Using this new registration technique, the foreign agents in the local and/or regional area provide mobility services to the mobile node and allow some degree of independence from the home agent. The foreign agents are arranged hierarchically in the regional topology, and the mobile node is then allowed to move from one local area of the regional topology to another area of the same regional topology without requiring approval by or rebinding at the home agent.

As before, when a mobile node changes its point of attachment to the Internet, it is said to *move*. Thus, a change in point of attachment is a movement. It is possible to make improvements by allowing a mobile node to inform only local mobility agents each time it moves. However, the local agents must then cooperate to allow the home agent to have incomplete knowledge of the mobile node's true point of attachment. For example, if the mobile node is currently located at one care-of address, but the home agent stores another care-of address in the mobile node's binding, then the foreign agents offering those two care-of addresses in question must cooperate to make sure all datagrams tunneled to the latter care-of address are actually delivered to the mobile node.

One approach to this problem is to allow the mobile node to send registration requests to a regional foreign agent that tracks its regional movements but does not forward the mobile node's request to its home agent. If the regional foreign agent is the tunnel endpoint for datagrams encapsulated by the home agent, then the regional foreign agent can make further arrangements for delivery of the datagram. This regional handling is further enhanced by effectively allowing subregions of regions and so on, and structuring as a hierarchy the foreign agents that manage each region.

Since agent advertisements can contain multiple care-of addresses, a natural implementation of the hierarchy suggests itself. Each foreign agent simply includes its ancestors in the tree of regional foreign agents in the list of care-of addresses in the agent advertisement. To maintain compatibility with mobile nodes that do not implement any processing for the foreign agent hierarchy, each foreign agent must advertise its own care-of address first in the list.

In this specification, the mobile node will reregister using a new registration request that includes all the fields of the existing registration request, but also includes more care-of addresses and places a different meaning on the address found in the home agent field in the existing registration request. Put briefly, the home agent address is replaced by the address of the nearest regional foreign agent in the hierarchy that has a previous registration with the mobile node.

To summarize, the main idea is to make registration requests go only as far as needed up a hierarchy of foreign agents. To understand how to do that, the following are important to keep in mind.

- Security needs careful attention. A registration key should be established as detailed in Section 6.1.3.

- Each ancestral foreign agent considers the mobile node to be registered at the foreign agent just below it in the hierarchy.

- Regional registration requests are passed from level to level.

- Regional registration replies are also passed from level to level.

- Agent advertisements show the complete regional hierarchy of cooperating foreign agents.

- A colocated care-of address can be used once a cooperating foreign agent has been found.

7.7.2 Operation

Conceptually the mobile node attempts to minimize the amount of tracking required to maintain its traffic flow by identifying the smallest region for which the mobile node has not traversed any regional boundary. That amounts to finding the closest common ancestor between its current and previous foreign agent. The mobile node may do this as described in the following pages.

Finding the Right Foreign Agent

Each time a mobile node determines that it has moved, it keeps track of the hierarchy of foreign agents serving its new point of attachment, called its *lineage*. At least the first care-of address will be different in the agent advertisements detected at the mobile node's new point of attachment.

When a mobile node moves to a new point of attachment, it checks the list of care-of addresses starting with the last one. If the last care-of address is the same as the previous last care-of address, it looks at the next-last care-of address. If that one is also the same as the next-last care-of address at its previous point of attachment, the mobile node checks the next-next-last care-of address, and so on until a care-of address is found that is different than the corresponding care-of address in the list that was advertised at the mobile node's previous point of attachment.

Once the mobile node finds out the highest level of the hierarchy that has a different care-of address, it registers with the foreign agent at the next higher level of the hierarchy. That foreign agent is the nearest common ancestor to the care-of addresses at the new and previous points of attachments, and becomes the targeted mobility agent of the registration. The registration is done by the new regional registration request message. The foreign agent nearest the mobile node (the first care-of address) relays the new registration request to the next higher level of the hierarchy and thus along toward the target of the registration request, just as if the targeted mobility agent were the home agent.

If the targeted mobility agent approves the regional registration request, it returns a registration reply similar in format to the base Mobile IP specification, but with a different type number.

The processing of the regional registration request and registration reply requires further refinement compared with the registration processing in the base Mobile IP specification. When the foreign agent receives the request from the mobile node, it must pass the request along to its next nearest ancestor in the hierarchy along the way to the agent listed as the home agent. In this way, each foreign agent in the hierarchy between the mobile node and the home agent will be able to maintain a binding for the mobile node. Similarly, regional registration replies are passed down from one level of the hierarchy to the next along the way to the mobile node, so that each foreign agent can determine the status of the corresponding registration request and create the appropriate binding for the mobile node. Note that each foreign agent's binding will be for the care-of address at the next lower level of the hierarchy, not necessarily the care-of address of the foreign agent advertising the care-of address hierarchy to the mobile node.

Figure 7.5 illustrates a hierarchy of cooperating foreign agents, and a wireless mobile node moving from the area of FA_7 through the area of FA_8 and into the area of FA_9. This example, for simplicity, does not show the distinction between the IP addresses of the foreign agents and their own care-of addresses that they advertise. When first entering the range of FA_7, the mobile node receives advertisements containing the lineage $< FA_7, FA_4, FA_2, FA_1 >$, which represents the ordered list of foreign agents under consideration from the mobile node's current care-of address to the top of the regional hierarchy. Therefore, the mobile node transmits a regional registration request targeted at its home agent, which will have the effect of causing the home agent to create a binding showing the mobile node at care-of address FA_1. At the same time, FA_1 will bind the mobile node to care-of address FA_2, FA_2 will bind it to care-of address FA_4, and FA_4 will insert the mobile node into its visitor list.

When the mobile node moves to FA_8 it will detect the advertisement of a new lineage, $< FA_8, FA_4, FA_2, FA_1 >$. Then, the mobile node will detect that FA_4 is the nearest common ancestor and will send a regional registration request to FA_4, which will cause FA_4 to change its binding for the mobile node to FA_8. At the same time, if the mobile node created a registration key to do so, FA_7 can be sent a previous foreign agent notification, which will allow it to release any resources allocated to the mobile node and to set up a binding cache entry for datagrams in flight.

Finally, when the mobile node moves to FA_9, it will detect the advertisement of the new lineage, $< FA_9, FA_6, FA_3, FA_1 >$. FA_1 is the nearest common ancestor, and the mobile node sends it a regional registration request. The request will cause FA_1 to change its binding for the mobile node to FA_3, FA_3 to create a binding for care-

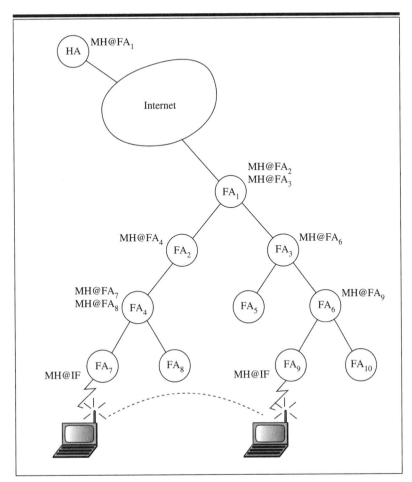

Figure 7.5 Hierarchical foreign agents.

of address FA_6, FA_6 to create a binding for FA_9, and FA_9 to put the mobile node into its visitor list. FA_1 can also forward the previous foreign agent notification to FA_2, FA_4, and FA_8.

Notice that both registrations proceed without the assistance of the home agent. Also, even though Figure 7.5 shows that the mobile node always attaches to care-of addresses at the leaves of the hierarchy, this is only a coincidence in the drawing. All of the foreign agents in the hierarchy should be equally able to manage regional registrations for the mobile node as needed.

Security

Note that each home agent can be considered a *universal root* for all such hierarchies of foreign agents as described. In fact, considered as an implicit care-of address, the home agent's address is an ancestor of every other care-of address, and the mobile node is guaranteed of never straying from the boundaries of the region defined by the home agent's care-of address, since it's the whole Internet.

Thought of in this way, there is the same clear threat posed by illicit regional registration requests, and thus the same need for authenticating registration requests. Unfortunately, the mobile node and the home agent currently share keys that are configured manually. Such manual configuration is unrealistic with the regional registration request. Fortunately, the problem is solvable using the same techniques in the route optimization protocol specification, wherein a mobile node's current foreign agent establishes a registration key with the mobile node for as long as the mobile node is on the foreign agent's visitor list.

As outlined in this section, when a mobile node registers with its home agent, it registers with all the foreign agents in the hierarchy between the home agent and the mobile node. When it registers the top-level care-of address with its home agent, the mobile node acquires a registration key, using one of the extensions for route optimization (Section 6.4). Suppose that each foreign agent in the hierarchy shares the same registration key that the home agent sent to the foreign agent at the top level of the hierarchy.

Subsequent moves by the mobile node may require reregistration with some (or all) of the foreign agents in the hierarchy without causing any change to the home agent's binding for the mobile node. Since each foreign agent between the mobile node's previous care-of address and the home agent shares the same registration key, when the mobile node reregisters an intermediate care-of address with an unchanged care-of address immediately above it in the hierarchy, the mobile node already shares a registration key with the care-of address that didn't change. To authenticate the binding update, then, the mobile node just has to send the registration key along with its registration through the changed parts of the hierarchy. When the reregistration occurs at the lowest level care-of address that has not changed and that is handled by a foreign agent that shares the same registration key with the mobile node, it need not go any further up the hierarchy.

Since each regional registration request is passed to every foreign agent between the mobile node and the *closest* foreign agent that didn't change, when the regional registration reply comes back, the targeted mobility agent processing the request can encode the registration key for each new foreign agent that will handle the reply. Thus, the hierarchy of foreign agents is presumed to share sufficient trust to allow encoding of such keys.

Forwarding Datagrams to the Mobile Node

At each level of the hierarchy, the foreign agent advertising the care-of address at that level has visitor-list entries for mobile nodes within its region of the hierarchy.

The mobile node's entry shows that it is regionally registered at the care-of address at the next lower level of the hierarchy.

Thus, a datagram arriving at the top of the hierarchy from the home agent will (figuratively speaking) be decapsulated and reencapsulated with a new tunnel endpoint—namely, the care-of address at the next lower level of the hierarchy. This decapsulation and reencapsulation occurs at each level of the hierarchy until the datagram reaches the last tunnel endpoint, which is either the mobile node itself (in case of a colocated care-of address) or a foreign agent that can deliver the decapsulated datagram to the mobile node with no further special Mobile IP handling.

Note that the actual decapsulation need not occur at each step of the hierarchy. Instead, the foreign agent at that level can typically merely change the source and destination IP addresses of the encapsulating IP header.

7.7.3 Agent Advertisements

A foreign agent wishing to participate in a hierarchy of foreign agents advertises its services using the mobility extension to the ICMP Router Advertisement, which is defined in base Mobile IP. However, a strict ordering is imposed on the list of care-of addresses. The first care-of address is associated with the advertising agent, and each successive care-of address must be associated with the next higher foreign agent in the hierarchy.

In addition, a new bit (the I bit, for "hierarchical") is defined in the flags field of the agent advertisement, so that the mobile node can be assured that the advertising agent is indeed equipped to handle the regional registration request. The format is illustrated in Figure 7.6 and contains the following fields (all other fields not defined here are unchanged from the definitions given in Section 4.3).

I   If the I bit is set, the foreign agent is advertising a hierarchy of care-of addresses and can properly process a regional registration request.

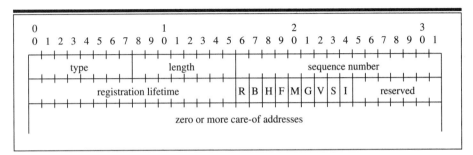

Figure 7.6 Hierarchical agent advertisement.

7.7.4 Regional Registration Request

A mobile node can register with all of the hierarchical mobility agents between itself and its home agent using a regional registration request message, as illustrated in Figure 7.7. When using a colocated care-of address as the lowest level care-of address of the foreign agent hierarchy, the mobile node may reregister with its previous care-of address if that care-of address wasn't a colocated care-of address.

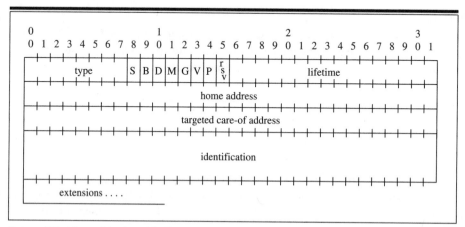

Figure 7.7 Hierarchical registration request format

Each mobility agent receiving the request relays it to the next higher level care-of address in the hierarchy. For each pending regional registration request, in addition to the information stored for the processing of registration requests as required by base Mobile IP, each foreign agent stores the care-of address of the next-lower foreign agent in the hierarchy. This address is available in the request message.

The regional registration request and the conventional registration request are very similar. All processing of regional registration requests by mobility agents is the same as the processing by mobility agents in base Mobile IP. The UDP fields are also the same as in the base Mobile IP.

- **IP fields:**

    Source address   Typically the interface address from which the message is sent

    Destination address   Typically that of the mobility agent at the next higher level of the hierarchy of mobility agents

- **UDP fields**

    Type   8 (regional registration request)

Targeted mobility agent	The IP address of the targeted mobility agent, which is the closest common ancestor between the mobile node's previous and current points of attachment
Extensions	What follows the fixed portion of the regional registration request

All fields not listed here are defined just as in the base Mobile IP registration message (see Section 4.3). The home agent field is replaced by the targeted mobility agent field.

The regional registration request always has to include an authentication extension appropriate to the targeted mobility agent (either a mobile-home authentication extension, or a mobile-foreign authentication extension). In the case of the mobile-foreign authentication extension the mobile node may use the mobility security association set up when it obtained a registration key (for example, using key request extensions as defined in Section 6.1.3) from previous regional registrations it transacted with its home agent and all intervening foreign agents at that time.

The same rules apply to the regional registration request as to the registration request regarding the relative order in which different extensions, when present, appear in the registration message.

Each foreign agent that receives a regional registration request compares its offered care-of address with the targeted mobility agent listed in the request. If they are the same the foreign agent determines whether or not to accept the request, and returns a regional registration reply with the appropriate status code. Otherwise, the foreign agent delivers the registration request to the next higher care-of address in the hierarchy. The registration key extension selected by the mobile node is processed appropriately at each level of the hierarchy, if necessary. Foreign agents in the hierarchy between the mobile node and the home agents can share the same registration key.

Each foreign agent makes note of the next-lower level care-of address in its list of pending registration requests for future association with the mobile node's home address. The formulation here assumes that the authentication extension supplied by the mobile node can be validated by the targeted foreign agents in the hierarchy. If this assumption is unable to be realized, additional authentication steps will be necessary as the registration is delivered up the hierarchy toward the targeted mobility agent.

When the mobile node first issues a regional registration request in a new hierarchy of cooperating foreign agents, the closest common ancestor will be the mobile node's home agent. In that case the targeted care-of address will be the address of the home agent, and the mobile node will need to use one of the key request extensions described in Section 6.4. That key should be acquired by each of the hierarchical foreign agents on return of the regional registration reply from the home agent to the mobile node.

7.7.5 Regional Registration Reply

A mobility agent returns a regional registration reply message to a mobile node that has sent a regional registration request message by way of the foreign agent at each intermediate level of the hierarchy between itself and the mobile node. Each foreign agent above the mobile node in the hierarchy will receive the regional reply from the mobility agent at the next higher level of the hierarchy. The regional reply message contains the necessary codes to inform the mobile node about the status of its request, along with the lifetime granted by the targeted agent. This lifetime is not allowed to be great enough to outlive the bindings at the home agent or at foreign agents above the targeted agent in the hierarchy. The lifetime at the mobile node's home agent is known from the original lifetime granted by the home agent in the last registration request (or regional registration request) approved by the home agent.

When the foreign agent receives a successful regional registration reply, it updates its visitor-list entry for the mobile node using the next-lower care-of address in the hierarchy as the care-of address of the mobile node.

The foreign agent is not allowed to increase the lifetime selected by the mobile node in the regional registration request, since the lifetime is covered by an authentication extension. The targeted mobility agent is not allowed to increase the lifetime selected by the mobile node in the regional registration request, since doing so could increase it beyond the maximal registration lifetime allowed by the intermediate foreign agents. If the lifetime received in the regional registration reply is greater than that in the regional registration request, the lifetime in the request is required to be used. When the lifetime received in the regional registration reply is less than that in the regional registration request, the lifetime in the reply is required to be used.

Note the similarity between the regional registration reply and the conventional registration reply message. The only difference is that the home agent's IP address is replaced by the more general notion of the targeted mobility agent's IP address. Processing of regional registration replies by mobility agents is similar to the processing by mobility agents in base Mobile IP. This includes determining the validity of the registration request and selecting the appropriate status code for the reply. The IP fields and UDP fields are chosen just as with the registration reply message in base Mobile IP. The UDP header is followed by the following reply fields, as shown in Figure 7.8.

Type	9 (regional registration reply)
Code	A value indicating the result of the regional registration request. The code values are similar to those for the base Mobile IP registration reply.

Targeted care-of address	The IP address of the registering mobility agent
Identification	A 64-bit number used for matching registration requests with registration replies, and for protecting against replay attacks of registration messages (see Section 7.7.6).
Extensions	What follows the fixed portion of the regional registration reply. An authentication extension is required to be included in all registration replies returned by the mobility agent.

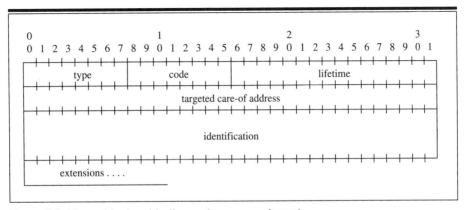

Figure 7.8 Hierarchical registration reply message format.

The values available for use within the code field are the same as for the standard registration reply field as listed in Section 4.4, but also include error codes 144 and 145 for the broadcast and multicast preference extensions described earlier in this chapter.

Note that processing of the identification field is significantly different than in base Mobile IP when nonces are to be used. Each foreign agent receiving a successful regional registration reply from the foreign agent immediately above it in the foreign agent hierarchy is required to replace any identification stored and associated with the mobile node, with the fresh identification in the received reply message.

Note also that when the targeted mobility agent is unknown, the regional registration request works as well as the base Mobile IP registration request in helping the mobile node to discover its home agent's address. In that case, however, the mobile node would probably prefer to use the base registration request, since the request cannot be accepted anyway until the home agent's address is known.

7.7.6 Replay Protection

The identification field is used to let the targeted mobility agent verify that a registration message has been freshly generated by the mobile node, not replayed by an attacker from some previous registration. Two methods are described in the base Mobile IP (Section 4.9.6): timestamps (mandatory) and nonces (optional). All mobile nodes and mobility agents using regional registration messages are required to implement timestamp-based replay protection. These nodes may also implement nonce-based replay protection.

The style of replay protection in effect between a mobile node and its mobility agents is part of the mobile security association. A mobile node and its mobility agent must agree to which method of replay protection will be used. The interpretation of the identification field depends on the method of replay protection as described in the following subsections.

All requirements of Section 4.9.6 regarding replay protection must be followed by mobile nodes using the regional registration procedures. There is no change to the replay procedures when timestamps are used. However, for nonce-based replay protection additional refinements must be instituted by the mobile node. Other mobility agents process nonces as in the base protocol specification. If no agreement is made to use nonces, then timestamps are used by default.

The identification in a new registration request is not allowed to repeat while the same security context is being used between the mobile node and the targeted care-of address. Retransmission, as described in Section 4.6.4, is allowed.

7.7.7 Replay Protection Using Nonces

The basic principle of nonce replay protection does not change from that described in the base Mobile IP specification. However, since there can now be multiple mobility agents all registering the same mobile node, the mobile node must maintain a vector of nonces, possibly one for each mobility agent in its current hierarchy.

Whenever a targeted mobility agent receives a regional registration request, it selects a new nonce using the same methods described for home agents selecting a new nonce in the base Mobile IP specification. The mobility agent then inserts the resulting identification in the appropriate field of the regional registration reply. Each mobility agent at lower levels of the hierarchy copies, when it receives the reply, the new identification for possible use in receiving future regional registration requests from the mobile node. In other words, new nonces from higher in the hierarchy supersede existing nonces stored by intermediate foreign agents in the hierarchy.

When a mobile node receives a regional registration reply, it in turn associates the nonce from the identification field with every intermediate foreign agent between itself and the targeted mobility agent to which it had sent the regional registration request.

If a registration message is rejected because of an invalid nonce, the reply always provides the mobile node (and each other intermediate foreign agent at lower levels than the targeted mobility agent) with a new nonce to be used in the next registration. Thus the nonce protocol is self-synchronizing.

7.8 Summary

Techniques for allowing Mobile IP to coexist with firewalls are not well developed, but include manual configuration of keys between the firewall and mobile node, and creation of special topologies within foreign visited domains that are cut off from the sensitive part of the visited domain.

Ingress filtering is motivating the introduction of reverse tunneling techniques into Mobile IP, whereby the mobile node even further imitates the model of operating on its home network even though it has moved to a new point of attachment on the Internet.

Broadcast and multicast preference extensions are proposed that allow the mobile node to specify exactly which broadcasts are of interest to the mobile node. This has the benefits of reducing traffic through the tunnel, reducing bandwidth over the wireless link, and simplifying configuration requirements for the mobile node. The multicast extension goes further to specify certain behavior on the part of the foreign agent.

A mobile node can use several methods for determining when to register with a new care-of address. The best methods are still to be developed in the future, and thus are not described in this book. They involve comparing the signal strength of the available advertisement packets to select the advertisement with the best signal. When such methods are not available, the mobile node has a choice of several methods that do not rely on such physical-layer indications. ECS is likely to be the best method when mobile nodes travel through wireless domains in trajectories that change direction rarely compared with the transit time through a cell. LCS is likely to be better when a mobile node changes directions multiple times compared with the cell transit time. Using prefix lengths, when available, is likely to be better when the network broadcast range is well defined, for instance with wired mobility.

When a mobile node moves rapidly through a large number of foreign agents, additional steps should be taken to minimize the number of registration messages that have to be sent across the Internet back to the mobile node's home agent. The method proposed in this chapter involves arranging the foreign agents in a hierarchy and using a currently underspecified feature in agent advertisements to advertise a bottom-up view of the hierarchy at each new point of attachment. This method fits naturally with the Mobile IP model. A number of tedious adjustments are needed to allow the registration procedures to remain reliable in some way that does not require an explosion of key distribution steps. Similarly, tunneling becomes a multistep phenomenon with more intermediate tunneling agents. Experience will determine whether further optimizations in the tunneling or registration fabric are needed.

Recent discussion indicates that the methods outlined for regional registration are also likely to be useful for handling registrations through security agents in foreign domains. The security domains represented by these security agents are typically arranged hierarchically, but not in class correspondence with the physical network topology. Similar advertisements and tunneling techniques are applicable.

CHAPTER EIGHT

IP version 6

This chapter describes the leading proposal for supporting mobile computer operation with IP version 6 (*IPv6*). IPv6 already defines useful minimal standards for security, and nice methods for attaching to the Internet. In IPv6, the mobile node can get a care-of address and inform its partners about each new care-of address in a secure fashion. A new destination option, the *binding update*, serves to notify correspondent nodes about the mobile node's care-of address. With just those mechanisms, the mobile node is assured of the availability of most of the basic protocol operations it needs for mobility support. In addition, a *binding acknowledgment* helps assure the mobile node of the delivery of its binding updates in certain special cases, for instance to make sure its home agent has received the most recent binding update.

The aspects of IPv6 are described that are particularly relevant to Mobile IP, as well as relevant IPv6 operations that are used in typical scenarios to support mobile nodes. Lastly, to put the protocol operations in a suitable context, the additional requirements placed on IPv6 nodes and routers to support the coming wave of mobile computing are listed.

8.1 An Overview of IPv6

IPv6 is a new protocol that has been under development within the IETF as a future replacement for the current version of IP (which is IP version 4, or *IPv4*). Several working groups are involved with various aspects of the development, and the Mobile IP Working Group has been involved with developing some support for mobile computers within IPv6, which is (like IPv4) a network-layer protocol.

Of course, IPv4 is eminently serviceable, as shown by the fact that it is the network-layer protocol that underpins the entire Internet. Even so, since the Internet has been growing by a factor of two every year, the underlying assumptions by which IPv4 has been designed and administered are starting to become invalid. What was sufficient for a few thousand or a few million users, or a few tens of thousands of networks, will no longer be feasible in a world with tens of billions of addressable network nodes and hundreds of millions of networks.

8.1.1 Motivation for Developing IPv6

There are two chief constraints that current IPv4 addressing may place on the continued growth of the Internet:

1. Limited number, 2^{32}, of available addresses

2. Difficulty in managing routing tables

One can reasonably ask why 2^{32} IP addresses do not suffice for the foreseeable future. After all, it will be a very long time before there are actually four billion Internet nodes that are assigned IP addresses of any sort. However, it turns out that IP addresses are usually allocated very sparsely from the available IP address space that has been parceled out to the various agencies and administrative entities that together constitute the Internet. Thus, from the portion of the IP address space that is already allocated (and, effectively, almost unrecoverable) only a few percent of the addresses are assigned to nodes in active use. The rest of the addresses are wasted, or in some cases reserved for future expansion. For a long time, no one cared about this problem because IP addresses are, in a sense, only numbers. With billions of numbers available to the first users of the Internet, there was no sense of urgency about conserving the address space.

The manner in which IP addresses have been allocated in the past has had another more pernicious effect, however. Since the Internet grows mainly by the creation of new networks, and new networks are made accessible by adding information to routing tables in existing routers, these existing routers have been faced with ever-increasing workloads. Today's backbone routers must handle more than thirty thousand routes, and there are not many products that can handle that workload. For years, new routes were added to the routing tables with little regard for the additional workload presented to the routers by each new entry. Since the Internet grows mainly by the creation of new networks, and new networks are made accessible by adding information to routing tables in existing routers, these existing routers have been faced with ever-increasing workloads. Router vendors have complained that they will not be able to keep up with the rapid pace of expansion.

The problem of large, unwieldy routing tables has been aggravated especially by the original design of the Internet address space, which partitioned the space into class A, class B, class C, and multicast or class D addresses (Stevens 1994). In each class, every network was of the same size. This strategy leads directly to a highly fragmented address space where addresses are spread far apart in the address space. For instance, if two organizations needed 500 addresses each, they would have possibly each requested their own separate class B addresses, each with 65,536 addresses. Even if the organizations were neighboring in the Internet topology (defined by the connections between routers), there was no real demand that their address spaces be closely associated. Thus, two of the now precious slots in the backbone routers would have been taken up to handle only 1,000 (out of more than 130,000 possible) addressable Internet nodes.

Recognizing this problem, the IETF has spent a great deal of effort to rectify the network sizing problem by eliminating the address space classes and moving toward a new routing strategy known as CIDR, mentioned briefly in Section 1.5.2. In CIDR, the remaining address space is allocated in sizes that more closely approximate the needs of the requester. Since the IP address of all nodes on a particular network share the same leading bits, the size of a network is typically indicated by the number of leading bits defining the network, or the length of the IP address prefix shared by all nodes on that network. For instance, a network with 512 nodes will have a prefix that is 23 bits long and could be denoted according to CIDR conventions as 119.224.130/23. And, for example, the two organizations mentioned with needs for networks with 500 nodes could have address space allocated to them that closely matches their needs.

Also, by use of newer network protocols such as BGP-4 (Rekhter and Li 1995), closely associated networks are able to be *aggregated* and appear as a single, larger network outside of an administrative domain. Thus, the previously unruly growth of the number of networks constituting the Internet has been slowed to a much more manageable rate. With thoughtful address administration, an organization with thousands of networks can organize their internal routers so that only a single network prefix needs to be published to the rest of the Internet backbone routers. For instance, two networks with prefixes 119.224.130/23 and 119.224.132/23 could be aggregated internally to an administrative domain and advertised to the rest of the Internet as a single network 119.223.132/22.

Nowadays, protocols are deployed to simplify the aggregation of route table information and thus to minimize the required dissemination of route table entries throughout the backbone of the Internet. Because of that, IP address allocation in the future will present proportionately less burden on the routers than it did in the past. Unfortunately, the theoretical advantage of good future route management comes only after the present reality of overburdened routers and sparsely assigned address space. With luck, the future development of routing protocols will point the way toward ever more efficient aggregation of routes, even from separate administrative domains.

In any case, starting over with a new address space (as the Internet will do when deploying IPv6) will enable a significant reduction in the number of routes required to be maintained by the backbone routers. Until new routing protocols really become available, this will be the main hope for improvement of the situation. As long as the existing IPv4 routes have to be maintained, however, no savings can be realized in the size of existing routing tables. Only if the Internet moves toward universal adoption of IPv6 could the routing table size decrease, unless some networks are relinquished or become unroutable.

8.1.2 Initial Development of IPv6

As momentum began to build toward the development of a replacement for IPv4, several protocols were proposed as contenders for the role (Callon 1992, Francis 1994, Hinden 1994, McGovern and Ullmann 1994). A special directorate was convened, and the decision was made that only a single replacement protocol could be supported in any successful manner. White papers were solicited and a number of requirements were placed that had to be satisfied by the various developers. After all, the directorate agreed, if the Internet was going to have to undergo the convulsions expected during adoption of a new network protocol, it might as well be done right this time. Some of the important requirements were as follows:

- Plenty of addresses
- Reduced administrative overhead
- Opportunity for better routing
- Support for address renumbering
- Improved header processing
- Reasonable security
- Support for mobility

Each of these requirements was driven by real needs and the understanding that the Internet would continue along its exponential growth curve, fueled largely by an ever-increasing number of mobile nodes operated by people who in large measure were not expected to be familiar with protocol or administrative details.

The protocol that has developed from the intense efforts within the IETF does in fact meet these requirements, given support for the mobility messages that are defined in this chapter.

Some of the important protocol differences between IPv4 and IPv6 are discussed in the following subsections, especially as they relate to the fulfillment of the last requirement—namely, support for mobility.

8.1.3 Bigger Address Space

IPv6 certainly manages to achieve the requirement for bigger address space. Over the objections of experts who wanted the new IP to have variable-length addresses, and thus a truly unbounded address space, the decision was made to make IPv6 address space statically sized with 128 bits of address space. With 128 bits in each IPv6 address, there are enough IPv6 addresses to assign a separate address to nodes on every square inch of every planet in the solar system. It remains to be seen how sparsely this address space will be assigned to active Internet nodes.

The IPv6 address space is certainly large enough to offer addressability for every existing node that today uses other network protocols. So, for instance, a portion of the IPv6 address space is reserved for computer systems using Novell's Internet packet exchange (*IPX*) network-layer protocol, Appletalk, as well as the Connection-Less Network Protocol (*CLNP*).

8.1.4 Reduced Administrative Overhead

One of the biggest technical hurdles facing the continued deployment of IPv4 is the need for understanding administrative techniques that seem inconvenient or even daunting for many users. These administrative requirements are evolving toward added complexity as the need for efficiency increases with the size of the growing Internet. For instance, search techniques and database update mechanisms that were sufficient for small networks are unthinkable in many of today's enterprise networks.

Much of the administrative load for IPv4 nodes involves allocating and managing their IPv4 addresses and their connectivity to the network. One clear requirement for IPv6 was the reduction or elimination of this administrative work. Protocols such as Stateless Address Autoconfiguration (Thomson and Narten 1996) and Neighbor Discovery (Narten, Nordmark, and Simpson 1996) have fulfilled this requirement, allowing new IPv6 nodes to get an address and the address of one or more default routers to effect their connection to the global Internet. IPv6 nodes are able to configure their addresses automatically based on their individual characteristics and the existing network configuration as disseminated by routers on the networks.

8.1.5 Support for Address Renumbering

Experience has shown that Internet nodes cannot, in general, expect to keep the same IP address for their entire useful lifetime. Commonly, a network or an enterprise intranet will need to renumber based on a topological change involving a wholesale reconnection to a different ISP or other point of presence on the Internet backbone. On a more individual basis, a computer may be moved to a new permanent location as offices are reorganized or the user embarks on new career phases.

Care has been taken to enable support for deprecating and finally invalidating IPv6 addresses as needs indicate. An IPv6 node discovers the need for configuring a new IPv6 address for itself by means of messages defined as part of Neighbor Discovery (Narten, Nordmark, and Simpson 1996), which also provides the means for performing the reconfiguration.

8.1.6 Improved Header Processing

The biggest improvement in header design involves the redefinition of IP options. Other significant improvements involve eliminating the need to calculate checksums and the inclusion of a flow label. Higher level protocols are assumed to perform their own checksums if any are needed. The flow label is expected to help improve the routability of packets making up high-capacity data flows.

IPv6 options are improved in two ways. First, the format of the options is improved for quicker processing by intermediate and end nodes. Second, options are now classified in such a way that in most cases they can be ignored by intermediate nodes (routers). In other words, in such cases options do not have any affect on the performance of intermediate nodes.

A relatively minor artifact has been removed from IPv4 source route option processing that has an important effect on support of mobility. In IPv4, the recipient of a datagram with a source route option is required to route any return traffic back through the intermediate nodes specified in the received source route. This has some security implications, because with source routing any node anywhere in the Internet can attempt to spoof any particular IP node just by claiming to be an intermediate node in a source-routed data flow between the spoofed endpoint and the victim endpoint. For this reason, many routers in today's Internet do not perform any forwarding functions for source-routed datagrams, thus effectively prohibiting them. See further discussion of the problems with source routing in IPv4 in Sections 1.5.3 and 5.14.

8.1.7 Reasonable Security

Among the greatest threats to the current Internet is the lack of almost any deployment of security technology. Almost all security today results from fortuitous physical circumstances. People can't see datagrams without computer equipment, and so for the most part the data is as physically secure as the wires and nodes that are connected by the wires, providing some measure of confidence. Of course, with wireless equipment even this minimal assurance is likely to evaporate, as someone in your neighboring enterprise's parking lot may be able to capture your data if it is sent over a radio frequency carrier.

With the growth and popularization of the Internet also has come a corresponding increase in the number of miscreants, who not surprisingly are becoming ever more technically competent in perpetrating their mischief. Even some backbone routers of the Internet have fallen to attacks by hackers. These attacks have made it clear that physical security, in the form of minimizing the number of physical links that the datagrams traverse, is no longer sufficient. There are now just too many links that can be vulnerable.

Making the Internet a better communications medium for transacting business is a huge task that lies before the Internet engineering community. Clearly, business will not expose its transactions to the vagaries and uncertainties that currently characterize the infrastructure making up the Internet. There are too many billions of dollars at stake. But there is hope. A software solution is available from the technology of cryptography, which has grown up over the last two decades. Public key cryptography and other advances now make it feasible to send data that is received exactly as sent but still cannot be understood by anyone except those who share a mutually agreed-on secret.

These technologies, which are available in rudimentary form today, are being standardized for use in the ancillary security protocols associated with IPv6. Several such authentication and privacy protocols have to be implemented as part of any IPv6 product before that product can claim to be compliant with the standards. In addition, any IPv6 product will need to support some (as-yet incompletely specified) protocol for key distribution. Today, the only universally agreed-on method is manual key distribution (for example, one could make a phone call).

This matter of improved security for IPv6 could eventually be seen as the biggest advance of all of the many advances promulgated as part of the IPv6 deployment. It will certainly usher in a new age of confidence and business reliance on the Internet. Clearly, there are other wide-ranging social impacts with implications that are not fully understood. For instance, with the ubiquitous availability of untraceable digital cash, the entire economic fabric of society could take unpredictable turns, lurching from one instability to the next. National governments and local police departments may find themselves hard pressed to follow the money or prove wrongdoing. For instance, kidnappers could deliver ransom notes by authentic personal videos of the victims and demand payment into one of the billions of untraceable accounts of the future. On the brighter side, people should all be able to manage their financial affairs with complete auditability and integrated account management, as well as having digital financial services available at the click of a mouse.

8.2 Overview of Mobility Support in IPv6

Mobility for IPv6 borrows the general ideas of a home network, home agent, and care-of address from Mobile IP for IPv4. A mobile node should always be reachable by sending packets to its home address. If the mobile node is no longer attached to its home network, the home agent again is charged with the responsibility for sending datagrams to the mobile node. This again implies that the home agent and mobile node cooperate to make sure that the home agent is always aware of the care-of address of the mobile node. That process of cooperation can be thought of as registration; and again, registration occurs whenever the mobile node acquires a new care-of address.

Again, as in IPv4 and illustrated in Figure 8.1, there are home networks, foreign networks, and home agents. Notably absent are the foreign agents. In the figure, the entities formerly serving as foreign agents are now thought of merely as *access points*, or points at which the wireless mobile nodes may connect to the IPv6 Internet.

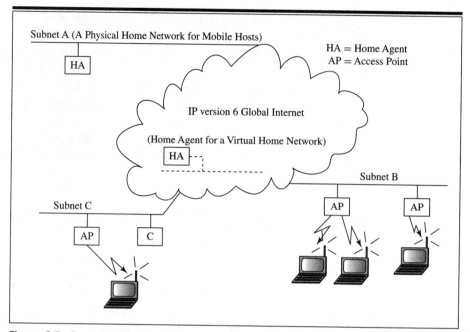

Figure 8.1 Overall picture for IPv6.

The design of IPv6 is much improved for mobile networking. In its broadest aspect, mobility is supported by the action of the mobile node, which takes the responsibility of supplying location information to each of its corresponding nodes. By correcting the problems associated with earlier implementations of source routing, IPv6 is able to make use of the previous elegant approaches that practical considerations made unsuitable for IPv4. The methods of IPv6 for automatic address configuration are perfect for allowing mobile nodes to configure their new care-of addresses at each new point of attachment. And, lastly, the presumed ubiquity of security options for IPv6 means that correspondents receiving location information from mobile nodes can confidently accept them without fear that subsequent data to the mobile node will be hijacked.

IPv6 requires every node to support address autoconfiguration (Thomson and Narten 1996) and Neighbor Discovery (Narten, Nordmark, and Simpson 1996). The latter is a much improved protocol substituting for ARP in IPv4. Using these protocols, a mobile node is able to determine the network prefix at any new point of attachment it might select, and subsequently create or obtain a globally routable IPv6 address appropriate for that point of attachment. Only those steps are necessary for obtaining a care-of address. So by using natural features available in IPv6, mobile nodes can perform for themselves most or all of the services for which foreign agents were needed in IPv4. Therefore, in this proposal, foreign agents are not specified for use with mobility in IPv6.

When the mobile node moves, it informs its correspondent nodes about its new location. The intermediate nodes between the mobile and the correspondent nodes do not need to know about the mobile node's new location, so it is useful to encode the location information as one of IPv6's new *destination options*. Such options can be included with any normal data packet that the mobile node would send to a correspondent node. In this way, information about the current location of the mobile node is transmitted at lowest cost to the mobile, the correspondent, and all intermediate nodes.

When a correspondent node wishes to deliver a packet to a mobile node, it does so by the simple expedient of including a routing header in the packet, with the care-of address used as the address of the intermediate node in the routing header. In fact, this technique can even be combined with other (nonmobile) uses of the routing header, as long as the care-of address is used as the last intermediate address (and in LSR mode).

The home agent, while not usually a node with which the mobile node maintains active connections, must nevertheless always be aware of any change in the care-of address by the mobile node as soon as possible. Although the home agent discovers and maintains the care-of address information from the mobile node in a manner identical in almost all respects to that of any correspondent node, the home agent uses the information differently.

First, when the home agent discovers that the mobile node has moved, it uses techniques from Neighbor Discovery to indicate a new MAC-layer address for the mobile node to all the mobile's correspondent nodes on the home network. This is similar to the operation of proxy ARP in IPv4. Second, when the home agent receives a packet destined for the mobile node, it must usually assume that the datagram is not to be modified in any way. Thus, the home agent uses IP6-in-IP6 encapsulation (Conta and Deering 1997) to deliver the datagram to the care-of address. When the mobile node receives such an encapsulated datagram, it will know to inform the correspondent node about its care-of address. Lastly, since it is so important for reachability of the mobile node, the home agent must always acknowledge receipt of any care-of address information from the mobile node.

Note that the mobile node is under no obligation to inform its correspondent nodes about its care-of address. The mobile node may choose to hide such information for reasons of privacy.

Mobility is supported in IPv6 by the use of new destination options, each containing fields that specify the type and length of the option. Destination options are preferable for this purpose, since there is no need for intermediate routers to do any processing of the option en route. Extensions to mobility support destination options may be included after the fixed portion of the option. The presence of such extensions will be indicated by the option length field. When the option length is greater than the number of octets taken up by the predetermined part of the header, the remaining octets are interpreted as extensions. Currently, no extensions have been defined.

The three highest order bits of each destination option type are encoded to indicate specific processing of the option (Deering and Hinden 1995). For the mobility support destination options, these three bits are set to 110, to indicate the following processing details.

- The data within the option cannot change en route to the packet's final destination.

- When the destination is a multicast address, any node processing this option that does not recognize the option type must discard the packet

- When the destination is a unicast address, any node processing this option that does not recognize the option type must discard the packet *and* return an ICMP parameter problem (code 2) message to the packet's source address.

As currently defined, the mobility support destination options will not appear in a multicast packet.

8.3 Binding Update Option

As mentioned earlier, a mobile node uses a new destination option (called the *binding update* option) to inform its home agents and its correspondents about its care-of address. In this section, the new option is described in detail with the packet layout shown and the meaning of each field in the header explained.

Any packet that includes a binding update option is required to meet the following two requirements.

1. The source address in the IP header of the packet has to be the home address for the binding, since the option does not contain a field to carry the mobile node's home address separately.

2. The packet must include an IPv6 authentication header to protect against forged binding updates.

As shown in Figure 8.2, the binding update option is encoded in TLV format. The fields are as follows:

Option Type   192

Option Length   Eight-bit unsigned integer: length of the option, in octets, excluding the option type and option length

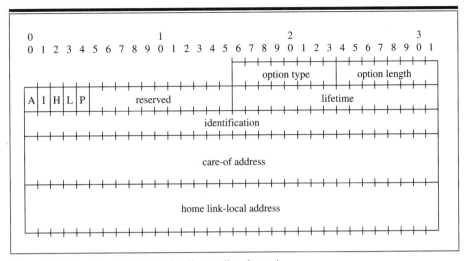

Figure 8.2 Binding update destination option format.

fields. For the current definition of the binding update option, this field must be set to 24 if the home link-local address present (L) bit is not set, and must otherwise be set to 40.

A   The A (acknowledge) bit is set by the sending node to request that a binding acknowledgment message be returned on receipt of the binding update option.

H   The H (home registration) bit is set by the sending node to request the receiving node to act as this node's home agent. The destination address in the IPv6 header of the packet carrying this option is required to be that of a router sharing the same network prefix as the source address in the IPv6 header of the packet.

L   The L (home link-local address present) bit indicates the presence of the home link-local address field in the binding update. This bit is set by the sending node to request the receiving node to act as a proxy (for participating in the Neighbor Discovery protocol) for the node while it is away from home. This bit is not allowed to be set unless the home registration (H) bit is also set.

Reserved	Sent as 0; ignored on reception
Lifetime	A 16-bit unsigned integer; the number of seconds remaining before the binding must be considered expired. A value of all ones (65,535) indicates infinity. A value of 0 indicates that the binding cache entry for the mobile node should be deleted.
Identification	A 32-bit number used by the receiving node to sequence binding updates, and by the sending node to match a returned binding acknowledgment message with this binding update. The identification field also serves to protect against replay attacks for binding updates.
Care-of address	The care-of address of the mobile node for this binding. When set equal to the home address of the mobile node (the source address of the packet carrying this binding update), the binding update option instead indicates that any existing binding for the mobile node should be deleted; no binding for the mobile node should be created in this case.
Home link-local address	The link-local address of the mobile node used by the mobile node when it was last attached to its home network. This field in the binding update is optional and is only present when the home link-local address (L) bit is set.

As it turns out, a distinction has to be made between sending binding updates depending on whether the intended recipient is expected to be the mobile node's home agent. If so, the recipient is expected to perform proxy neighbor advertisements on behalf of the mobile node. Suppose there are multiple home agents on the home network, and one of them is maintaining communication with a mobile node for which it is not the home agent, purely in the role of a correspondent node. Since only one home agent should provide the proxy advertisements, the binding update needs to be acted on differently by the other home agent, which is only acting as a correspondent node. The mobile node would not set the H bit for the binding update sent to the other home agent when it is acting as a correspondent node.

If the mobile node ever takes up residence on its home network, it is likely that the home agent will observe its presence and make the proper association between the mobile node's link-local address and its (global) home address. In this case, no binding updates will ever need to be sent to the home agent with the L bit set, because the home agent will always have a record of the link-local address.

However, the mobile node may never yet have been in operation on its home network. In this case, the mobile node can still permit the home agent to perform proxy advertisements and duplicate address detection (*DAD*) (Thomson and Narten 1996) on its behalf by setting the L bit and including its link-local address in its first binding update to the home agent.

The P bit and I bit are not fully described in this book because their definitions are not finished. Roughly speaking, the I bit is to be used in the same way as the I bit in previous foreign agent notification extensions, defined in Section 6.3.1. The P bit has to do with using the binding update option to manage renumbering of the mobile node, as well as possibly redirecting sessions aimed at anycast addresses or multihome nodes.

8.4 Binding Acknowledgment Option

In this section, the binding acknowledgment destination option is described in detail. In most cases, acknowledgment is not required for binding updates. The mobile node will know that the correspondent node has received the update, because the correspondent node will no longer send datagrams to the older address. However, the mobile node has to be sure right away that the home agent has received binding updates, so the home agent must always acknowledge the receipt of binding updates.

Any packet that includes a binding acknowledgment option is required to meet the following two requirements.

1. The packet destination address in the IP header is required to be sent back to the node sending the binding update. Only the mobile node is authorized to send the binding update. This means that the binding update will be sent to the mobile node. The acknowledgment is delivered to the mobile node at its home address by way of a routing header containing the mobile node's care-of address.

2. The packet is also required to include an IPv6 authentication header (Atkinson 1995a) in order to protect against forged binding acknowledgments.

The binding acknowledgment option is encoded in TLV format as shown in Figure 8.3. The fields are as follows:

Option type   193

Option length   Eight-bit unsigned integer; length of the option, in octets, excluding the option type and option length fields. For the current definition of the binding acknowledgment option, this field must be set to 8.

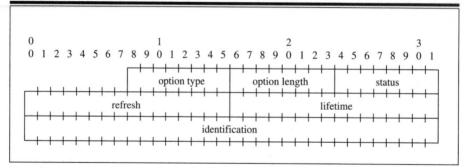

Figure 8.3 Binding acknowledgment destination option format.

Status	Eight-bit unsigned integer indicating the disposition of the binding update. Values of less than 128 indicate that the binding update was accepted by the receiving node. One such status value is currently defined as

>   0   Binding update accepted

Values greater than or equal to 128 indicate that the binding update was rejected by the receiving node. The following such status values are currently defined:

>   128   Reason unspecified
>   129   Poorly formed binding update
>   130   Administratively prohibited
>   131   Insufficient resources
>   132   Home registration not supported
>   133   Not home network
>   134   Identification field mismatch
>   135   Unknown home agent address

Up-to-date values of the status field are to be specified in the most recent *Assigned Numbers* (Reynolds and Postel 1994).

Refresh   The recommended period at which the mobile node should send a new binding update to this node to *refresh* the mobile node's binding in this node's binding cache, in case the node fails and loses its cache state.

Lifetime   The granted lifetime for which this node will attempt to retain the entry for this mobile node in its binding cache. If the node sending the binding acknowledgment is serving as the mobile node's home agent, the lifetime period also indicates the period for which this node will continue this service. If the mobile node requires home agent service from this node beyond this period, the mobile node is required to send a new binding update to it before the expiration of this period to extend the lifetime.

Identification   The acknowledgment identification is copied from the binding update option, for use by the mobile node in matching the acknowledgment with an outstanding binding update.

The three highest order bits of the option type are 110, to indicate the necessary option processing. The refresh period is determined by the node sending the binding acknowledgment (the node caching the binding), typically the mobile node's home agent. The refresh value may be set, for example, based on whether the node stores the mobile node's binding in volatile storage or in nonvolatile storage. If the node sending the binding acknowledgment is not serving as the mobile node's home agent, the refresh period should be set equal to the lifetime period in the binding acknowledgment. Even if this node loses this cache entry due to a failure of the node, packets from it can still reach the mobile node through the mobile node's home agent, causing a new binding update to this node to allow it to recreate this cache entry.

8.5 Binding Request Option

In most cases the mobile node will send updates to its correspondent nodes without any need for action on their part. The updates will be sent some number of round-trip times before the binding expires at the correspondent node, or as needed when the mobile node acquires a new care of address and the old address becomes stale or deprecated.

However, in some cases it may be possible that the mobile node and one of its correspondent nodes have sufficiently different clock rates such that the correspondent node finds its binding is imminently scheduled to expire (say, within only a few round-trip times). In this case it would be useful to allow the correspondent node to ask the mobile node directly for a binding update. This will presumably allow smoother communication even in anomalous cases when the two nodes' clocks work at different rates over long periods of time. The binding request destination option is used for just this purpose.

The binding request option is encoded in TLV format as shown in Figure 8.4.

Option type   194

Option length   Eight-bit unsigned integer; length of the option, in octets, excluding the option type and option length fields. For the current definition of the binding request option, this field must be set to 0.

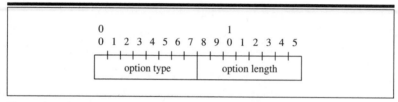

Figure 8.4 Binding request option format.

The three highest order bits of the option type are 110, to indicate processing as before.

8.6 Movement Detection in IPv6

IPv6 mechanisms offer just about the right mix of discovery mechanisms so that a mobile node can keep track of its connectivity status to its point of attachment, even though the mechanisms were really designed with the static desktop computer in mind. Since wireless connectivity is often asymmetrical, it is important to remain aware of that fact when considering the interactions of mobile nodes with Neighbor Discovery (Narten, Nordmark, and Simpson 1996).

Medium-specific mechanisms below the network layer can often provide hints about the status of the link connection. It is fair game for any mobile node to use such status information when considering whether or not it still has a physical link to its current point of attachment. Nevertheless, in this discussion we must focus instead on ways to determine link status using only IPv6 protocol operations. Most of this discussion will be based on operations defined by Neighbor Discovery.

Just as before, a mobile node listens for Router Advertisements to determine that the link is operational in the direction from the router to the mobile node. The advertisements indicate which default router or routers should be used by the mobile node, as well as give prefix information to inform the mobile node about those networks on which it is residing. Each such prefix has a lifetime. When the lifetime of the prefix expires, addresses using that network prefix are deprecated, and addresses formed by newer prefixes must be preferred by the node. This expiration date is typically pushed further into the future on reception of each new Router Advertisement. If the mobile node is impatient, it can transmit (multicast) a router solicitation message.

While away from home, a mobile node should select one router from its *default router list* (Narten, Nordmark, and Simpson 1996) to use as its default router, and one network prefix advertised by that router from its list of prefixes to use as the network prefix in its primary care-of address. Note that it is possible for the mobile node to receive packets at as many care-of addresses as it likes, but only one care-of address can be handled for the mobile node by any particular home agent. The mobile node configures the new care-of address using this prefix and registers it with its home agent as its primary care-of address, as described in Section 8.3. A mobile node may have care-of addresses using other network prefixes from its prefix list. Some wireless nodes will find it advantageous, for smoother transitions between adjacent points of attachment, to accept packets at previous care-of addresses even after receiving the acknowledgment for their new care-of address from their home agent. This is natural in IPv6 because every IPv6 node is a multihomed node, often with link-local and site-local addresses in addition to its globally routable IPv6 address.

A mobile node uses neighbor unreachability detection (NUD) (Narten, Nordmark, and Simpson 1996) to detect when its default router becomes unreachable. While the mobile node is actively sending packets by way of its default router, it can detect that the router has become unreachable in two ways:

1. Through indications from upper layer protocols on the mobile node that a connection is not making forward progress (for example, TCP is timing out while waiting for an acknowledgment after a number of retransmissions)

2. Through the failure to receive a neighbor advertisement message from its default router in response to explicit neighbor solicitation messages retransmitted to it

So, IPv6 NUD is sufficient for the mobile node to determine when it cannot send packets to its default router.

On the other hand, NUD is not sufficient to allow the mobile node to detect efficiently when it cannot receive packets from its default router. The network overhead would be prohibitively high in many cases for a mobile node to probe its default router continually with solicitation messages unless it is otherwise already sending data packets to it. Instead, a mobile node should consider receipt of any IPv6 packet from its current default router as an indication that it is still reachable from the router. Since the router should be sending periodic multicast router advertisement messages (Narten, Nordmark, and Simpson 1996), the mobile node will have frequent opportunity to check if it is still getting packets from its default router, even in the absence of other packets to it from the router. On some types of network interfaces, the mobile node may also supplement this by at times setting its network interface into promiscuous receive mode, so that it is able to receive all packets on the link, including those not link-level addressed to it. The mobile node will then be able to detect any packets sent by the router, to detect reachability from the router. Both packets from the router's IP address and (IPv6) packets from its link-layer address (for example, those forwarded but not originated by the router) should be considered.

If the above means do not indicate that the mobile node is still reachable from its current default router (that is, the mobile node receives no packets from the router for a period of time), then the mobile node should actively probe the router with solicitation messages, even if it is not otherwise actively sending packets to the router. If the solicitation elicits an advertisement message from the router, then the mobile node can deduce that it is still reachable. The mobile node should typically be able to determine its reachability from the router by listening for packets from the router; and thus, such extra NUD probes should rarely be necessary.

8.7 Home Agent Discovery

For IPv4, Mobile IP defines a method (using directed broadcast; see Section 4.6.3) by which a mobile node can discover the IP address of one of its home agents in case its configured home agent address fails to respond. However, there is not (yet) any feature in IPv6 analogous to the directed broadcast address. Several schemes have been proposed to handle this lack.

8.7.1 Ubiquitous Home Agents

First, it is possible to require that all nodes be able to serve as home agents. This would be okay as far as the required protocol operations go, because the operations are simple enough that router manufacturers would not complain. However, home agents are more likely to need nonvolatile storage than other routers. In particular, it would be very nice if a home agent could remember the care-of addresses of its mobile nodes across momentary power outages. As an outage goes on longer and longer, the care-of address information becomes more and more stale, and therefore less useful. However, until power failures become a thing of the past, the inconvenience of lost bindings at the home agent is something that should be prevented. One way to prevent this problem is to have home agents keep a record of current bindings for emergency use. Thus, there will be some routers that are more appropriate than others to serve as home agents.

If all routers are assumed to be equally serviceable as home agents, then the all-routers-on-link anycast address can be used as a directed broadcast address for the home agents on the home network. That anycast address is formed in a conventional way by appending all zeros to the advertised network prefix available from router advertisements.

8.7.2 Special Handling by Routers

Unfortunately, as just described, it seems likely that not all routers will make equally good home agents. If so, one possible next step would be to require that every router perform some special action to help find a home agent when needed. For instance each router, on receipt of a binding update issued to the all-routers anycast address, could be required to retransmit the binding update to the all-home-agents multicast address on the appropriate network interface.

8.7.3 Home Agents Anycast Address

A new anycast has been requested on every subnet. This anycast address is configured by all home agents on the subnet. When a registration request is received at the anycast address the home agent receiving it can follow the same method used in IPv4 to send a registration reply to the mobile node.

This method is the leading proposal, even though it consumes one more IPv6 address for every subnet.

8.8 Smooth Handoffs

Routers (just as any IPv6 node) should be able to accept authenticated binding updates for a mobile node and, subsequently, act on the cached binding by encapsulating packets for intermediate delivery to the care-of address specified in the binding. In cases when a mobile node moves from one care-of address to another without being able to maintain simultaneous connectivity at both care-of addresses, the mobile node should send a binding update to the router servicing the previous care-of address so that packets for the mobile node can be delivered to the new care-of address immediately. For example, a mobile node may move from one radio link to another on a different channel and may be unable to monitor packets transmitted over both channels at once. In this example the mobile node should send a binding update to the previous router (which is the entity delivering packets to the mobile node over the previous radio channel) so that those packets will instead be delivered via its new care-of address. This binding update associates the mobile node's (immediately) previous care-of address with the mobile node's new care-of address, and is authenticated using the IPv6 authentication header with whatever security association the previous router had with the mobile node's previous care-of address.

Note that the previous router does not necessarily know anything about the mobile node's home address as part of this sequence of events. The previous router only knows about the care-of address used by the mobile node at its previous point of attachment. The mobile node, in effect, requests the previous router to serve as a temporary home agent for its own previous care-of address. The mobile node treats its new care-of address as the primary care-of address of its previous care-of address. Thus, in the binding update to its previous router, the mobile node sets the home agent (H) bit if it wishes to ask the router to serve as a home agent, and sets the acknowledge (A) bit to request a binding acknowledgment from the router. The H bit should be set in case the mobile node is in communication with any correspondent nodes on its previous networks. Those nodes would have neighbor cache information for the mobile node's care-of address. To continue communications with the mobile node requires the router on its previous network to perform proxy neighbor advertisement for the mobile node's previous care-of address. In this case the router should only accept the binding update if the mobile node's care-of address is still present in its neighbor cache. Moreover, the previous router should retain the security association for the mobile node's previous care-of address for a brief time, in case the mobile node loses the acknowledgment and retransmits the binding update (with the same new care-of address).

The previous router then operates in the same way as when the mobile node's home agent (for its home address) receives a binding update from the mobile node. That is, the previous router must intercept any packets destined for the home address indicated in the binding update (the mobile node's previous care-of address) and tunnel any such intercepted packets to the care-of address indicated in the binding update (the mobile node's new care-of address). This tunneling is done using IPv6 encapsulation (Conta and Deering 1997) in the same way packets are tunneled from any home agent. Once the mobile node receives the encapsulated packet, it can then typically follow the routing header contained in the decapsulated packet (that the correspondent node used to route the packet to the mobile node's previous care-of address) and send a binding update to this correspondent node giving its new care-of address.

This process of smooth handoff is illustrated in Figure 8.5. In the figure, the mobile node has configured NewCOA at a new point of attachment and sends a binding update for OldCOA to its previous default router on its previous network. Then, consider a packet sent from the correspondent node to its previous care-of address (that is, OldCOA). With the binding update, the mobile node's previous router can then encapsulate the datagram from the correspondent node with a new

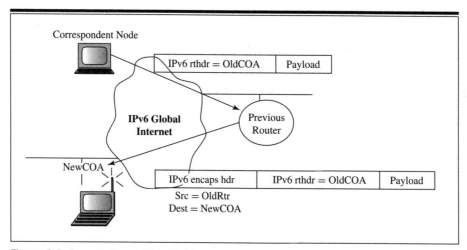

Figure 8.5 Smooth handoffs in IPv6.

IPv6 header using NewCOA as the tunnel endpoint. Since the mobile node is decapsulating tunneled packets sent to NewCOA, it will get the packet sent from the correspondent node. This process should enable fewer packets to be dropped as the mobile node moves to new points of attachment to the Internet. Notice that for wireless nodes it will also be helpful to continue to accept packets (whenever possible) at both OldCOA and NewCOA during the travel time through the overlap of two wireless cells.

8.9 Renumbering the Home Subnet

IPv6 Neighbor Discovery specifies a mechanism by which all nodes on a subnet can gracefully autoconfigure new addresses; for example, when the home subnet changes its Internet service to a different service provider and must change its network prefix (and thus the network prefix of all nodes on the home subnet). As currently specified, this mechanism works when the nodes are on the same link as the router issuing the necessary multicast Router Advertisement packets to advertise the new routing prefixes appropriate for the subnet.

However, for mobile nodes not currently attached to the same link as their home agent, special care must be taken to allow the mobile nodes to renumber gracefully along with the rest of its home subnet. The most direct method of correctly extending the renumbering to mobile nodes away from home is for the home agent to tunnel the multicast Router Advertisement packets used for renumbering to the care-of address of each mobile node for which it is serving as the home agent. The rules for this are as follows.

- A mobile node assumes that its home network prefix has not changed until it receives an authenticated Router Advertisement message with a new prefix.

- When the mobile node is at home, the home agent does not tunnel Router Advertisements to it.

- When a home network prefix changes, the home agent tunnels the Router Advertisement messages to each mobile node that is currently away from home using a home address with the affected network prefix. Such tunneled Router Advertisements must be authenticated using an IPv6 authentication header (Kent 1997a).

- When a mobile node receives a tunneled Router Advertisement containing a new home network prefix, it must perform the standard autoconfiguration operation to create its new home address.

- When a mobile node returns to its home subnet, it must again perform IPv6 DAD at the earliest possible moment after it has registered with its home agent.

- A mobile node may send a router solicitation message to its home agent at any time, within the constraints imposed by rate control in IPv6 Neighbor Discovery (Narten, Nordmark, and Simpson 1996).

8.10 Requirements for Supporting Mobility

In this section the requirements for mobility support are recounted. There are three distinct kinds of requirements: for correspondent nodes, for mobile nodes, and for routers that wish to offer home agent services. None are particularly onerous, and the mobile node assumes most of the burden for initiating action.

8.10.1 Requirements for Correspondent Nodes

For an IPv6 node to provide mobility support as described in this chapter, the requirements are really fairly minimal. Most functions are performed using mechanisms already required as part of the IPv6 protocol suite. For instance, IPv6 nodes are supposed to be able to use routing headers and maintain a destination cache that can also be used to store care-of address information for mobile nodes.

The additional work, to be performed by an IPv6 node that supports mobility, is that of processing the binding update option. This means in practice that the node creates or modifies an entry in its destination cache for the mobile node whenever a binding update arrives that specifies a new care-of address for that mobile node. Destination cache entries for mobile nodes are handled differently in the following ways.

- The neighbor information in such an entry refers to a nonlocal neighbor.

- The route is managed by insertion of a routing header in addition to the neighbor's link address.

- Such entries have a lifetime that on expiration, must cause removal of the entry.

The value of the type of the binding update destination option carries along with it the meaning that any correspondent node that does not recognize the option is required to return an ICMP Parameter Problem, Code 2, message to the source of the packet. The packet containing the option must then be discarded. However, it is to be hoped that all IPv6 nodes will recognize binding update options.

8.10.2 Requirements for Mobile Nodes

To be mobile, an IPv6 node has to perform several additional functions, all involving transmission of the binding update. First, the mobile node has to be able to detect when it needs a new care-of address. This care-of address, naturally, has to be formed in addition to its permanent home address. The home address needs to be maintained even in the absence of all Neighbor Discovery packets that nodes usually receive while attached to their home networks.

The main additional requirement for mobile nodes is determining when to transmit binding updates to their correspondent nodes and their home agent. This requires paying careful attention to the list of active correspondent nodes and keeping records to detect when a correspondent node has a valid (unexpired) binding in its destination cache for the mobile node. Other than that, the only additional destination option processing by the mobile node is that needed for the binding acknowledgment and binding request destination options, and this is quite simple to implement.

Lastly, the mobile node has to be able to decapsulate packets sent to it by the home agent in those cases when correspondent nodes have no valid binding for the mobile node.

8.10.3 Requirements for Home Agents

Mobility support for IPv6 places few requirements on routers that wish to offer home agent services. The requirements are so few, that it is reasonable to expect that in the future all routers will be home agents. In addition to processing binding updates (as described, and as needed for *all* IPv6 correspondent nodes), a home agent must perform the following functions to serve the mobile node:

- Encapsulation
- Proxy neighbor advertisements

These two functions, however, can hardly be described as overhead due to mobility support, since all routers will often need to perform the same functions in circumstances unrelated to mobility.

For better availability in the face of home agent crashes (or, for instance, power outages) it is advisable for the home agent to maintain in nonvolatile storage a list of the current bindings for mobile hosts on its home network. Otherwise, in these circumstances, mobile nodes would in some respects get "lost" or become unavailable for the purposes of conversations initiated by correspondent nodes. In other words, correspondent nodes that are not otherwise notified of the mobile node's current care-of address would not be able to have their packets delivered to the mobile node by the home agent. This, of course, is already true for home agents in IPv4.

Lastly, home agents (as with any routers expected to perform encapsulation) should maintain some soft state as indicated in the encapsulation draft (Conta and Deering 1997). The need for doing so, however, may be diminished by the fact that all IPv6 implementations are required to support an MTU of at least 576 bytes.

8.11 Summary

IPv6 has been designed to offer a huge address space useful for the foreseeable future to enable better routing technology and to clean up various architectural details that are seen as deficiencies in IPv4. Option processing in IPv6 is able to be done without the loss of performance associated with IPv4 options. Security is a required feature for every compliant IPv6 node, and this has the effect of allowing a much cleaner specification for supporting mobility because of the requirement to authenticate remote redirects. The binding updates that provide the care-of addresses (remote redirects) to home agents and correspondent nodes are in destination options, and the needed authentication is also in a destination option. Thus, IPv6 mobility offers all the good features, and more, of IPv4 mobility, with less additional protocol code and a natural fit with the rest of the base IPv6 protocol.

IPv6 mobility uses movement detection and care-of acquisition address techniques available with the base IPv6 protocol, and thus mobility places few additional requirements on IPv6 nodes. The main detail is the specification of the binding update destination option, and the rest of the needed protocol amounts to a few minor details supporting the reliable delivery of the binding update whenever it is needed.

Renumbering and home agent discovery techniques are available, but the latter is currently underspecified. Smooth handoffs, which require additional complication in IPv4, are done without additional machinery in IPv6.

8.12 Addendum: Home Address Option

As a result of developments in the IPv6 mobility support specification that occurred while this book was going to press, a new destination option has been defined for use between mobile nodes and correspondent nodes. The new option is called the *home address option*, and it is currently specified to be included with every data packet sent from the mobile node to the correspondent node. This new option informs the correspondent node that it is required to consider the packet as originating from the address contained within the option, instead of the IPv6 address found in the actual source IP address field of the IPv6 header. The mobile node inserts its home address in the option, and uses its care-of address in the source IPv6 field of the header. This allows better compatibility with expected ingress filtering operations (see Section 7.1.1). There is no need for authentication for the home address option, as can be seen by careful consideration of the various scenarios. The disadvantage of the new option is that it requires another 144 bits in the header of each data packet, but it is hoped that header compression (Degermark 1997) can eliminate that disadvantage.

DHCP

This chapter takes a quick look at DHCP. DHCP will be a very popular source of care-of addresses for use with Mobile IP. The client/server model captures the essence of the protocol, and a discussion of that model as applied to DHCP is followed by enough technical details to understand the way it would be used by mobile clients. There are two modes of use: one for portable computing and another for mobile computing which uses Mobile IP and is much more convenient for nomadic users.

Before discussing the details of using DHCP with Mobile IP, an overview of the DHCP protocol itself is first presented. This is done by describing an overall model of its architecture and by outlining the general operation of a client using DHCP. Once the basic protocol is understood along with the purposes for which it is generally applied, several approaches for portable and mobile computing become evident. These approaches are compared and contrasted, including a proposed new mobile home address option. The proposed new DHCP option would allow mobile nodes to operate correctly without having a preconfigured home address.

This chapter concludes with some basic observations about the likely ways that DHCP will be administered in general and also ways to provide support for mobile computers. DHCP's interesting relationship with DNS will be described, as well as necessary modifications to DNS to support an expected mode of portable operation for mobile computers. Lastly, some observations will be made to emphasize the important role that security should eventually play in any installation using DHCP.

9.1 Overview of DHCP

DHCP is enjoying widespread deployment to alleviate administrative requirements for the installation and initial configuration of new Internet computers. Generally speaking, DHCP is used by clients to obtain necessary information like their IP address, DNS server addresses, domain names, subnet prefixes, and default routers, as well as many other kinds of similarly useful information. In general, DHCP is supposed to provide all the necessary configuration that a stationary system needs to establish itself as a viable Internet citizen. Whether this lofty goal can ever be completely achieved in practice is still debatable (Veizades et al. 1997), but there is no question that DHCP can go a long way toward making life easier for system administrators.

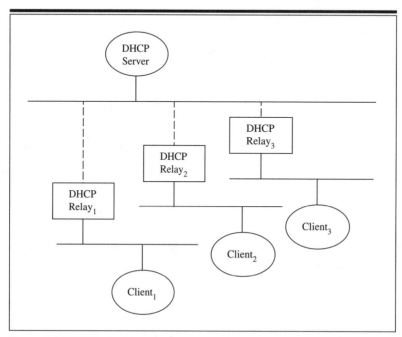

Figure 9.1 DHCP client/server model.

DHCP is specified in a general way to allow a very flexible relationship between DHCP servers and DHCP clients. For instance, the DHCP server on one enterprise network link can serve clients on an arbitrary number of other networks by way of auxiliary functional units known as *DHCP relays* (see Figure 9.1). Even more generally, multiple DHCP servers could offer their services to multiple DHCP clients on any reasonable collection of connected networks, and the clients are more or less free to select service from any server that meets their needs (and answers their requests), as shown in Figure 9.2.

To see how the protocol works, imagine that a client starts up and needs to get an IP address. It first broadcasts a request on the network to which it is attached. This broadcast can only be received by other hosts on the same network, so there has to be some other DHCP agent on the same network as the client or the protocol fails. If there is a DHCP server on the same network, all is well and good; the server and the client proceed to negotiate further protocol details. If,

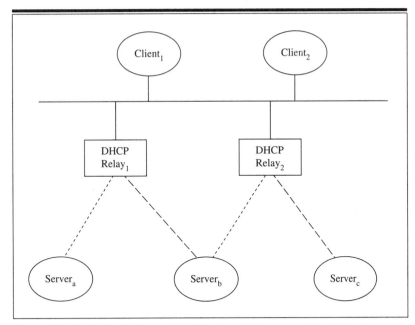

Figure 9.2 Multiple clients and multiple servers.

on the other hand, there is only a DHCP relay on the network, the relay then proceeds to rebroadcast the request to other networks or, alternatively (and better), to send the client's request for service to whatever DHCP servers the relay has been configured to contact. In this case it is of particular importance to note that the server must depend on the DHCP relay to include information about the network to which the client is connected. The client does not typically have any way to identify the network to which it is attached; it doesn't even have an IP address yet!

Once the server finds out that a client wants service (and how to contact the client) it formulates a message offering the desired service to the client. In particular, it may offer the client an IP address and other needed information. However, the server does not know that its offer has been accepted by the client until it subsequently receives another message from the client confirming its desire to accept the DHCP server's offer. At that point, the server commits the allocation of the IP address and other information to the client, finally acknowledges that fact to the client, and the protocol is done.

Of course, it's not really all that simple. There are various timeouts and other service parameters associated with DHCP, and for full details one should consult the DHCP standard specification documents (Droms 1997, Alexander and Droms 1997). In particular, DHCP associates a lease time with the IP address it allocates to a client. Handling the lease time correctly is of crucial importance to the correct operation of the protocol, and some fairly precise bounds are placed on it by the protocol specification. After a while, to avoid having the lease expire while the client is still using the IP address, the client is expected to renew the lease with a DHCP server, probably the same server from which the address was received.

9.2 Client/Server Protocol Description

This section describes in more detail the ways in which DHCP clients and servers interact with each other.

9.2.1 Startup

When a DHCP client first starts, it needs to find a DHCP server with which to communicate. For this purpose, it broadcasts a DHCP discover message to port 67. This broadcast message will be received by any DHCP servers or DHCP relays on the same link as the client. DHCP servers on the link can respond directly to the client with a DHCP offer message. Servers not on the same link have to be notified by the DHCP relay that receives the client's discover message. When a relay on the same link as the client further transmits the client's discover message to the appropriate DHCP servers, the relay also indicates within the relayed DHCP discover message the link from which the message emanated. This indication is inserted in the giaddr field of the discovery message. Since the message transmitted by the client typically includes the client's MAC address, the relay can use the giaddr and the MAC address to identify the client uniquely and transmit messages back to it at some later time.

If any servers respond to the client's DHCP discover message by sending a DHCP offer message to the relay, that message (from the server) will also include the giaddr for use by the relay and, typically, the client's MAC address.

Once the client has a selection of offers from DHCP servers, it can select the configuration data it wants. To do so, the client sends a DHCP request message to the server offering the configuration data it wants and waits for the server to reply with a DHCP ack message. The client, to be polite, should also send the same message to the other servers with offers that it is rejecting. When other servers receive the message they will be able to offer the reserved configuration data to other clients. These operations are illustrated in Figure 9.3.

Note that it is theoretically possible for a client to receive the same configuration data in multiple, different DHCP offer messages. This might be a normal course of events in an installation where multiple DHCP servers are coordinating their configuration services by way of a DHCP server-to-server protocol. Unfortunately, there are no standards yet for such a server-to-server protocol, and the prospects for quick convergence seem uncertain at this time.

As a result, DHCP servers are generally administered so that they serve disjointed, nonoverlapping ranges of IP (IPv4) addresses. This leads to undesirable address space fragmentation, and thus puts additional pressure on the existing IP address space, partially defeating the purpose of the original creation of DHCP in the first place.

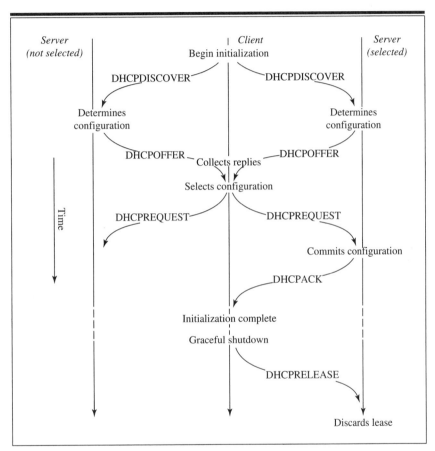

Figure 9.3 DHCP client/server startup timelines.

9.2.2 Leases and Renewals

When a client gets an IP address from a DHCP server, it is typically granted the use of that address for a limited time, known as the *lease time*. When the lease is about two thirds over, the client is expected to request that the DHCP server reallocate the address for its continued use (assuming that the client still needs the address). This process of lease renewal does not need to go through the entire DHCP configuration procedure, because the client already knows the server from which it obtained the IP address in the first place.

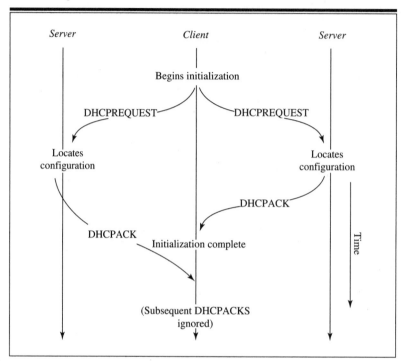

Figure 9.4 DHCP client/server lease renewal timelines.

For that reason, an abbreviated DHCP handshake (as illustrated in Figure 9.4) is permitted whereby the client simply transmits (by unicast) a renewing DHCP request message to the original DHCP server. Presumably the server will then renew the client's lease and indicate the result (with a new lease time) in a DHCP ack message. However, it is possible that the client will fail to hear back from the server. If that happens, the client has to begin again from scratch, even though it is still possible to request the use of the particular address that it already has.

A state machine (as in Figure 9.5) provides a complete representation of the client's behavior. From the standpoint of state machine operation, the DHCP server is simpler because it basically only operates in response to DHCP client messages and to handle timeouts. However, with all the client configuration handling and administrative user interface requirements, the DHCP server is a far more complicated program.

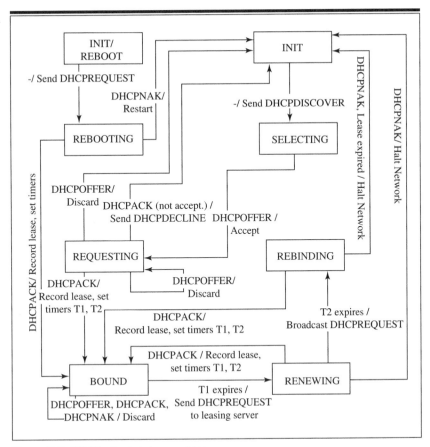

Figure 9.5 DHCP client state machine.

9.3 DHCP Option Handling

This section describes a number of important DHCP options, along with the necessary details about the way they may be used by DHCP clients and servers, including

- Default router
- Netmask
- NTP timeserver
- SLP directory agent
- DNS options

DHCP options have an eight-bit type code at the beginning of the option, followed by an eight-bit length. Thus, options can be no longer than 255 bytes.

Generally a server is likely to provide the first two options to each client without being asked. The other two options in the list (along with many other possible options) are typically requested by the client in a parameter request option, which is DHCP option type 55.

9.3.1 Default Router

A DHCP client finds its default router by receiving the router option, DHCP option type 3. The format of this option is just a list of 32-bit router IP addresses, listed in order of preference.

9.3.2 Netmask

A DHCP client discovers its subnet mask by receiving the subnet mask option, DHCP option type 1. This option is required to precede the router option. The mask is specified as a single 32-bit quantity, with the significant bits indicated as ones. Almost all subnet masks have all the one bits contiguously located in the high-order bits of the mask. So, for instance, a host with IP address 9.2.46.53, which is located on a subnet with 256 IP addresses, will have subnet mask 255.255.255.0 in conventional notation.

9.3.3 Timeserver

A DHCP client can get nearby timeservers from the NTP option (Mills 1992), DHCP option type 42. Note that this is different than information that might be received if option type 4 were requested by the client, since the latter option refers to time-servers following the specification in RFC 868. The 32-bit IP addresses of the NTP timeservers are listed in order of preference.

9.3.4 SLP Directory Agent

A DHCP client can get a directory agent for use with the SLP by requesting the directory agent option, DHCP option type 79. This option will typically also include any necessary scope configuration information useful to the SLP client. Use of SLP will reduce the need for the increasing consumption of DHCP option numbers. Moreover, SLP offers clients the ability to specify the service characteristics they need, whereas DHCP options do not typically allow specification of service attributes.

9.3.5 DNS Options

A DHCP client can obtain the addresses of DNS servers from the domain name server option, which is option type 6. The domain name server options specifies a list of domain name system (Mockapetris 1987b) name servers available to the client. The 32-bit IP addresses of the DNS servers should be listed in order of preference. The client can also get it local domain name by using option 15, and its host name by using option 12.

9.4 Using DHCP for Portability

Since DHCP servers are seen to provide methods by which a newly attached computer can obtain an IP address, it is natural to try to use DHCP to enable the operation of computers as they move from place to place. One might naturally expect that given an appropriate IP address, a mobile computer should be able to operate wherever it is attached. This section examines that model of operation, examining its advantages, disadvantages, and the additional technologies that are likely to be required for its successful deployment.

Suppose, then, that a mobile computer has just begun its operation, and establishes a link to the Internet (or an intranet) at some particular point of attachment. As already seen, the computer can broadcast a DHCP discover message, carry out the appropriate protocol operations described in the previous sections, and receive a workable IP address from some cooperative DHCP server. Let us also suppose for the sake of simplicity that the mobile node has also requested and received all the other information it needs for operation in its current environment, from DHCP and any other relevant protocols.

Figure 9.6 illustrates a typical scenario. In the figure, a wireless mobile DHCP client (Finesse) has obtained an IP address 9.2.46.53 from a local DHCP server. Also illustrated is a likely wireless configuration, in which the access points are also bridges as well as DHCP relays. These three functions are all independent. Currently, wireless manufacturers are already combining the access point with a bridge function in some cases, so that the wireless stations appear to reside on a LAN (for instance, an Ethernet link). Hopefully, as the use of DHCP spreads, more manufacturers will see the benefits for also providing DHCP relay functionality in their access points. If not, then in the figure one would have to migrate mentally the relay function into another entity (perhaps the default router) connected to the same network link as the access point/bridge.

Once Finesse has its IP address and other associated configuration parameters, Internet operation can begin. All the necessary local demons can be started and interface parameters configured. However, the IP address may only be valid at the particular access point selected by Finesse to provide connectivity to the wired network. When Finesse moves to a new access point, it is likely that all network operations will have to be interrupted and restarted.

After the mobile node has detected, by some means (Section 7.5), that it has changed or lost its point of attachment to the network, the task becomes that of

making a new connection. This can proceed by performing the usual DHCP operations of broadcasting DHCP discover datagrams and waiting for an answer from
another DHCP relay (or server). If the DHCP relay address indicates that the node
can use its previously allocated address, then all is well and the operation can stop
without going through the rest of the steps. Otherwise, the node has to get a new IP
address. This new address will not work with any existing connections. In fact, the
support programs inetd, nfsd, and so forth, will have to be terminated and restarted.
For many users the typical strategy will be to reboot the machine and start over.

This state of affairs is obviously not acceptable or conducive to any sort of seamless mobility. However, in actuality the situation is quite a bit worse. A problem
arises precisely because of the dynamic (and hence unpredictable) nature of the
DHCP address assignment. Since the address allocated to the mobile node is not
known to any other computer with which it might wish to communicate, the mobile
computer can only initiate connections. No other system can initiate a connection
that the mobile node can accept until the mobile node's address is more widely
known. The typical means by which the mobile node's address is known is by
association with the mobile node's domain name, managed by some DNS server
that participates in the global hierarchy of DNS name resolution.

For other computers to be able to contact the mobile node at its new address,
the mobile node would have to be able to make modifications to the association

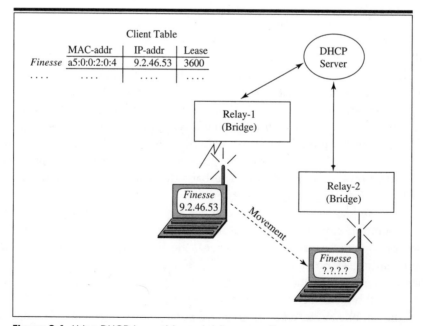

Figure 9.6 Using DHCP to enable portable computing.

between its name and its IP address as stored in the DNS server administering the domain name indicated by the mobile system's configured name. For instance, my office machine (finesse.corp.sun.com) is administered to resolve to the IP address 129.145.210.105, which naturally resides on a subnet of Sun's network 129.145. To make such modifications, a mobile node would have to be given enough authority to do so, and a means of authenticating the updates would have to be put into place. If a DNS server ever accepted bogus new resolutions on behalf of the mobile node, it would have the effect of cutting the mobile node off from any communication with other systems trying to resolve the mobile node's name—in other words, from almost every system trying to initiate a communication with the mobile node.

It remains to be seen whether any DNS administrators will provide such services for users desiring to use DHCP to aid portability in this manner. Any experienced system administrator would harbor a natural fear of the danger associated with frequent modification to the enterprise DNS data. DNS is, after all, at the heart of the enterprise TCP/IP computing capability.

9.5 Using DHCP for Mobility

Given an existing DHCP service available for prospective mobile clients using Mobile IP, it is possible to use the locally acquired IP address as the care-of address on the new point of attachment. This avoids the need to reinitialize existing connections, which can proceed to use the same home address as was used when they were first started.

Referring again to Figure 9.6, suppose that Finesse instead uses the allocated IP address as a care-of address. Then, each new point of attachment will involve the same set of operations as far as the DHCP server is concerned. In fact, the client DHCP state machine can be operated in basically the same way as always, except that when the IP address is received the client must be careful not to configure its interface in such a way as to lose its home address information. One typical strategy is to use the new IP address obtained by DHCP as an *alias* IP address for the (wireless) interface. Another point of interest is that the DHCP server should allow the mobile node to have more than one IP address assigned to it, especially in cases when the mobile node can exist within range of more than one wireless access point at the same time.

The detailed operation is as follows. The mobile client detects (using any mechanism) that it needs to make a new point of attachment to the Internet. If it wishes to acquire a care-of address from DHCP, it follows the normal mechanism of broadcasting a DHCP discover message and waiting to receive any DHCP offer. If at least one offer is received (and is acceptable), the mobile node proceeds to complete the DHCP request and awaits the DHCP ack. After the reply is received, the mobile node then initiates a Mobile IP registration request with the newly acquired address used as its new care-of address. The mobile node uses the care-of address as the source address on the registration request and receives the registration reply from the home agent, of course without the intervention of any foreign agent.

In this circumstance, the mobile node must be prepared to perform the normal operations otherwise done by the foreign agent. In particular, it must decapsulate all datagrams sent to the care-of address by the home agent.

There are some special considerations which must be observed when registering the care-of address acquired from DHCP. In particular

- The mobile node should set the D bit in the registration request, especially if it needs to get broadcast or multicast packets sent by the home agent

- The mobile node is required to register its care-of address by way of a foreign agent, if any advertisements with the R bit set are being received from local foreign agents

9.5.1 Lease Renewal and Binding Lifetimes

When the mobile node has registered its DHCP-allocated care-of address, it has two address expiration events of which to keep track. First, the DHCP server can deallocate the address after the lease expires, unless the mobile node renews the lease in time. Second, the home agent will expire the binding unless the mobile node renews its registration before the lifetime is over. A natural choice would be to choose these expiration times to be the same. In fact, the mobile node should probably adjust its DHCP request so that the lease time is appropriate to the natural lifetime of the binding. This lease time may be considerably less than the lease times normally associated with the configuration by DHCP for desktop or other stationary devices on the same network as the mobile computer.

9.6 Dual-Mode Operation

Suppose a mobile node is equipped to handle the additional operations to allow it to acquire a care-of address from an available DHCP server. This includes having mechanisms to detect disconnection from the local link. Even so, the mobile node should continue to detect any incoming agent advertisements that may be broadcast by foreign agents in the area. For one thing, the foreign agents are allowed to require registration from mobile nodes that use any local DHCP service. As mentioned in Section 3.6.1, this is done (by setting the R bit) when a network administrator wishes to control the registration of mobile nodes by way of foreign agents (perhaps for billing purposes or for interactions with firewalls). If a mobile node is within range of several foreign agents, all of them should agree on the setting of the R bit. Any two foreign agents that offer conflicting information should be scheduled for necessary administrative reconfiguration. Either all such nearby foreign agents have to set the R bit or none of them may set that bit. Moreover, if a mobile node tries to register a DHCP allocated care-of address with its home agent when foreign agents are advertising the R bit, the visited enterprise border routers may disallow datagrams from the mobile node to emanate from the enterprise.

If the mobile node receives an agent advertisement after initiating the DHCP care-of address acquisition, it will normally switch over to using the care-of address offered by the foreign agent (even without the R bit set). This is because foreign agents offer several advantages compared to the DHCP mode of operation, among them

- Less address maintenance is required when using a care-of address advertised by a foreign agent (no lease renewal is required with the DCHP server)

- The foreign agent is likely to be equipped to handle decapsulation efficiently

- Foreign agents can cooperate to provide smooth handoffs as described in Section 8.8

- Packets for the mobile node will be decapsulated before transmission over the wireless medium, taking up less bandwidth

Consequently, mobile nodes should usually prefer to use foreign agents as often as possible, even when they are also equipped to use DHCP. This requires a flexible mode of operation on startup, awaiting mobility agent advertisements (from home agents, too!) at all times.

9.7 DHCP Home Address

This section describes a new DHCP option that should enable mobile hosts to configure themselves automatically even when they are not preconfigured with a home address. The option enables a mobile host to derive a mobile home address and determine the subnet mask for the home network. The purpose of this option is to allow a mobile node to obtain a home address temporarily when the node does not have a permanent home address assigned to it. To use this method of autoconfiguration, a mobile host must also be a DHCP client; it must be capable of sending and receiving DHCP packets.

When a mobile node expects to use the Mobile IP protocol, the address that the node obtains by using the DHCP option has to be from a subnet where a home agent resides. However, a node will not always be able to connect to a home network where such an agent resides, especially if the home network is only a virtual network. Therefore, it is necessary that the node inform the DHCP server of the node's expectation to "go mobile" so that the DHCP server can properly select a home address to allocate to the node (that is, an IP address for a subnet where a home agent is known to reside). The other DHCP options are not sufficient for this purpose.

If the mobile node using the new option is not attached to a subnet where its home agent resides, that node will detect that it is not on its home network and immediately start a Mobile IP registration, thereby establishing communications. As described in previous sections, this may involve a new (but independent) transaction with a DHCP server in the area to obtain a care-of address.

How a node figures out that it needs to go mobile, and thus knows to signal its intentions to the DHCP server, is not completely determined. Possible schemes include

- A configuration parameter on the node

- Always asking for such an address

- Letting the user indicate this when the node starts

The term *mobile home address* explicitly refers to an address on a subnet that is known to contain a home agent. The new DHCP option is called the *mobile home address option*.

9.7.1 Mobile Home Address Option

When the option (illustrated in Figure 9.7) is present in a DHCP discover message, the DHCP server is asked to send an appropriate home address to the mobile host. The DHCP server, in its corresponding DHCP offer message, will insert the requested address into the usual place for requested IP addresses, namely the yiaddr field. The code for the mobile home address option is 68. The length is four octets multiplied by the number of home agents supplied in the option, which may be zero or more. The DHCP server will typically include the address of (one of) the mobile host home agents, configured by the local administrator to be associated

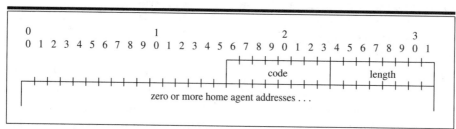

Figure 9.7 DHCP mobile home address option format.

with the address given to the mobile host. That home agent's IP address is inserted in the data field of the mobile home address option.

Many installations may configure several home agents to serve the same mobile home addresses for redundancy or load sharing. For this reason it is possible for the DHCP server to insert multiple home agent addresses in the mobile home address option. On the other hand, the DHCP server may be configured to send out mobile home addresses and expect that the mobile host discover the home agent's address by using a directed broadcast (Section 4.6.3). In that case, there may not be any home agent addresses at all included in the option returned by the DHCP server.

9.7.2 Using DHCP to Acquire Mobility Configuration Information

To retrieve any option of interest, a DHCP client is required to request the return of this information when a DHCP Discover or DHCP Request message is sent. This option is requested by including in a DHCP Discover or DHCP Request message the parameter request list option containing the appropriate option codes. According to the DHCP specification, the server must return an option that is explicitly requested (assuming a value has been configured in the database).

In particular, to acquire a mobile home address, a DHCP client is required to request the return of option 68 in a DHCP Discover and DHCP Request message. On receiving a reply from a server, a client uses the 32-bit (IPv4) address returned in the yiaddr field as its home address. The client then proceeds to register, using that home address along with a care-of address obtained by whatever means, with its associated home agent. The associated home agent's address is typically derived from the data returned in the mobile home address option.

In Figure 9.8, the operations illustrated are analogous to the earlier operations depicted in Figure 9.6. The server delivers to the mobile node an IP address that is a mobile home address on subnet D (the home network). The server maintains a list of home agents (in this case, only one home agent) for subnet D, which will be inserted into the *DHCP offer* message for outgoing mobile home address option requests by mobile nodes.

In this case, however, it is also illustrated that for access points explicitly designed to support Mobile IP, the access point should also provide the foreign agent function for use by the mobile nodes. Then, by the time the mobile node gets a home address back from the DHCP, it is likely to have detected some agent advertisements by the foreign agent residing in the access point unit. There is no reason why foreign agents cannot supply care-of addresses for use by mobile nodes that have obtained their home address from DHCP. If the mobile node moves into the vicinity of foreign agent 1, it will operate in the same way as any other node using Mobile IP to register the new care-of address with the home agent with the address that it initially received from DHCP. Note that the mobile node will probably never make

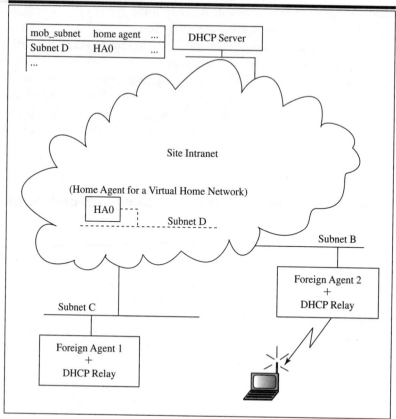

Figure 9.8 Mobile node using a mobile home address.

any registration lifetime larger than its DHCP home address lifetime, although these numbers are logically independent.

9.8 Multihoming

As indicated, wireless mobile nodes can be DHCP clients at more than one point of attachment. This mode of operation may become very popular, especially when wireless nodes can maintain communications using more than one kind of network interface to the Internet. For instance, one might plug into an Ethernet outlet as long as one is available, but when leaving the area switch to a CDPD (CDPD Consortium 1993) wide area wireless modem connection.

Mobile IP works fine in such circumstances. The only requirement for continued operation when switching to new network media is that the mobile node be able to accept datagrams from each such interface using the same IP address (that is, the mobile node's home address). This is quite reasonable, as shown by Katz (1994), and really just involves issuing an *ifconfig* command whenever the node detects the switchover to a new medium.

For DHCP-allocated care-of addresses, however, the requirements are even lower. The mobile node just has to manage its (perhaps wireless) interfaces so that it can respond to care-of addresses at each such point of attachment. Since the incoming datagrams are expected to be encapsulated, the encapsulating header is removed to expose the IP header containing the mobile node's home address, and thus there is no requirement to associate the home address with more than one network interface. However, in the case when several care-of addresses are to be acquired from a DHCP server, the administration has to be careful to make sure that the server can associate more than one IP address with the mobile node.

9.9 Administration and Security

No chapter on DHCP would be complete without at least some mention of current security concerns about the enterprise use of DHCP. The root of the problem is a basic inconsistency between the needs of security and the design goals of automatic configuration.

9.9.1 Denial of Service: Address Space Depletion

Suppose for the moment that a DCHP server is configured to allocate an IP address to any computer that requests one (for instance, a mobile node). Then the server would be vulnerable to a denial-of-service attack, wherein a bogus DHCP client asks for IP addresses one after another until all the addresses for the particular subnet are exhausted. Afterward, any DHCP client on that subnet would be unable to get the configuration information it needed.

It does not help much for the DHCP server to limit the allocated addresses to one per customer. In that case, the bogus DHCP client would only have to change its apparent MAC address with every new request, and the DHCP server would not be able to easily detect that successive requests were from the same bogus client.

One possible solution would be for the server to keep track of all the possible MAC addresses that are allowed to obtain IP addresses, but this introduces a burdensome requirement for managing the MAC address list. Collecting and maintaining this information is not yet a commonly deployed procedure. Moreover, it makes it much more difficult for mobile hosts (say, from friendly external enterprises) to acquire care-of addresses by using the techniques described in the previous sections. Again, such requirements have the effect of working against the design goals of DHCP, which was created just for the purpose of avoiding such tedious record keeping and user administration.

9.9.2 Server Spoofing

Suppose, instead, that a malicious node acquires a valid IP address by any means (say, by correctly and innocuously following the DHCP protocol). Then that host could, unless safeguards are in place, pretend to be a DHCP server. It could listen for all DHCP discover messages broadcast on a subnet—or, indeed, to all such multicast messages that may be bound for any DHCP server in the area. Then any client unlucky enough to respond to DHCP offer messages from the server would be effectively incapacitated. The bogus server could take any of a wide range of malicious actions. The effects of the bogus information would be different for each of the dozens of DHCP options that are currently defined.

9.9.3 Securing the DHCP Home Address Option

When using the DHCP home address option, it is more difficult to secure Mobile IP registrations confidently, especially given the current state of key distribution protocols within the Internet. For instance, if you get a key from the DHCP server, how can you trust the DHCP server? This difficulty is inherited from a much larger and more serious problem; namely, that securing or authenticating any information whatsoever from a DHCP server (or client!) is not possible in common DHCP deployments.

9.10 Summary

DHCP (Alexander and Droms, 1997, Droms 1997) provides portability and mobility for mobile computers. As always, mobility is likely to be a preferred mode of operation when available. The advantage of using DHCP is that it enables a mobile computer to establish operation at a care-of address without the need for the presence of a foreign agent.

The new *DHCP* home address option allows a mobile node to start operation with the minimal amount of preconfiguration, but this option is only useful in environments that can survive without the authentication available by using a mobility security association between the mobile node and the home agent on its dynamically acquired home network.

Simple but fatal attacks on DHCP clients and servers are easy to demonstrate, and emphasize the importance of security in the administration of DHCP. Enterprises deploying DHCP must be able to take appropriate countermeasures. This will be ever more important in the future as the technical sophistication of malicious users increases and as reliance on DHCP for the convenience of providing care-of addresses for nomadic users becomes more widespread. When a large fraction of an enterprise's computing assets are handled by DHCP, then security techniques will naturally be considered essential in the protection of those assets.

CHAPTER TEN

Summary and Future Work

Mobile IP answers many questions about how to implement network mobility and creates many more questions about how to improve the basic protocol further. Although it is now known how to move from one network to another in the classically connected Internet, it is not well understood how to move similarly when other realistic constraints such as firewalls are placed on the classic model. On the one hand, it is known how to use home networks to avoid the need for modifying existing hosts that communicate with mobile nodes. On the other hand, however, the best techniques for route optimization are not as well understood, even though the correspondent nodes are assumed to be willing to help. On the one hand, mobile nodes and home agents can cooperate well enough with sufficient attention paid to the needed configuration details. On the other hand, filtering out unwanted broadcasts, establishing security associations, or getting home addresses in the first place are configuration items that will have to be made much easier before mobile nodes can assume their eventual dominant position in the Internet. Protocols for mobile computers are far less mature than corresponding protocols for mobile telephones used in telephone networks. On the other hand, those protocols have had frightening security problems even after decades of engineering and development. Wireless mobile computers will not be allowed the luxury of this style of deployment.

As mentioned in the first chapter, Mobile IP is likely to hold a prominent place in the support of nomadic computing, but it is hardly the sole means of such support. Every assumption made about networking over the life of the Internet needs to be examined closely. Often, as in the case of both IP and TCP, the assumptions are no longer true, and repairing the errors caused by the outdated assumptions will take years of engineering, marketing, and administrative effort. In fact, the very location transparency offered by Mobile IP has to be examined closely to see where it fits or does not fit the needs of nomadic users. For instance, although IP and thus Mobile IP hides the nature of the physical link from the nomadic user, nomadic applications will be developed that can better adapt to user needs if they have access to information about the current link conditions. Devising the architecture for the information flow between the various application and network protocols is a challenge for the future, and may have major implications on the network interfaces with which Internet designers have grown comfortable.

Every configuration procedure, in particular, should be examined closely for suitability to mobile computing. It is no longer enough to imagine that a system administrator can configure a mobile node for interconnection to a specific set of network resources, because the available set of network resources can change with every move. Moreover, movements by wireless computers between various points of attachment to the Internet will occur more rapidly due to the changing nature of the attachment points themselves. One can easily imagine that a nomadic user would simply refuse to use any computer that required manual reconfiguration on every cell switch, and wouldn't even consider for a nanosecond the possibility of calling an administrative expert for help. Reconfiguration has to be made automatic.

To maximize the available wireless bandwidth, network administrators will try to shrink the cells to a size determined by the budget available for infrastructure creation and installation. Some wireless technologies, notably infrared, can make that budget go a long way. The wireless cells will coexist with a hoped-for increase in wired bandwidth, as more installations move to 100Mb-per-second Ethernet, ATM, or even 1,000Mb-per-second Ethernet wired infrastructures. The more rapid movement between cells, and the faster response time available for registrations with home agents, would have the effect of creating demand for a reduction in some basic Mobile IP parameters, in particular the minimal time between registrations and the minimal time between successive solicitations for foreign agent service.

This increased mobility will also favor increased deployment of more sophisticated techniques for determining signal strength at the link layer. Recent results from the University of Alabama (personal communication with Tracy Camp, May 1997) indicate that only with such indications can a mobile node make the right decision about when to change cells. Moreover, making the right decision is likely to be the most important factor for avoiding packet loss. Avoiding packet loss offers immediate improvements in the perceived interactivity of Internet computers, as noted in Chapter 1 (Caceres and Iftode 1995). Until such signal-strength indications are available, choosing between ECS versus LCS techniques for cell switching will depend on two factors:

1. How many cells are traversed before a change of direction

2. How sharply the direction is changed

If the cells are very large compared to the trajectory of the mobile node, or if the movement is oscillatory and characterized by sharp changes of direction, any advantages offered by ECS can be completely wiped out and LCS should be considered. If the speed of the mobile node is fast, then waiting two seconds for LCS to figure out that a cell switch is needed may be out of the question, and ECS should be used if available.

Aside from these, there are many other interactions begging for further investigation, suggested by the existing work with Mobile IP. As an example, *RSVP*, the Resource ReSerVation Protocol is being standardized (Braden, Zhang, and Berson 1996, Zhang et al. 1993) for the purpose of reserving routing resources between two Internet nodes. Such reservations are often crucial for the satisfactory performance of applications transporting voice and video data between the endpoints. Making RSVP work with Mobile IP would be one way to offer good multimedia services to mobile nodes, but no one really knows how to do that effectively yet. For an initial approach and analysis, see Talukdar, Badrinath, and Acharya (1997).

Each mobile node has a home address, which it uses in many ways as its network identity. This corresponds to the classic Internet model and is a basic underpinning of the architecture of Mobile IP. However, in many cases this identity is irrelevant to the nature of the network transaction. For instance, when the nomadic user clicks a button on a Web page, it usually doesn't matter what the user's home address is. Similarly, when the mobile computer is retrieving information by using the anonymous FTP, the home address is irrelevant. With NAT (Network Address Translation) boxes, the IP address itself becomes subject to strange manipulations. Moreover, for a number of reasons there have already been protocols developed (for example, the Post Office Protocol for mail retrieval (Myers and Rose 1996)) to reduce the importance of the exact IP address of the node that is used to access the nomad's information.

As a result, sometimes the home address of the mobile node will be important and sometimes it will not. For applications for which the mobile node's home address is not important, it should be possible for the mobile node to use its care-of address instead of its home address, because then the home agent is surely not involved, and the correspondent node can be correspondingly unaware of any binding for the mobile node's home address. This programming model, however, is not necessarily easy to provide for with today's mobile nodes. It's difficult even to imagine how a foreign agent could do it effectively, without traveling into the uncultivated field of generalized proxy definition for mobile computing. Today's proxies are very special purpose, and likely to remain that way. Therefore, this flexible use of the care-of address, when it becomes available, will almost certainly be restricted to mobile nodes that use a colocated care-of address. In that case, the mobile node effectively has two Internet identities—one that is permanent and one that is quite evanescent. The ease with which IPv6 handles this latter case may indeed become an opportune bit of protocol synergism which will lead to the faster deployment of both protocols.

No book on mobile computing should be considered complete without at least mentioning the general area of ad hoc networking—that is, the creation of networks as they are needed, whether or not there is any supporting Internet infrastructure. Early work in ad hoc networks came about because of Defense Advanced Research and Projects Agency (*DARPA*) interest in packet radio, especially in defense scenarios. Some description of this may be found in Steenstrup's book (1995). Other applications for ad hoc wireless networking may be discovered for disaster relief, wireless conferencing, and whenever nomadic users may chance to meet. After all, ad hoc networking is good for whatever networking is good for, but it can be applied in more situations. Moreover, techniques that enable ad hoc networking with sufficient performance may inspire further improvements in the routing technology used in the global Internet. Our own initial work details a refinement on classic distance-vector routing, called *destination sequenced distance vector* (DSDV) routing (Perkins and Bhagwat 1994). DSDV has been further refined to reduce broadcasts, and to acquire the relevant topological information only when needed (Perkins and Bhagwat 1997).

This burgeoning field of ad hoc networking rises up somewhat independently of Mobile IP, but not at all independently of the technology that motivates Mobile IP. Since both technologies are important for overlapping populations of wireless mobile Internet nodes, it is likely that the wireless nodes will eventually implement some merged version of the two. We have found, however, that for Mobile IP to coexist gracefully with ad hoc networks certain protocol assumptions and techniques for route installation require modification (Lei and Perkins 1997).

Mobile IP is at once an established building block for mobility, an ongoing area of protocol engineering, a first step toward supporting a new paradigm of mobile computing, a challenge for network administration and security, a rich source of questions about the future of networking, a new market opportunity for computer vendors, and the subject that has motivated me to expend many hours in the production of this first book. I hope you have found it worthwhile.

Several freeware implementations of various versions of Mobile IP are available on the World Wide Web. Please look up the following URLs for more information.

- `http://www.monarch.cs.cmu.edu/`   (Dave Johnson)

- `http://www.cs.pdx.edu/research/SMN`   (Portland State)

- `http://mip.ee.nus.sg`   (University of Singapore)

- `http://www.mcl.cs.columbia.edu/source.html`   (JI's Mach code)

- `ftp://ftp.it.kth.se/pub/klemets/klemets.tar.gz`   ("MINT")

- `http://anchor.cs.binghamton.edu/~mobileip/`   (Linux MH and "agent")

- `http://mosquitonet.stanford.edu/software/mip.html` (MosquitoNet)

This glossary contains terms and acronyms that might be unfamiliar to the reader, especially since many of them are new terms defined as part of the Mobile IP specification.

access point

a point of attachment to the Internet. For wireless nodes, an access point often provides bridging functions between the wireless medium and another wired network.

agent advertisement

an ICMP Router Advertisement, modified by attaching an extension specially defined for advertising the presence of mobility agents

agent discovery

the process by which a mobile node detects the presence of any prospective mobility agents

agent solicitation message

a message sent in hopes of receiving an agent advertisement

anonymous FTP

free access to files by using FTP, without needing a password

API

applications programming interface

ARP

Address Resolution Protocol (Plummer 1982)

AS

autonomous system; commonly an independent administrative domain or intranet

ASN.1

Abstract Syntax Notation 1; a grammar for indicated fields needed for object identifiers

attributes

a name that specifies the meaning of the value for some characteristic of a network entity (for instance, the attribute IP-address might have the value 129.92.29.1)

authenticated

known to be authentic, typically by passing a test that can only be performed correctly by an entity sharing the restricted access to a shared secret

247

authentication header	a protocol element of an IP (or IPv6) packet that contains the necessary information enabling a receiver to be assured that the sender has access to a shared secret (and, thus, that the identity of the sender is assuredly known)
base protocol	the Mobile IP protocol as described in RFCs 2002, 2003, 2004, 2005, and 2006
beacon	a message sent from a foreign agent (or base station) advertising its presence along with some other configuration information for prospective customers (e.g., mobile nodes)
BGP	Border Gateway Protocol (Rekhter and Li 1995)
binding acknowledgement	a message indicating that a correspondent node received a particular binding update
binding cache	a cache of mobility bindings of mobile nodes maintained by a node for use in tunneling datagrams to those mobile nodes
binding update	a message indicating a mobile node's current mobility binding and, in particular, its care-of address
BOF	birds of a feather; a somewhat informal, unstructured meeting for people who have a common agenda
care-of address	the termination point of a tunnel toward a mobile node for datagrams forwarded to the mobile node while it is away from home (See Section 2.3 for more discussion about the two types of care-of addresses defined for use with Mobile IP.)
catenet	a model for an collection of networks, by which the networks are mutually joined together at connection points (routers) in a hop-by-hop fashion. The routers transfer information between one network and the next.
CDPD	cellular digital packet data (CDPD Consortium 1993)

cell	a wireless point of attachment to the Internet
checksum	a computed value that depends intimately on characteristics of a particular set of data, and that changes if the data changes
CIDR	classless inter-domain routing (Fuller et al. 1993, Rekhter and Li 1993)
CLNP	Connection-Less Network Protocol; the ISO's answer to IP
configuration variables	variables that take different values according to the administrative needs in a particular situation. For instance, the IP address of a network node is one of its configuration variables.
correspondent domain	the administrative domain in which a correspondent node is attached
correspondent node	a peer with which a mobile node is communicating; may be either mobile or stationary
DA	directory agent
DAD	duplicate address detection; part of the Stateless Address Autoconfiguration Protocol (Thomson and Narten 1996)
default router	the router to which a node typically forwards all outgoing packets for further delivery toward the ultimate destination
default router list	a list of default routers, typically supplied as part of a Router Advertisement ICMP message
descriptor	a term that—possibly along with a value for the descriptor—describes an entity under discussion
destination option	a protocol element present in IPv6 packets that only needs to be interpreted by the destination of the packet, not any of the intermediate routers that may participate in the delivery of the packet
DF	don't fragment; a bit in the IP header

DHCP	Dynamic Host Configuration Protocol (Droms 1997, Alexander and Droms 1997)
DHCP Relay	nodes (often, routers) that pass along DHCP messages between DHCP clients and DHCP servers
directory agent	a network entity that registers, maintains, and grants access to service information
DNS	Domain Name System (Mockapetris 1987a, Mockapetris 1987b)
DoD	(United States) Department of Defense
DSDV	Destination Sequenced Distance Vector; a routing algorithm for ad hoc networks of mobile nodes
ECS	eager cell switching; accepting service from a new point of attachment to the Internet as soon as the service is offered
entry point	the point at which encapsulation occurs and the tunnel is thought of as being created
environment manager	a proposed entity whose task is to provide relevant information about the computing environment for the use of mobile nodes
environment variable	a variable that symbolizes one characteristic of the environment, and whose value describes specific information about that characteristic
exit point	the node at which a tunneled packet is considered to have departed from the tunnel, because the node decapsulates the packet
fidelity	degree of faithfulness to the desired standard
firewall	protection from the raging hell of the Internet
foreign agent	a router on a mobile node's visited network that provides routing services to the mobile node while registered; an agent that detunnels and delivers datagrams to the mobile nodes that were tunneled by the mobile node's home agent; selected as a default router by registered mobile nodes

foreign domain	the administrative domain in which a foreign network is located
foreign network	any network other than the mobile node's home network.
FTP	File Transfer Protocol
GPS	global positioning system (Berry 1995)
gratuitous ARP	a broadcast, unrequested ARP reply to initiate the resolution of a mobile node's home address, expecting that nodes receiving the broadcast will update their ARP caches
GRE	Generic Record Encapsulation (Hanks et al. 1994b, Hanks et al. 1994b)
hidden terminal	another network node that is undetectable by a particular node of interest, but which nevertheless interferes with transmissions from that node to a third party
Home Address	an IP address that is assigned for an extended period of time to a mobile node; the address remains unchanged regardless of where the node is attached to the Internet
home agent	a router on a mobile node's home network that tunnels datagrams for delivery to the mobile node when it is away from home and maintains current location information for the mobile node
home domain	an administrative domain in which a mobile node's home network is located
home network	a network, possibly virtual, that has a network prefix matching the mobile node's home address.
IAB	Internet Architecture Board
IANA	the Internet Assigned Numbers Authority
ICMP	Internet Control Message Protocol (Postel 1981a)
IEEE	Institute of Electrical and Electronic Engineers

IETF	the Internet Engineering Task Force
IGMP	Internet Group Membership Protocol (Deering 1989), a common way for nodes to join multicast groups
IHL	Internet Header Length
IMHP	Internet Mobile Host Protocol (Perkins, Myles, and Johnson 1994); a forerunner of Mobile IP
ingress	in the direction toward the big Internet cloud, and away from a leaf node or leaf domain
ingress filtering	filtering (selective discard) of packets before they transit across a border router from an administrative domain into the rest of the Internet
IP	the Internet Protocol (Postel 1981b)
IPAE	Internet Protocol for Address Encapsulation
IPv4	IP version 4
IPv6	IP version 6 (Deering and Hinden 1995, Bradner and Mankin 1996), a replacement for IP, currently under development within the IETF
IPX	Internet packet exchange; Novell's layer-3 protocol (Novell Inc. 1986)
isochronous	roughly, synchronous; used to indicate that (relatively tight) delay bounds are in effect
ISP	Internet service provider; an enterprise that sells connectivity to the Internet along with, possibly, some value-added services
KDC	a key distribution center
keyword	similar to an attribute, a keyword indicates a distinctive characteristic of a network entity, but does not require the specification of a value
LAN	local area network (for example, Ethernet or token ring)
LCS	lazy cell switching; waiting as long as possible to change to a new point of attachment
LD	Location Directory

lease time	the time for which an address allocated by DHCP will be valid for use by the requesting DHCP client
link	a facility or medium over which nodes can communicate at the link layer; underlies the network layer
link-layer address	the address used to identify an endpoint of some communication over a physical link; typically, an interface's media access control address
LRU	Least Recently Used; often a good cache-entry replacement algorithm
LSR	Loose Source Route
MAC	(1) media access control; (2) message authentication code; particular algorithm for producing an authenticator (such as a digital signature) for security purposes
MAC address	media access control-layer address; commonly the physical address of the card on the LAN; often a 48-bit IEEE address
macro	large scale
managed objects	objects responding to management according to the SNMP
MD5	message digest 5 (Rivest 1992)
message digest	the result of performing some computation on data, often for purposes of authentication
MHRP	Mobile Host Routing Protocol (Johnson 1994); a forerunner of Mobile IP
MIB	Management Information Base (for SNMP)
MICP	Mobile Internet Control Protocol
middleware	software that fills the space between what the applications are willing to see and what the harsh world of the Internet actually looks like
mobile network	a network that is itself mobile

mobile node	a host or router that changes its point of attachment from one network or subnetwork to another. A mobile node may change its location without changing its IP address; it may continue to communicate with other Internet nodes at any location using its (constant) IP address, assuming link-layer connectivity to a point of attachment is available.
mobile subnet	a mobile network that is decomposed from a larger network, typically defined by using a netmask
mobility	the ability to remain connected to the Internet while moving from one point of attachment to another
mobility agent	either a home agent or a foreign agent
mobility binding	the association of a home address with a care-of address, along with the remaining lifetime of that association
mobility security association	a collection of security contexts, between a pair of nodes, that may be applied to Mobile IP protocol messages exchanged between them. Each context indicates at least an authentication algorithm and mode (as described in Section 4.9.1), a secret (for example, a shared key or appropriate public/private key pair), and a style of replay protection (Section 4.9.6).
MSR	mobility support router (Ioannidis, Duchamp, and Maguire 1991, Ioannidis and Maguire 1993)
MTU	maximum transfer unit; the biggest size packet that can be transmitted on a link without fragmenting
NDIS	Network Device Interface Standard
netizen	a catchy moniker for a citizen (denizen?) of the Internet
netmask	a bit pattern defining the part of an IP address (typically some initial and contiguous bits) that is to be used for routing purposes

node
: a host or a router

nomadic architecture
: a system organization of nomadic services intended to respond to the needs of nomadic computer users

nomadic services
: services especially intended for use of nomadic computer users

nonce
: a randomly chosen value, different from previous choices, inserted in a message to defend against replays

NTP
: Network Time Protocol (Mills 1992)

NUD
: neighbor unreachability detection; part of the Neighbor Discovery protocol (Narten, Nordmark, and Simpson 1996); alternatively, a good way to sit in a hot tub

OID
: Object Identifier

opaque identifier
: an identifier without discernible substructure

pad
: useless bits serving only as filler, so that other useful data can be located after an expected field boundary

PDA
: personal digital assistant

PMTU
: path MTU; the biggest size packet that can be transmitted over the path from one network endpoint to another endpoint without fragmenting; the minimum of all the MTUs for all links along the path

pocket
: a domain in a foreign enterprise that is segregated from the main foreign network to protect the foreign enterprise assets and yet provide a host network for nomadic computer users

policy routing
: routing using a route selection algorithm depending upon parameters decided by local policy rather than typical hop-count or shortest-time-delay

port
: a number assigned to a data packet to enable demultiplexing by a higher-level protocol for handling by the correct application process

portability
The ability to initiate a connection to the Internet after establishing a link at a new point of attachment

PPP
Point-to-Point Protocol (McGregor 1992, Simpson 1994)

preference level
a number used by a recipient to indicate a preferred selection between several otherwise equivalent choices

profile manager
a network entity responsible for managing the profile (that is, personal configuration variables) for a computer user

protocol control block
state information used by a higher-level protocol to maintain correct processing for a network connection

proxy ARP
use of ARP by one network node to impersonate some other network node by pretending to own a MAC address that is associated to the other's IP address (Postel 1984).

quadrilateral routing
routing that follows four distinct legs (phases) of hop-by-hop forwarding to and from a destination, as opposed to triangle

readdressing
modifying the address of an IP packet that is visible to infrastructure routers

registration
the process that occurs when a mobile node is away from home and it registers its care-of address with its home agent. Depending on its method of attachment, the mobile node will register either directly with its home agent or through a foreign agent, which forwards the registration to the home agent.

registration key
a secret key shared between a mobile node and a foreign agent that may optionally be established during registration with that foreign agent. When later moving and registering a new care-of address elsewhere, the mobile node uses the registration key shared with its previous foreign agent to send it an authenticated binding update to this foreign agent.

registration lifetime	the time duration for which a binding is valid.
relaying	passing data along to another designated IP address known to the relaying node but not indicated directly in the IP header
remaining registration lifetime	the amount of time remaining for which a registration lifetime is still valid, at some time after the registration was approved by the home agent
remote redirection	from a remote location, causing a modification to an entity's route table
reverse tunneling	tunneling from the care-of address to the home agent, instead of vice versa
RFC	request for comments
route optimization	reducing or eliminating unnecessary intermediate hops from the path followed by a packet from its source to its final destination
router discovery	the process of determining the IP address of a router available to a node on its link
router solicitation	a message issued by a node in order to attempt router discovery
routing prefix	the part of an IP address used for routing purposes as opposed to identifying a particular node on a network; possibly obtained by applying a netmask to an IP address
RSA	Rivest, Shamir, and Adelmann; the three inventors of a popular public key cryptosystem (Rivest, Shamir, and Adelmann 1978)
RSVP	Resource reSerVation Protocol
RTP	the Real-time Transport Protocol (Schulzrinne et al. 1996)
seamless roaming	mobility, transparent to the user (thus not presenting any inconvenience)
security parameters index (SPI)	an index identifying a particular security context between a pair of nodes

SEN

Student Electronic Notebook, envisioned as a way to simplify note-taking and submission of classwork

service advertisement

a message containing service information for use by prospective clients

service agent

a network entity handling requests for a network service, and possibly issuing service advertisements

service reply

a message sent in reply to a service request to a prospective client (a user agent) for a network service

service request

a message sent to a service agent or a directory agent by a client wishing to access a service agent

shadow directories

directories containing replicated data for quicker or somehow more convenient access compared to the original or authoritative data

silently discard

when a datagram is discarded without further processing and without indicating an ICMP error to the sender. Nevertheless, an error should be logged (perhaps by way of SNMP [see, for example, Case et al. 1993], or some other network management protocol) and the event should be recorded in a statistics counter.

SLP

Service Location Protocol (Veizades et al. 1997)

SNMP

the Simple Network Management Protocol (Case et al. 1993)

sockets API

a conventional interface for programmed utilization of sockets

source routing

routing specified by the source of a packet instead of by the routers that would otherwise manage the hop-by-hop forwarding of the packet

special tunnel   a method of tunneling a datagram in which the outer destination address (when encapsulating the datagram) is set equal to the inner destination address (the original destination address of the datagram); used in route optimization for returning a datagram addressed to a mobile node to the mobile node's home agent without knowing the home agent's address

SPI   security parameters index

SRE   source route entry (used with GRE); an intermediate routing point along a (not necessarily IP) routing path

TCP   Transmission Control Protocol (Postel 1981c)

timestamp   data included to indicate the time at which a protocol element was created or first transmitted

TLV   type-length-value; a seemingly ubiquitous idea for organizing data into a collection of functional compartments or protocol options

topology advertisement   a theoretical message that would indicate to its recipients the local network topology of the administrative domain to which they are attached

TOS   type of service; an underutilized set of bits in the IP header

triangle routing   a routing anomaly caused by the requirement that the home agent be in the path of all packets sent from a correspondent node to a mobile node, whereas packets sent by the mobile node do not need to be handled by the home agent

TTL   see type-length-value

tunnel   the path followed by a datagram while it is encapsulated. The conceptual model is such that, while it is encapsulated, a datagram is protected from normal Internet routing until it reaches a knowledgeable decapsulating agent

tunneling	bypassing the normal Internet routing of a packet by enclosing (encapsulating) the packet within a new IP header containing an alternate destination IP address
tunnel soft state	information tabulated about a tunnel to enable more timely use of the tunnel, especially including management of transient tunnel error conditions
type-length-value	a seemingly ubiquitous idea for organizing data into a collection of functional compartments or protocol structures. The first field of the protocol element is the type, which defines the structure of the rest of the data. The second field is the length of the data, and the rest of the protocol structure is the data being communicated.
UDP	the User Datagram Protocol (Postel 1980)
universal root	a node that appears to be the root node of any hierarchy
user agent	an agent acting on behalf of a user's application to obtain access to a service agent
VIP	Virtual Internet Protocol (Teraoka and Tokoro 1993); a way of associating a virtual IP address (for example, a care-of address) to a physical IP address (for example, a home address)
virtual network	a network with no physical instantiation beyond a router (with a physical network interface on another network). The router (for example, a home agent) generally advertises reachability to the virtual network using conventional routing protocols
visited network	a network other than a mobile node's home network to which the mobile node is currently connected; a foreign network
visitor list	the list of mobile nodes visiting a foreign agent
XIWT	Cross-Industry Working Team

REFERENCES

Alexander, Steve, and Ralph Droms. *DHCP Options and BOOTP Vendor Extensions*. RFC 2132. March 1997.

Amir, Elan, Steve McCanne, and Hui Zhang. "An Application Level Video Gateway." In *Proceedings of ACM Multimedia '95*. November 1995.

Aziz, A., T. Markson, and H. Prafullchandra. *Simple Key-Management For Internet Protocols (SKIP)*. (Work in Progress) draft-ietf-ipsec-skip-07.txt. August 1996.

Baker, F., ed. *Requirements for IP Version 4 Routers*. RFC 1812. June 1995.

Bantz, D. F. and F. J. Bauchot. "Wireless LAN Design Alternatives." *IEEE Network* (March 1994): 43–53.

Bellovin, Steven M. "Security Problems in the TCP/IP Protocol Suite." *ACM Computer Communications Review* 19 (March 1989).

Berry, Joseph K. "Put Things in Their Proper Places with GPS." *GIS World* 8 (1995): 31–32.

Bhagwat, Pravin, and David Maltz. *MSOCK: An Architecture for Supporting Mobility at the Transport Layer*. IBM Technical Report. IBM, March 1997.

Bharghavan, V., A. Demers, S. Shenker, and L. Zhang. MACAW: "A Media Access Protocol for Wireless LANs." *SIGCOMM '94: Computer Communications Review* 24 (October 1994).

Bhattacharya, P., B. Patel, and C. Perkins. *Preference for Multicast Datagram Support with Mobile IP*. (work in progress) draft-partha-mobileip-mcastpref-00.txt. February 1996.

Bird, Ray et al. "A Family of Light-weight Protocols for Authentication and Key Distribution." *IEEE Transactions on Networking* 3 (February 1993): 31–41.

Braden, R., L. Zhang, and S. Berson. *Resource ReSerVation Protocol (RSVP)—Version 1 Functional Specification*. (work in progress) draft-ietf-rsvp-spec-14.txt. November 1996.

Bradner, Scott O., and Allison Mankin. *IPng Internet Protocol Next Generation*. IPng Series. Reading, MA: Addison Wesley Longman, 1996.

Caceres, Ramon, and Liviu Iftode. "Improving the Performance of Reliable Transport Protocols in Mobile Computing Environments." *IEEE Journal on Selected Areas in Communications* 13 (June 1995): 850–857.

Callon, R. *TCP and UDP with Bigger Addresses (TUBA), A Simple Proposal for Internet Addressing and Routing*. RFC 1347. June 1992.

Case, Jeffrey D., Mark Fedor, Martin Lee Schoffstall, and James R. Davin, *A Simple Network Management Protocol (SNMP)*. RFC 1157. May 1990.

Case, J., K. McCloghrie, M. Rose, and S. Waldbusser. *Introduction to version 2 of the Internet-standard Network Management Framework.* RFC 1441. May 1993.

CCITT. *Specification of the Abstract Syntax Notation One (ASN.1).* Recommendation X.208. 1988.

CDPD Consortium. *Cellular Digital Packet Data Specification.* July 1993.

Cerf, V., "The Catenet Model for Internetworking." *IEN* 48 (July 1978).

Cheshire, S., and M. Baker. "Internet Mobility 4x4." In *Proceedings of the ACM SIGCOMM '96 Conference.* August 1996.

Cheswick, William R., and Steven M. Bellovin. *Firewalls and Internet Security.* Addison-Wesley Professional Computing Series. Reading, MA: Addison Wesley Longman, 1994.

Comer, Douglas E. *Principles, Protocols, and Architecture.* Vol. 1 *Internetworking with TCP/IP.* 3rd ed. Englewood Cliffs, NJ: Prentice-Hall, 1991.

Cong, D., M. Hamlen, and C. Perkins. *The Definitions of Managed Objects for IP Mobility Support using SMIv2.* RFC 2006. October 1996.

Conta, A., and Stephen Deering. *Generic Packet Tunneling in IPv6.* (work in progress) draft-ietf-ipngwg-ipv6-tunnel-07.txt. December 1996.

Corporation for National Research Initiatives (CNRI). *XIWT: Cross industry working team.* 1994. http://www.cnri.reston.va.us:3000/XIWT/public.html.

Deering, Stephen, and R. Hinden. *Internet Protocol, Version 6 (IPv6) Specification.* RFC 1883. December 1995.

Deering, Stephen. *Host Extensions for IP Multicasting.* RFC 1112. August 1989.

Deering, Stephen E., ed. *ICMP Router Discovery Messages.* RFC 1256. September 1991.

Degermark, Mikael, Bjorn Nordgren and Stephen Pink. *Header Compression for IPv6.* (Work in progress) draft-degermark-ipv6-hc-03.txt. July 1997.

Diffie, W., and M. Hellman. "New Directions in Cryptography." *IEEE Transactions on Information Theory* 22 (November 1976): 644–654.

Droms, Ralph. *Dynamic Host Configuration Protocol.* RFC 2131. March 1997.

Eastlake, Donald E., Stephen D. Crocker, and Jeffrey I. Schiller. *Randomness Recommendations for Security.* RFC 1750. December 1994.

Fenner W. *Internet Group Management Protocol, Version 2.* (work in progress) draft-ietf-idmr-igmp-v2-02.txt. February 1996.

Ferguson, P. *Ingress Filtering in the Internet.* (work in progress) draft-ferguson-ingress-filtering-01.txt. November 1996.

Francis, P. *PIP Near-term Architecture.* RFC 1621. May 1994.

Fuller V., T. Li, J. Yu, and K. Varadhan. *Classless Inter-Domain Routing (CIDR): An Address Assignment and Aggregation Strategy.* RFC 1518. September 1993.

Gilligan R., E. Nordmark, and B. Hinden. *IPAE: The SIPP Interoperability and Transition Mechanism.* Internet Draft (work in progress) March 1994.

Hanks Stan, Tony Li, Dino Farinacci, and Paul Traina. *Generic Routing Encapsulation (GRE).* RFC 1701. October 1994a.

————. *Generic Routing Encapsulation over IPv4 networks.* RFC 1702. October 1994b.

Hellman, M.E., W. Diffie, and R. C. Merkle. *Cryptographic Apparatus and Method.* U.S. Patent 4,200,770. April 1980.

Hinden B. *Simple Internet Protocol Plus White Paper.* RFC 1710. October 1994.

IEEE 802.11 Committee. *Draft Standard, Wireless LAN MAC and PHY Specifications*, Rev. D1. IEEE Document P802.11/D1-94/12. Alpha Graphics #35. 1997.

Ioannidis, John, and Matt Blaze. "The Architecture and Implementation of Network-layer Security under UNIX. Presented at the *4th USENIX Security Workshop.* Santa Clara, CA. October 1993.

Ioannidis, John, Dan Duchamp, and Gerald Q. Maguire Jr. "IP-based Protocols for Mobile Internetworking." In *Proceedings of the SIGCOMM '91 Conference: Communications Architectures & Protocols.* 1991.

Ioannidis, John, and Gerald Q. Maguire Jr. "The Design and Implementation of a Mobile Internetworking Architecture." In *Proceedings of the Winter USENIX Conference.* January 1993.

Jacobson, Van. *Compressing TCP/IP Headers for Low-Speed Serial Links.* RFC 1144. February 1990.

Johnson, David B. "Scalable and Robust Internetwork Routing for Mobile Hosts." In *Proceedings of the 14th International Conference on Distributed Computing Systems.* June 1994.

Katz, Randy H. "Adaptation and mobility in wireless information systems." *IEEE Personal Communications Magazine* 1 (1994): 6–17.

Kent, Stephen and Randall Atkinson. *IP Authentication Header.* Work in progress. July 1997.

Kent, Stephen and Randall Atkinson. *IP Encapsulating Security Payload (ESP).* Work in progress. July 1997.

Kleinrock, Leonard. "Nomadic Computing—An Opportunity." *ACM SIGCOMM Computer Communications Review* 25 (January 1995): 36–40.

Knowles, Steve. *IESG Advice from Experience with Path MTU Discovery.* RFC 1435. March 1993.

Kraster, Barbara. *Magic Cap Complete Official Guide.* Addison Wesley Longman, Reading, MA: 1995.

Lei, Hui, and Charles Perkins. "Ad-hoc networking with mobile IP." In *Proceedings of the The Second European Personal Mobile Communications Conference.* October 1997.

Mankin, Allison, and K. K. Ramakrishnan. *Gateway Congestion Control Survey.* RFC 1254. August 1991.

McCloghrie, Keith, and Marshall T. Rose. *Management Information Base for Network Management of TCP/IP-based internets: MIB-II.* RFC 1213. March 1991.

McGovern, Michael, and Robert Ullmann. *CATNIP: Common Architecture for the Internet.* RFC 1707. November 1994.

McGregor, Glenn. *The PPP Internet Protocol Control Protocol (IPCP).* RFC 1332. May 1992.

Maughan, Douglass, Mark Schertler, Mark Schneider, and Jeff Turner. *Internet Security Association and Key Management Protocol (ISAKMP).* (Internet draft) draft-ietf-ipsec-isakmp-08.txt, .ps. July 1997.

Metcalfe, Robert M., and David R. Boggs. "Ethernet: Distributed Packet Switching for Local Computer Networks." *Communications of the ACM*, 19 (July 1976): 395–404.

Mills, David L. *Network Time Protocol (Version 3): Specification, Implementation and Analysis.* RFC 1305. March 1992.

Mockapetris, P. *Domain Names—Concepts and Facilities.* RFC 1034. November 1987a.

————. *Domain Names—Implementation and Specification.* RFC 1035. November 1987.

Mogul, Jeffery, and Stephen Deering. *Path MTU Discovery.* RFC 1191. November 1990.

Montenegro, G. *Reverse Tunneling for Mobile IP.* (work in progress) draft-ietf-mobileip-tunnel-reverse-00.txt. January 1997.

Myers, John G., and Marshall Rose. *Post Office Protocol—Version 3.* RFC 1939. May 1996.

Myles, Andrew, and David Skellern. "Comparing Four IP Based Mobile Host Protocols." *Computer Networks and ISDN Systems* (November 1993): 349–356.

Narten, T., E. Nordmark, and W. Simpson. *Neighbor Discovery for IP version 6 (IPv6).* RFC 1970. August 1996.

Novell Inc. *Advanced Netware v2.1 Internetwork Packet Exchange Protocol (IPX) with Asynchronous Event Scheduler (AES).* Novell Inc., October 1986.

Patel, B., and Charles E. Perkins. *Preference for Broadcast Datagram Support with Mobile IP.* (work in progress) draft-perkins-mobileip-bcastpref-00.txt. February 1996.

Perkins, Charles E. "Providing Continuous Network Access to Mobile Hosts Using TCP/IP." *Computer Networks and ISDN Systems* (November 1993): 357–370.

Perkins, Charles E., ed. *IPv4 Mobility Support.* (outdated draft) ietf-draft-mobileip-protocol-10.txt. May 1995.

Perkins, Charles E. *IP Encapsulation within IP.* RFC 2003. October 1996a.

Perkins, Charles E., ed. *IPv4 Mobility Support.* RFC 2002. October 1996b.

Perkins, Charles E. *Minimal Encapsulation within IP.* RFC 2004. October 1996c.

Perkins, Charles E., and Pravin Bhagwat. "A Mobile Networking System Based on Internet Protocol (IP)." In *USENIX Symposium on Mobile and Location-Independent Computing.* August 1993.

Perkins, Charles E., and Pravin Bhagwat. "Routing over Multi-hop Wireless Network of Mobile Computers." *SIGCOMM '94: Computer Communications Review* 24 (October 1994): 234–244.

Perkins, Charles E., and Pravin Bhagwat. "Ad-hoc on-demand distance vector routing." Mobicom '97 (submitted for publication), September 1997.

Perkins, Charles E., and David B. Johnson. "Mobility Support in IPv6." In *ACM Mobicom 96*. November 1996.

Perkins, Charles E., and Andrew Myles. "Mobile IP." In *Proceedings of International Telecommunications Symposium*. (August 1994): 415–419.

Perkins, Charles E., Andrew Myles, and David B. Johnson. "IMHP: A Mobile Host Protocol for the Internet." *Computer Networks and ISDN Systems* 27 (December 1994): 479–491.

Perlman, Radia. *Interconnections: Bridges & Routers*. Reading, MA: Addison Wesley Longman, 1994.

Plummer, David C. *An Ethernet Address Resolution Protocol: Or Converting Network Protocol Addresses to 48-bit Ethernet Addresses for Transmission on Ethernet Hardware*. RFC 826, November 1982.

Postel, J. B. *User Datagram Protocol*. RFC 768. August 1980.

Postel, J. B., ed. *Internet Control Message Protocol*. RFC 792. September 1981a.

Postel, J. B., ed. *Internet Protocol*. RFC 791. September 1981b.

Postel, J. B., ed. *Transmission Control Protocol*. RFC 793. September 1981c.

Postel, J. B. *Multi-LAN Address Resolution*. RFC 925. October 1984.

Rappaport, Theodore S. *Wireless Communications: Principles and Practice*. Upper Saddle River, NJ, Prentice-Hall: 1996.

Rekhter, Yakov, and Tony Li. *An Architecture for IP Address Allocation with CIDR*. RFC 1518. September 1993.

———. *A Border Gateway Protocol 4 (BGP-4)*. RFC 1771. March 1995.

Reynolds, Joyce K., and Jon Postel. *Assigned Numbers*. RFC 1700. October 1994.

Rivest, Ronald L. *The MD5 Message-Digest Algorithm*. RFC 1321. April 1992.

Rivest, R. L., A. Shamir, and L. Adleman. "A Method for Obtaining Digital Signatures and Public Key Cryptosytems." *Commun. ACM* 21 (1978): 120–126.

Rose, Marshall T. *The Simple Book: An Introduction to Internet Management*. Prentice-Hall, 1991.

RSA Laboratories. *RSAREF: A Cryptographic Toolkit*, Version 2.0. RSA Laboratories, 1994. http://www.consensus.com/rsaref/index.html.

Samara, C. S. et al. *Webexpress: A Client/Intercept-based System for Optimizing Web Browsing in a Wireless Environment*. (submitted for publication), July 1997.

Satyanarayanan, M. "Mobile Information Access." *IEEE Personal Communications* 3 (February 1996): 26–33.

Schneier, Bruce. *Applied Cryptography: Protocols, Algorithms, and Source Code in C.* 2nd ed. New York: John Wiley and Sons, 1995.

Schulzrinne, H., Stephen Casner, Ron Frederick, and Van Jacobson. *RTP: A Transport Protocol for Real-Time Applications.* RFC 1889. January 1996.

Simpson, William Allen, ed. *The Point-to-Point Protocol (PPP).* RFC 1661. July 1994.

———. *IP in IP Tunneling.* RFC 1853. October 1995.

SNMPv2 Working Group, J. Case, K. McCloghrie, M. Rose, and S. Waldbusser. *Structure of Management Information for Version 2 of the Simple Network Management Protocol (SNMPV2).* RFC 1902. January 1996.

Stardust Technologies. *NetDev Specification for WinSock Version 2.* http://www.stardust.com/ wsresource/winsock2/netdev.html. Stardust Technologies, July 1996.

Steenstrup, Martha. *Routing in Communications Networks. Internetworking with TCP/IP.* 1st ed. Upper Saddle River, NJ: Prentice Hall, 1995.

Stevens, W. *TCP Slow Start, Congestion Avoidance, Fast Retransmit, and Fast Recovery Algorithms.* RFC 2001. January 1997.

Stevens, W. Richard. *TCP/IP Illustrated, Volume 1: The Protocols.* Addison-Wesley Professional Computing Series. Reading, MA: Addison Wesley Longman, 1994.

Talukdar, Anup K., B. R. Badrinath, and Arup Acharya. "On Accommodating Mobile Hosts in an Integrated Services Packet Network." In *Proceedings of the Infocom 97.* April 1997.

Teraoka, Fumio, and Mario Tokoro. "Host Migration Transparency in IP Networks." *Computer Communication Review* (January 1993): 45–65.

Thomson, Susan, and Thomas Narten. *IPv6 Stateless Address Autoconfiguration.* RFC 1971. August 1996.

Veizades, J., E. Guttman, C. Perkins, and S. Kaplan. *Service Location Protocol.* (work in progress) draft-ietf-svrloc-protocol-17.txt. April 1997.

Vixie, Paul, Sue Thompson, Yakov Rekhter, and Jim Bound. *Dynamic Updates in the Domain Name System (DNS).* RFC 2136. April 1997.

Wada, Hiromi, Takashi Yozawa, Tatsuya Ohnishi, and Yasunori Tanaka. "Mobile Computing Environment Based on Internet Packet Forwarding." In *Proceedings of the Winter USENIX Conference* (January 1993): 503–517.

Want, Roy, Andy Hopper, Veronica Falcao, and Jonathan Gibbons. "Active Badge Location System." *ACM Transactions on Information Systems* 10 (January 1992): 91–102.

Waters, G. *User-Based Security Model for SNMPV2.* RFC 1910. February 1996.

Zhang, L., S. Deering, D. Estrin, S. Shenker, and D. Zappala. "RSVP: A New Resource ReSerVation Protocol." *IEEE Network* (September 1993).

The Addison-Wesley Wireless Communications Series

Dr. Andrew J. Viterbi, Consulting Editor
http://www.awl.com/cseng/wirelessseries/

0-201-63374-4
272 pages
Hardcover

CDMA
Principles of Spread Spectrum Communication
by Andrew J. Viterbi

CDMA, a wireless standard, is a leading technology for relieving spectrum congestion caused by the explosion in popularity of wireless communications. This book presents the fundamentals of CDMA so that you can develop systems, products, and services for this demanding market.

Andrew J. Viterbi is a pioneer of wireless digital communications technology. He is best known as the creator of the digital decoding technique used in direct broadcast satellite television receivers and in wireless cellular telephones, as well as numerous other applications. He is cofounder, Chief Technical Officer, and Vice Chairman of QUALCOMM Incorporated, a developer of mobile satellite and wireless land communication systems employing CDMA technology.

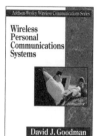

0-201-63470-8
448 pages
Hardcover

Wireless Personal Communications Systems
by David J. Goodman

Goodman presents the technology and underlying principles of wireless communications systems. He describes nine important systems: AMPS, IS-41, NA-TDMA, CDMA, GSM, CT-2, DECT, PHS, and PACS. Each system is described using a unified framework so the reader can easily compare and contrast the systems. Key features, such as architecture, radio transmission, logical channels, messages, mobility management, security, power control, and handoff are addressed. An analysis of such design goals as low price, wide geographical coverage, transmission quality, privacy, and spectrum efficiency helps the reader to understand why the various systems have such divergent designs.

David J. Goodman is the Director of the Wireless Information Networks LABoratory (WINLAB) and is a member of the faculty at Rutgers University. Previously, Dr. Goodman worked at Bell Laboratories for twenty-one years, where he did pioneering research in wireless communications.

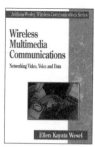

0-201-63394-9
336 pages
Hardcover

Wireless Multimedia Communications
Networking Video, Voice, and Data
by Ellen Kayata Wesel

This book is a comprehensive guide to understanding the design of wireless multimedia communication systems. *Wireless* is synonymous with *mobile*, enabling the computer user to remain connected while moving from one place to another. *Multimedia* denotes a mix of video, voice, and data information—each of which has different transfer requirements. The author has made significant contributions to the theory, design, standardization, and policies of several wireless multimedia systems. The book is comprehensive in scope, and addresses in detail each of the key elements of a complete wireless multimedia system, including propagation characteristics, modulation, intersymbol interface mitigation, coding, medium access protocols, and spectrum and standards networking, while defining their relationship to one another.

Dr. Ellen Kayata Wesel is a Senior Scientist at Hughes Communications, Inc. (HCI), where she designs next-generation wireless multimedia communication systems. Prior to joining HCI, she designed the physical and data link layers for high data rate wireless LANs at Apple Computer.